# SPANDA-KĀRIKĀS

## The Divine Creative Pulsation



JAIDEVA SINGH

MOTILAL BANARSIDASS INTERNATIONAL
• DELHI •

# SPANDA-KĀRIKĀS

## The Divine Creative Pulsation

*The Kārikās and the Spanda-nirnaya Translated into English by*

JAIDEVA SINGH

MOTILAL BANARSIDASS
INTERNATIONAL
DELHI

*Reprint Edition Delhi, 2020, 22*
*First Edition, Delhi, 1980*



ISBN : 978-81-944-3875-5 (Cloth)
ISBN : 978-81-944-3874-8 (Paper)

*Also available at*
MOTILAL BANARSIDASS INTERNATIONAL
41 U.A. Bungalow Road, (Back Lane)Jawahar Nagar, Delhi - 110 007
4261 (basement) Lane #3,Ansari Road, Darya Ganj, New Delhi - 110 002
203 Royapettah High Road, Mylapore, Chennai - 600 004
Samar Auddy 56/2, Ahiritola Street, Kolkata - 700 005
*Stockist :* Motilal Books, Ashok Rajpath, Near Kali Mandir, Patna - 800 004

Printed & Bound by
MOTILAL BANARSIDASS INTERNATIONAL

# DEDICATED

*With profound respects to Svamī Lakṣmaṇa Joo,*
*the doyen of Śaivāgama*

# PREFACE

The Spandakārikās are a number of verses that serve as a sort of commentary on the Śiva-sūtras. According to Śaivāgama, the Divine Consciousness is not simply cold, inert intellection. It is rather *spanda*, active, dynamic, throbbing with life, creative pulsation.

In Śiva-sūtras, it is the *prakāśa* aspect of the Divine that is emphasized; in Spandakārikās, it is the *vimarśa* aspect that is emphasized. Together, these two books give an integral view of *Śaiva* philosophy.

Kṣemarāja has written a commentary on Spandakārikās, titled *Spanda-nirṇaya*. He is fond of sesquipedalian compounds, long and windy sentences, but he is very profound in the comprehension of the subject and so cannot be ignored.

I have tried to provide a readable translation of both the kārikas and the Spanda-nirṇaya commentary.

Each *kārikā* (verse) is given both in Devanāgarī and Roman script, followed by its translation in English. This is followed by Kṣemarāja's commentary in Sanskrit. Then follows an English translation of the commentary. After this, copious notes are added on important and technical words. Finally, I have given a running exposition of each *kārikā* in my own words.

The text and commentary published in the Kashmir Series of Texts and Studies have been adopted. A few misprints that occurred in the above edition have been corrected with the assistance of Svāmī Lakṣmaṇa Joo. I am deeply indebted to him for his luminous exposition of this important text.

A long Introduction has been given in the beginning of the book, and a glossary of technical terms and an Index have been appended at the end.

Varanasi
12.4.1980

JAIDEVA SINGH

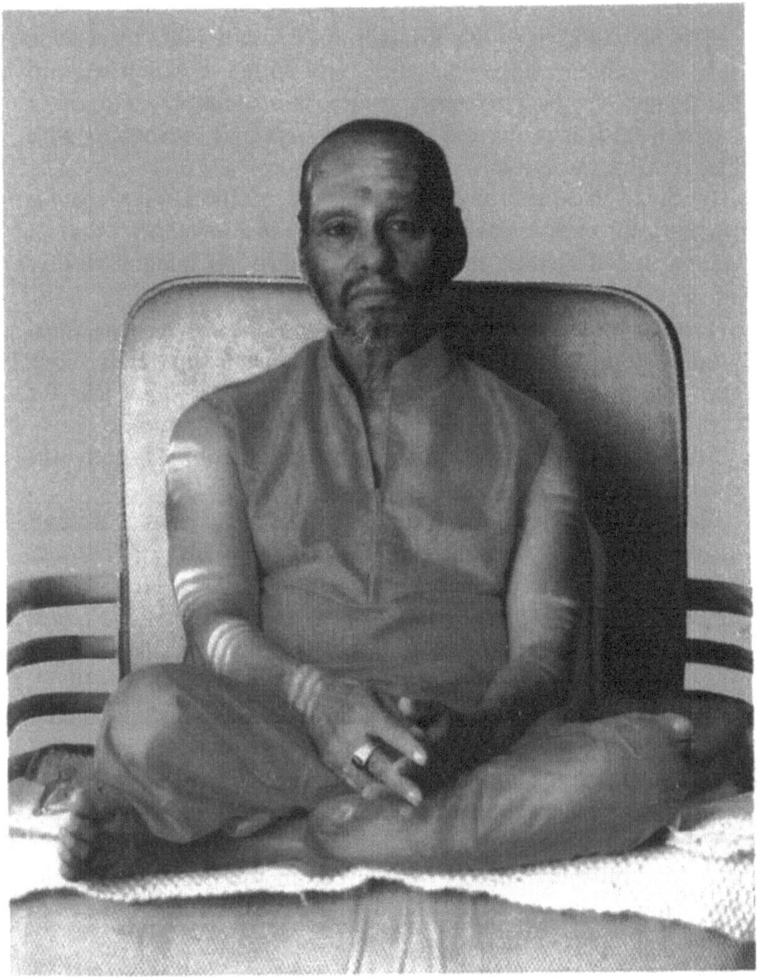

Sadguru Swami Muktananda

## BLESSINGS

*Spanda Kārikās* is one of the important works of Kashmir Śaivism. The doctrine of Spanda is scientific. Modern scientists have discovered that the world was created from the vibration of the first explosion and that the universe is still expanding. Yet so far they have not been able to find out how the first explosion occurred. However, the ancient scriptures of the Spanda doctrine have always contained the knowledge that this vibration is the Spanda or throb of the Absolute Reality, the Universal Consciousness which is also called Śiva. The world came into existence with the throb of His opening eye. Jñāneśvara Mahārāja has described Lord Śiva as having the mudrā of expanding universe.

It is a matter of great satisfaction to know that the work which reveals this truth is now available in English. Modern scientists will definitely make use of it to enhance their knowledge. In America when I meet with scientists, I always refer to the doctrine of Spanda. They express interest and desire to read about it.

I welcome Jaideva Singh, who helps to spread this supreme wisdom of Kashmir. In the company of great beings he has acquired the knowledge of the truth. He has also translated and explained in English such great works of Kashmir Śaivism as *Śiva Sūtras*, *Pratyabhijñāhṛdayam*, and *Vijñāna Bhairava*. In this way, he has helped the people of English speaking countries who desired to know this doctrine. I hope his work in this direction continues for a long time.

Let the humanity of the world benefit by the knowledge contained in this work.

Miami, USA — Swami Muktananda
15-4-1980

# CONTENTS

# INTRODUCTION

## *Spandakārikās—The importance of the book*

*Spandakārikās* are a sort of commentary on the Śiva-sūtras. The word *kārikā* means 'a collection of verses on grammatical, philosophical or scientific subjects.' The word *spanda* literally means a 'throb.' It connotes dynamism or the dynamic aspect of the Divine, the Divine creative pulsation.

The Self, according to Spandakārikās, is not simply a witnessing consciousness, but is characterized by both cognition and activity. He who is in communion with this active Self can alone rise to the status of his highest being.

### *The author of Spandakārikās*

The opinion regarding the authorship of Spandakārikās is divided. According to Bhāskara and Utpala Vaiṣṇava or Bhaṭṭa Utpala, both of whom flourished in the second and third quarters of the 10th century A.D., the author of these kārikās was Kallaṭa who was the chief disciple of Vasugupta.

Bhāskara says in his Śiva-sūtra-vārttika that Kallaṭa wrote a commentary, called *Spanda-sūtras* on the three sections of the Śiva-sūtras, and a commentary, called Tattvārtha-cintāmaṇi on the fourth section of the Śiva-sūtras.[1]

Bhaṭṭa Utpala, in his commentary, on the Spandakārikās, entitled Spandapradīpikā, says in the 53rd verse that Bhaṭṭa Kallaṭa duly versified the secret doctrine after receiving it from his *guru* (spiritual guide) Vasugupta who had clear insight into Reality.[2]

Kṣemarāja and Maheśvarānanda attribute the authorship of the kārikās to Vasugupta. Both refer to the following verse :

---

[1]व्याकरोत्त्रिकमेतेभ्यः स्पन्दसूत्रैः स्वकैस्ततः ।
तत्त्वार्थचिन्तामण्याख्यटीकया खण्डमन्तिमम् ॥ S. S. V. pp. 2-3.

[2]वस्तुगुप्तादवाप्येदं गुरोस्तत्त्वार्थदर्शिनः ।
रहस्यं श्लोकयामास सम्यक् श्रीभट्टकल्लटः ॥

लब्ध्वाप्यलभ्यमेतज्ज्ञानधनं हृद्गुहान्तःकृतनिहितेः ।
वसुगुप्तवच्छिवाय हि भवति सदा सर्वलोकस्य ॥

"As on the attainment of this treasure of knowledge which is difficult of attainment, and on its being well preserved in the cave of the heart, it has been for the good of Vasugupta, so also on the attainment and on its being well preserved in the cave of the heart, it would always be for the good of all."

This verse is, however, not found in the recension of Bhaṭṭa Utpala, Kallaṭa and Rāmakaṇṭha.

In his commentary on Spandakārikās, called vṛtti, Kallaṭa makes the following concluding remark :

दृब्धं महादेवगिरौ महेशस्वप्नोपदिष्टाच्छिवसूत्रसिन्धोः ।
स्पन्दामृतं यद्वसुगुप्तपादैः श्रीकल्लटस्तत्प्रकटीचकार ॥

On the basis of this verse, some writers have concluded that Kallaṭa was the author of the Spandakārikās. But Kallaṭa specifically says *Yat Spandāmṛtaṁ Vasuguptapādaiḥ dṛbdham,* i.e. 'the Spandakārikās which were composed by Vasugupta. spandāmṛtam is only another name for Spandakārikās. The word *dṛbdhaṃ* only means 'strung together, arranged, composed' and *Vasuguptapādaiḥ* only means 'by revered Vasugupta.' Regarding himself, Kallaṭa only claims to have brought it to the notice of the people. "Vasugupta-pādaiḥ dṛbdhaṃ" clearly shows that the Kārikās were composed by Vasugupta.

The truth, therefore, seems to be that Vasugupta actually composed the Kārikās, taught them to Kallaṭa, and Kallaṭa only publicized them.

*Commentaries*

Four commentaries are available on these *Kārikās,* viz., (1) the *vṛtti* by Kallaṭa, (2) the *Vivṛti* of Rāmakaṇṭha, (3) the *Spandapradīpikā* of Bhaṭṭa Utpala and (4) the *Spandasandoha* and *Spanda-nirṇaya of Kṣemarāja.*

Kallaṭa flourished in the second and third quarter of the 9th century A.D. On these *kārikās,* he has written a commentary, called *vṛtti.* It gives a simple meaning of these verses. He has divided the *kārikās* into three *niḥṣyandas* or sections. The first *niḥṣyanda* contains twentyfive verses, and is designated by him as *svarūpa-spanda*. It gives the essential nature of *spanda*. The second section is named by him *sahaja-vidyodaya* i.e. the emergence of *Sahaja-vidyā*. It contains seven *Kārikās* (verses) from 26 to 32. The third section is named *vibhūti-spanda* or supranormal powers acquired through *spanda*. It contains twenty verses from 33 to 52.

Râmakaṇṭha wrote a commentary, called *Vivṛti*. He calls himself a pupil of Utpaladeva, the grand teacher of Abhinavagupta. He, therefore, flourished in the second and third quarters of the 10th century A.D. He closely followed the *Vṛtti* of *Kallaṭa* in his interpretation of the *kārikās*. He himself says so in the colòphon of his commentary *Saṃpūrṇā iyaṃ vṛtyanusāriṇī spandavivṛtiḥ*. "This *Spanda-vivṛti* closely following the *vṛtti* (of Kallaṭa) is finished." His division, however, of the sections of the *Kārikās* is different. His first section includes sixteen verses and he names it *vyatirekopapatti-nirdeśaḥ* i.e. the section that points out the proved distinction of the knower from the known.

His second section includes eleven verses and is named *vyatirikta-svabhāvopalabdhiḥ* i.e. the acquisition of distinct nature.

His third section includes only three verses and is named *Viśva-svasvabhāva-śaktyupapattiḥ* i.e. the universe is only a manifestation of one's own essential nature.

His fourth section includes twenty-one verses and is named, *abhedopalabdhiḥ* i.e. realization of identity with the Divine. He adds one more verse to this section expressive of the obeisance of the writer to his *guru*.

Bhaṭṭa Utpala or Utpala Vaiṣṇava wrote a commentary entitled *Spandapradīpikā*. He flourished in the second and third quarters of the 10th century A.D. He says in his commentary that he was born in a place called Nārāyaṇa in Kashmir and that his father's name was Trivikrama. His commentary consists mostly of parallel quotations from other sources.

Kṣemarāja first of all wrote a commentary, called Spandasandoha only on the first verse of Spandakārikā. Later on, at the persistent request of his pupil, Śūra he wrote

Spandanirṇaya, a commentary on the whole book. He flourished in the last quarter of the 10th and first quarter of the 11th century. He was Abhinavagupta's cousin and pupil. His commentary on Spandakārikā is exceedingly scholarly and bears the stamp of his teacher's profundity. According to him, Bhaṭṭa Lollaṭa had also written a commentary on these *kārikās*, but that is not available now.

He has divided the *kārikās* into four sections. The first section consists of twenty-five verses. Like Kallaṭa he has named this section as *svarūpa-spanda*. His second section consists of seven verses, and like Kallaṭa, he names it *Sahaja-vidyodaya*.

His third section consists of nineteen verses, and like Kallaṭa, he names it *Vibhūtispanda*. Kallaṭa has added one more verse in this section which is only expressive of homage to the guru, and cannot, by any stretch of imagination, be included in *Vibhūti* (supernormal powers). Kṣemarāja has thrown this laudatory verse and one more verse descriptive of the fruit of this knowledge in a separate fourth section.

*What is Spanda ?*

*Spanda* is a very technical word of this system. Literally, it is some sort of movement or throb. But as applied to the Divine, it cannot mean movement.

Abhinavagupta makes this point luminously clear in these lines :

"स्पन्दनं च किञ्चिच्चलनम्। स्वरूपाच्च यदि वस्त्वन्तराक्रमणं, तच्चलनमेव, न किञ्चित्त्वम्। नोचेत्, चलनमेव न किञ्चित्। तस्मात्स्वरूप एव क्रमादिपरिहारेण चमत्कारात्मिका उच्छलता······ स्पन्द इत्युच्यते"। (परा०त्रि०वि०, पृष्ठ २०७)

"Spandana means some sort of movement. If there is movement from the essential nature of the Divine towards another object, it is definite movement, not some sort, otherwise, movement itself would be nothing. Therefore, *Spanda* is only a throb, a heaving of spiritual rapture in the essential nature of the Divine which excludes all succession. This is the significance of the word Kiñcit in *kiñcit calanam* which is to be interpreted as "movement as it were."

Movement or motion occurs only in a spatio-temporal framework. The Supreme transcends all notions of space and time. *Spanda*, therefore, in the case of the Supreme is neither physical motion, nor psychological activity like pain and pleasure, nor *prāṇic* activity like hunger or thirst. It is the throb of the ecstasy of the Divine I-consciousness (*vimarśa*). The Divine I-consciousness is spiritual dynamism. It is the Divine creative pulsation. It is the throb of Śiva's *svātantrya* or absolute Freedom.

If *Spanda* is not any kind of movement, how can the application of this word be justified to the activity of the Supreme, for the word *Spanda* means 'a somewhat of motion ?' This is the explanation offered by Abhinavagupta.

"स्पन्दनं च किञ्चित् चलनम्। एषैव च किञ्चिद्रूपता यद् अचलमपि चलम् आभासते इति, प्रकाशस्वरूपं हि मनागपि नातिरिच्यते अतिरिच्यते इव इति अचलमेव आभासभेदयुक्तमेव च भाति इति।"

(I. Pr. V. I. 5, 14, p. 208)

"*Spandana* means a somewhat of movement. The characteristic of 'somewhat' consists in the fact that even the immovable appears 'as if moving,' because though the light of consciousness does not change in the least, yet it appears to be changing *as it were*. The immovable appears as if having a variety of manifestation."

*Spanda* is, therefore, spiritual dynamism without any movement in itself but serving as the *causa sine qua non* of all movements.

The Infinite Perfect Divine Consciousness always has *vimarśa* or Self-awareness. This Self-awareness is a subtle activity which is spiritual dynamism, not any physical, psychological or *prāṇic* activity. As Utpaladeva puts it in Īśvarapratyabhijñā :

स एव विमृशत्त्वेन नियतेन महेश्वरः।
विमर्शं एव देवस्य शुद्धे ज्ञानक्रिये यतः॥ (I, 8. 11)

The Divine is termed the great Lord (Maheśvara) because of His ever-present, immutable Self-awareness (*vimarśa*). That Self awareness in its absolute Freedom constitutes Divine (śuddha—pure) knowledge and activity." *Spanda* is only another name of Self-awareness or *Vimarśa*. As Kṣemarāja puts it, *Spanda* also connotes the *svātantrya* or absolute Freedom of the Divine (*Bhagavataḥ svātantrya-śaktiḥ*). *Vimarśa, parāśakti, svātantrya, aiśvarya, kartṛtva, sphurattā, sāra, hṛdaya*, and *spanda* are synonymous in Śaivāgama.

*Sections of Spandakārikās*

While the verses of the text are practically the same in all the editions available, they have been divided under different sections somewhat differently by each editor and commentator. The topics under each section are given in this book as described by *Kṣemarāja.*

## I. SECTION

*Svarūpaspandaḥ or Spanda as the Essential Nature of Śiva*

1. The first verse of this section describes *Spanda-śakti* represented by the *unmeṣa* (emergence) and *nimeṣa* (submergence) of the *Śakti* (primal energy) of *Śiva.* As Kṣemarāja puts it, it is the essential nature of *Śiva* and also that of the empirical individual (*sphurattāsāra-spandaśaktimaya-svasvabhāva*).

*Unmeṣa and nimeṣa* are only figuratively spoken of as occurring one after the other. As a matter of fact, they occur simultaneously (*yugapadevonmeṣa-nimeṣobhayarūpām pratibhām bhagavatīṁ vicinvantu mahādhiyaḥ*).

In activity, there is no depletion of *Spanda-śakti* as there is of physical energy. *Lelihānā sadā devī sadā pūrṇā ca bhāsate* i. e. This goddess is always engaged in exercising her energy in withdrawal and yet always appears as replete."

वस्तुतस्तु न किञ्चिदुदेति व्ययते वा, केवलं स्पन्दशक्तिरेव भगवत्यक्रमापि तथातथाभासरूपतया स्फुरन्त्युदेतीव व्ययते इव च ।

(Commentary on the first Kārikā)

In reality, nothing arises, and nothing subsides. It is only the divine *Spandaśakti* which, though free of succession, appears in different aspects as if flashing in view and as if subsiding."

Kṣemarāja believes that there is close correlation between the *spanda* system and the *krama* system. In his *Spandanirṇaya* commentary, Kṣemarāja interprets the phrase *śakti-cakra-vibhava-prabhavam* as representing the *Mahārtha* or *Krama* ideal of five-fold functioning through the agency of the deities *Sṛṣṭi, Rakta Kālī*, etc. In explaining *vibhava*—he uses the very technical terms of *Krama Śāstra. Vibhava udyogāvabhāsana-carvaṇā-vilāpanātmā krīḍāḍambaraḥ—udyoga* meaning creative activity, *avabhāsana*, meaning maintenance, *carvaṇā* (absorption), and *vilāpana*, meaning the assumption of the indefinable state (anâkhyâ).

2. The second verse says that the world is contained in the *spanda* principle, and comes out of it. The world being contained in *spanda* and coming out of it does not mean that the world is anything different from *Śiva* as a walnut is different from the bag in which it is contained. Being contained in and coming out of, are only limitations of the human language. The world is *Śiva* as reflections in a mirror are the mirror itself. The world consisting of the subject, object and means of knowledge cannot really conceal Śiva, because without the light of Śiva, they themselves cannot appear. The world is inherent in *Spanda* just as a banyan tree exists as potency in the seed.

3. The third verse maintains that even in the differing states viz., waking, dream, and deep sleep, the *spanda* principle remains the same, viz., as the invariable of Experient of all the states.

4. While states of experience like pleasure, pain, etc. differ, the Experient cannot change; for it is the Experient that connects the differing states as the experience of the identical Experient.

5. Reality is neither psychological subject nor the psycho-physical experience, nor is it mere void. Reality or *Spanda* is the underlying basis of the psychological subject, it is the eternal Experient that can never be reduced to an object.

6 & 7. It is from the *Spanda* principle that the group of senses acquires its power of going forth towards the objects, maintaining them in perception for a while and then withdrawing them towards the centre.

8. It is not the will or desire of the empirical individual that moves the senses towards their objects. He derives this power from the spanda principle—the dynamism of *Śiva.*

9. It is on account of *āṇava*, *māyīya* and *kārma mala* that the empirical individual is unable to realize the *spanda* principle.

10. When the limited ego or *āṇava mala* of the individual is dissolved, he acquires the true characteristic of the *spanda* principle, viz., innate knowledge and activity.

11. When the *yogi* realizes the *spanda* principle, he knows that this is his essential Self, and not his empirical self.

12 & 13. The experience of void does not prove that there is no Experient, for without the Experient, even the experience of void would not be possible. This Experient is the *spanda* principle.

14, 15 & 16. *Spanda* or the Divine principle appears in two aspects, subject and object. It is only the object that changes and disappears, never the Subject. *Spanda* constitutes the eternal subject.

17. The fully awakened *yogi* or *suprabuddha* has an integral experience of the *Spanda* principle in all the three states of waking, dream and deep sleep, but the partially awakened individual has an experience of it only in the beginning and end of waking, dream, and deep sleep, not in the middle of these states.

18. To the fully enlightened *yogi*, the *spanda* principle appears as knowledge (*jñāna*) and objects of knowledge (*jñeya*) in the middle of the two states of waking and dream, fully integrated to the I-consciousness just as they appear to Sadāśiva and Īśvara. In the deep sleep, since there is no object, the *spanda* principle appears as sheer consciousness (*cinmaya*).

19. There are two aspects of *spanda-sāmānya* and *viśeṣa*. *Sāmānya* is the general principle of consciousness, *viśeṣa* is the manifestation of *Spanda* in constitutive aspects like *sattva*, *rajas* and *tamas* or objective experiences like blue, pleasure etc. Ordinary people consider the *viśeṣa spanda*, i.e. the particular manifestations as something entirely different from consciousness, but the fully enlightened *yogī* considers them only as forms of *Spanda*.

20. The particular forms of *spanda* appear as entirely different from consciousness to all those who are not awakened to their divine source. So they are doomed to a life of worldly existence.

21. One should, therefore, have constant awareness of the *spanda* principle even in the common work-a-day world.

22. In intense emotional state or a state of mental impasse, all the mental activities come to a dead stop. That is the time when one can have an experience of the *spanda* principle if one is properly oriented towards it.

23, 24, 25. When the *yogī* lays his grip firmly on the *spanda* principle, his *prāṇa* and *apāna* get merged in the *suṣumnā*; they mount up to Brahmarandhra and finally get dissolved in the ether of consciousness beyond it.

Thus by means of twenty five verses the essential nature of *spanda* together with the means for attaining it has been described from various points of view.

## II. SECTION

*Sahaja Vidyodaya*

The first section describes *spanda* principally as Śiva's dynamic aspect which is identical with the essential Self of each. In the first section, there is the stress on *nimīlana samādhi* (introvertive meditation,) for the realization of the *spanda* principle.

The second section describes *spanda* not only as identical with the essential Self but also with the whole universe. In order to realize this aspect of *spanda*, (there is the stress on *unmīlana samādhi* (extrovertive meditation). This is possible by the rise of *Sahaja vidyā* by which one experiences unity in the midst of diversity.

Verses 1 and 2 say that *mantras* whether taken in the sense of Mantra, Mantreśvara, and Mantramaheśvara or in the sense of sacred formulae derive their power from the *spanda* principle and are finally dissolved in it.

Verses 3 and 4 tell us that the individual through his knowledge of all objects feels his identity with all. Hence there is no state which is not *Śiva* to him.

Verse 5 tells us that one who has this realization views the entire world as the play of the Self identical with *Śiva*.

In verses 6 and 7, it is said that if one realizes his identity with the deity who is the object of his meditation, one becomes ultimately identified with *Śiva* and acquires immortality.

## III. SECTION

*Vibhūti Spanda*

This section describes mostly the supernormal powers gained by the realization of *spanda.*

Verses 1 and 2 tell us that as Śiva fulfils the desires of the embodied *yogī* in the waking condition, so also does He reveal his desired objects even in dream by appearing in *Suṣumnā.*

Verse 3 tells us that if the *yogī* is not alert, he will have the same common experience in waking condition and particular, personal experiences in dream as other ordinary people of the world have.

Verses 4 and 5 say that if the self of the *yogī* becomes identified with the essential nature of *Śiva,* he is endowed with the power of knowing everything in its essential form.

Verse 6 says that such a *yogī* can acquire full control over his hunger.

Verse 7 says that he can also acquire the power of omniscience.

Verse 8. Depression proceeds from spiritual ignorance. Depression can no longer remain when ignorance disappears.

Verse 9 describes the rise of *unmeṣa.* It occurs at the junction-point of two thoughts. It is that metempirical Self that relates all thoughts and runs through all as the underlying subject.

Verse 10. From the realization of *unmeṣa,* one experiences supernormal light in the middle of the two eye-brows, unstruck, spontaneous sound in the *suṣumnā, rūpa* i.e., a glow shining even in darkness and supernormal taste experienced on the tip of the tongue. They are, however, a disturbing factor in the realization of the *Spanda* principle.

11. When the *yogī* is established in the essential Self, he

can experience all objective reality right from earth upto Śiva.

Verse 12. One who is identified with the essential Self perceives all phenomena only as the form of *Śiva.*

Verse 13. The empirical individual is deprived of the real spiritual power of will, knowledge and activity and coming under the suzerainty of powers derived from the multitude of words, he is reduced to the status of paśu—a limited, bound soul.

Verse 14. The bound soul loses his independence on account of the rise of ideas which have their sphere in sense-objects.

Verse 15. The empirical individual becomes bound on account of ideas, and ideas are due to the power of words. So words have a tremendous influence on the empirical individual.

Verse 16. The power of ideation and verbalization is derived from *kriyā śakti.* When the empirical individual realizes that the *kriyā śakti* is only an aspect of *parāśakti* or *spanda*, he is liberated.

Verse 17 & 18. All our motivated desires and ideas remain in the form of residual traces in the subtle body or *puryaṣṭaka* consisting of the five *tanmātrās*, *manas*, *buddhi and ahaṃkāra.* The transmigratory existence can be stopped only by the extermination of the impurities of the *puryaṣṭaka*.

Verse 19. When the empirical individual is firmly rooted in the *spanda* principle, he brings the emergence and dissolution of the *puryaṣṭaka* under his control and can become the lord of the entire group of *śaktis*.

## IV SECTION

In this section, there are only two verses. The first one, by means of *double entendre*, lauds both the power of the spanda state and the power of the word of the *guru*.

The second one only points out the good that would accrue to all who carefully betake themselves to the *spanda* principle, and realize it.

JAIDEVA SINGH

## KṢEMARĀJA'S PROPITIATORY VERSES AND THE GENERAL PURPOSE OF HIS COMMENTARY, SPANDA-NIRṆAYA

### TEXT

सर्वं स्वात्मस्वरूपं मुकुरनगरवत्स्वस्वरूपात्स्वतन्त्र-
स्वच्छस्वात्मस्वभित्तौ कलयति धरणीतः शिवान्तं सदा या ।
दृग्देवी मन्त्रवीर्यं सततसमुदिता शब्दराश्यात्मपूर्णा
हन्तानन्त[१]स्फुरत्ता जयति जगति सा शाङ्करी स्पन्दशक्तिः ॥१॥

स्पन्दामृते चर्वितेऽपि स्पन्दसन्दोहतो मनाक् ।
पूर्णस्तच्चर्वणाभोगोद्योग एष मयाश्रितः ॥२॥

सम्यक्सूत्रसमन्वयं परिगतिं तत्त्वे परस्मिन्परां
तीक्ष्णां युक्तिकथामुपायघटनां स्पष्टार्थसद्व्याकृतिम् ।
ज्ञातुं वाञ्छथ [२]चेच्छिवोपनिषदं श्रीस्पन्दशास्त्रस्य त-
द्वृत्तावत्र धियं निधत्त सुधियः स्पन्दश्रियं प्राप्नुत ॥३॥

Sarvaṃ svātmasvarūpaṃ mukuranagaravat
svasvarūpātsvatantra-
svacchasvātmasvabhittau kalayati
dharaṇītaḥ śivāntaṃ sadā yā //
Dṛgdevī mantravīryaṃ satatasamuditā
śabdarāśyātmapūrṇāhantānantasphurattā
jayati jagati sā śāṃkarī spandaśaktiḥ //[1]
Spandāmṛte carvite'pi spandasandohato manāk /
Pūrṇastaccarvaṇābhogodyoga eṣa mayāśritaḥ. //[2]
Samyaksūtrasamanvayaṃ parigatiṃ tattve parasminparāṃ
Tīkṣṇāṃ yuktikathāmupāyaghaṭanāṃ spaṣṭārthasadvyākṛtim /
Jñātuṃ vāñchatha cecchivopaniṣadaṃ Śrīspandaśāstrasya tad-
vṛttāvatra dhiyaṃ nidhatta sudhiyiyaḥ spandaśriyaṃ prāpnuta//[3]

१. ग०पु० नन्देति पाठः । २. क०ख०ग०पु० चिदिति पाठः ।

## TRANSLATION

She, who is ever conscious of the vitality of mantra,[1] who is the endless flash of the perfect and complete I-consciousness whose essence consists in a multitude of letters,[2] who is the goddess embodying *jñāna*[3] (knowledge), ever knows the totality of categories from the earth upto Śiva, which is one in substance with Her own Self and is portrayed out of Her own nature on the canvas of Her own free, clear Self just as a city is reflected in a mirror (from which it is non-distinct). Hail to that Energy of creative pulsation (*spandaśakti*) of Śiva (*Śāṃkarī*) that exults in glory all over the world.

Though the ambrosia of *spanda* has been relished in a small degree from my work Spandasandoha,[4] I am now making an effort for providing complete enjoyment of that (*spanda*).

If you want to know the exact inter-connexion of the *sūtras* (i.e. of the *kārikās* or verses of this text), the most excellent ascertainment of the highest Reality, pointed and subtle statement of reasoning, the right application of means, exquisite exposition through clear sense and the secret doctrine of Śaivāgama, then, O intelligent people, apply your mind to this gloss of the Spandaśāstra and obtain the wealth of *spanda*.

## NOTES

1. The mantra referred to is the I-consciousness or *ahaṃ parāmarśa* of the Absolute.

2. This I-consciousness or aham contains all the letters of the Sanskrit alphabet from 'a' (अ) to 'ha' (ह)

3. Dṛgdevī as the goddess embodying *jñāna* or knowledge.

Actually there is only one Śakti, viz., *Svātantrya śakti*, the Absolute Freedom of the Divine. The initial appearance of *svātantrya* is known as *Icchā-śakti* or the power of Will. Its final appearance is known as *Kriyā-śakti* or the power of action. Its expansion is known as *jñāna-śakti* or power of knowledge. As Spandaśakti refers to the *svātantrya* or Freedom of Śiva in the form of the expansion of the universe, she is referred to as *dṛgdevī*. Dṛk means insight, vision, divine vision. Here it means jñāna. By the rule of *Sandhi*, *dṛk* has become *dṛg*.

4. Spandasandoha is the earlier work of Kṣemarāja in which he has expounded only the first verse of Spandakārikā at great length.

## INTRODUCTORY

### TEXT

(TRADITION)

इह हि विश्वानुजिघृक्षापरपरमशिवावेशोन्मीलितमहिमा स्वप्नोपलब्धोपदेशः श्रीमान्वसुगुप्ताचार्यो महादेवपर्वताद्गुरवविच्छय्यैव महाशिलातलोल्लिखितान्यति-रहस्यानि शिवसूत्राण्यासाद्य प्रसन्नगम्भीरैरेकपञ्चाशता श्लोकैरागमानुभवोपपत्त्यै-कीकारं प्रदर्शयन्संगृहीतवान् ।

### TRANSLATION

In this world, the excessive greatness of Self was revealed (*unmīlitamahimā*) to the exalted preceptor Vasugupta by Śiva's inspiration who is intent on conferring His grace on all. He (Vasugupta) received instruction in dream and thus, in Mahādeva mountain, he obtained through divine will the most esoteric Śiva-sūtras which were engraved on the surface of the great rock. He, by demonstrating the agreement of revelation, experience and reasoning, put together the import of the sūtras in an abridged form by means of fifty-one verses which were deep in sense but were expressed in a lucid form.

(*Synopsis of the Book*)

### TEXT

तत्र १ पञ्चविंशत्या स्वरूपस्पन्दः, २ सप्तभिः सहजविद्योदयस्पन्दः, ३ एको-नविंशत्या विभूतिस्पन्द उक्तः,—इति त्रिनिःष्यन्दमिदं स्पन्दशास्त्रम् ।

### TRANSLATION

In this book, the first twentyfive verses describe the *spanda* or creative pulsation which is the essential nature of Śiva (*svarūpaspanda*), the next seven refer to the *spanda* pertaining to the emergence of *Sahaja-vidyā*, the last nineteen give a glimpse of the *spanda* pertaining to supernormal powers (*vibhūti*). Thus this *spanda-śāstra* is arranged in three sections.

(*Contents of the first Section*)

## TEXT

तत्र प्रथमनिःष्यन्देऽस्मिन् स्तुतिपूर्वं प्रकरणार्थः श्लोकेनोपक्षिप्तः । ततश्चतुर्भिः श्लोकैः सोपपत्तिकं स्पन्दतत्त्वं व्यवस्थापितम् । ततः श्लोकाभ्यां साभिज्ञानं तत्प्राप्तावुपाय उक्तः । श्लोकेनोपायविप्रतिपत्तिर्निरस्ता । श्लोकेनोपाय एवोपेयप्राप्त्यानुरूप्यकथनेनोपोद्बलितः । तत एकेन तदुपायलभ्यं यादृगुपेयस्य स्वरूपं तदुपदर्शितम् । ततस्तदवष्टम्भात्संसाराभावः श्लोकेनोक्तः । द्वयेनाभाववादिमतं व्युदस्यता तद्वैलक्षण्यं स्पन्दतत्त्वस्योक्तम् । श्लोकेन तदुल्लासितस्य कार्यस्य क्षयित्वेऽपि तदक्षयमित्याख्यातम् । एतदेव श्लोकाभ्यामुपपाद्याभाववाद एवोन्मूलितः । तत एकेन सुप्रबुद्धस्य सदैवैतत्प्राप्तिः, प्रबुद्धस्य तु पूर्वापरकोटयोरित्यावेदितम् । एकेन सुप्रबुद्धस्य प्रतीतेर्विषयविभाग उक्तः । ततोऽन्येन सुप्रबुद्धस्यावरणाभावे युक्तिरुपक्षिप्ता । श्लोकेनाप्रबुद्धस्य स्थगितस्वरूपतोक्ता । तत एकेन सुप्रबुद्धतालाभाय सततमुद्यन्तव्यमित्युक्तम् । श्लोकेन व्यवहारावस्था एव काश्चित्तदितरसकलवृत्तिक्षयरूपा उद्योगस्य विषयाः इत्यावेदितम् । ततोऽपि प्राप्तप्रबोधेन सुप्रबुद्धतायै योग्युचितसौषुप्ततमोवरणविदलने प्रजागरितव्यमित्युक्तं श्लोकत्रयेण, —इति 'यस्योन्मेष' इत्यादेः 'प्रबुद्धः स्यादनावृत' इत्यन्तस्य तात्पर्यम् । अथ ग्रन्थार्थो व्याख्यायते ।

## TRANSLATION

Now in the first section of the book, the first verse begins with the laudation of Śiva and suggests the main purport of the treatise. By the next four verses, the true nature of *spanda* is established with valid reasoning: next by two verses, the means for attaining it with proper recognition is described. The eighth verse refutes the objection raised against the means, the ninth one supports the means referred to by describing its perfect suitability for attaining the goal. The tenth verse shows the real nature of the goal which is attainable by that means. The eleventh verse says that by close adherence to that goal, the delusion of the world as a thing separate from Śiva ceases. The twelfth and thirteenth, by discarding the view of the Nihilists bring into prominence the striking difference of the *Spanda*-principle from their doctrine.

The fourteenth establishes the indestructibility of the *spanda* principle as such, though the world of objects brought about by it is subject to destruction. The fifteenth and sixteenth so thoroughly expound this idea that Nihilism stands completely eradicated. The seventeenth declares that while the fully awakened always has the realization of the *spanda*-principle, the partially awakened has it only in the initial and final stages (of waking, dream and dreamless sleep). The eighteenth describes the sphere of objects experienced by the fully awakened. Then the nineteenth hints at the means for the removal of the veils in the case of the fully awakened. The twentieth says how the real nature of Self is veiled in the case of the unawakened one. The twentyfirst exhorts that one should always exert oneself in acquiring the state of the fully awakened. The twenty-second declares that there are certain states of the individual in practical life which by bringing about the total cessation of all other states than that (*spanda*) provide the occasion for the realization of *Spanda*. The last three (23rd to 25th) verses urge that one who has experienced enlightenment in order to maintain the state of complete enlightenment, should be (always) on the alert in tearing asunder in a manner befitting a *yogī* the sleep-like veil of (spiritual) darkness. This is the sum and substance of the first section, beginning with 'Whose opening and shutting of the eyelids, and ending with, 'The awakened one is unveiled.'

Now the purport of the book is being expounded.

## TEXT

यस्योन्मेषनिमेषाभ्यां जगतः प्रलयोदयौ ।
तं शक्तिचक्रविभवप्रभवं शङ्करं स्तुमः ॥ १ ॥

Yasyonmeṣanimeṣâbhyām jagataḥ pralayodayau/
Taṃ Śakticakravibhavaprabhavaṃ Śaṅkaraṃ stumaḥ//1

## TRANSLATION OF THE TEXT

We laud that Śaṅkara by whose mere opening and shutting of the eye-lids there is the appearance and dissolution of the world and who is the source of the glorious powers of the collective whole of the *śaktis* (the divine energy in various forms).

# COMMENTARY

## TEXT

'शम्' उपशान्ताशेषोपतापपरमानन्दाद्वयमयस्वचैतन्यस्फारप्रत्यभिज्ञापनस्वरूपमनुग्रहं करोति यस्तमिमं स्वस्वभावं शङ्करं स्तुमस्तं विश्वोत्कर्षित्वेन परामृशन्तस्तत्क्लृप्तकल्पितप्रमातृपदनिमज्जनेन समाविशामः, तत्समावेश एव हि जीवन्मुक्तिफल इह प्रकरण उपदेश्यः। बहुवचनमनुग्रहदृष्टिकटाक्षिताशेषानुग्राह्याभेदप्रथनाय। तमित्यनेन यदस्य निःसामान्यत्वमपि ध्वनितं तत्प्रथयति यस्येत्यर्धेन। इह परमेश्वरः प्रकाशात्मा महादेवः शब्दराशिपरमार्थपूर्णाहन्तापरामर्शसारत्वात् सदैवानन्दघनस्फुरत्तात्मकोभयविसर्गारणिपराशक्त्यात्मकपूर्णस्वातन्त्र्यस्वरूपस्तत एव चित्स्वाभाव्यादचलस्यापि श्रीभगवतः स्वातन्त्र्यशक्तिरविभक्ताप्यशेषसर्गसंहारादिपरम्परां दर्पणनगरवत्स्वभित्तावेव भावियुक्त्यानधिकामप्यधिकामिव दर्शयन्ती किञ्चिच्चलत्तात्मकधात्वर्थानुगमात्स्पन्द इत्यभिहिता, तेन भगवान्सदा स्पन्दतत्त्वसतत्त्वो न त्वस्पन्दः। यदाहुः केचित् 'अस्पन्दं परं तत्त्वम्' इति। एवं हि शान्तस्वरूपत्वादनीश्वरमेवैतद्भवेत्। स्फुरत्तासारस्पन्दशक्तिमयशङ्करात्मकस्वस्वभावप्रतिपादनायैव चेदं शास्त्रं समुचितस्पन्दाभिधानं महागुरुभिर्निबद्धम्। एतच्च व्यक्तीभविष्यति। सा चैषा स्पन्दशक्तिर्गर्भीकृतानन्तसर्गसंहारैकघनाहन्ता चमत्कारानन्दरूपा निःशेषशुद्धाशुद्धरूपा मातृमेयसंकोचविकासाभासनसतत्त्वा सर्वोपनिषदुपास्या युगपदेवोन्मेषनिमेषमयी। तथा हि—शिवादेः क्षित्यन्तस्याशेषस्य तत्त्वग्रामस्य प्राक्सृष्टस्य संहर्तृरूपा या निमेषभूरसावेवोद्भविष्यद्दशापेक्षया स्रष्टृरूपोन्मेषभूमिस्तथा विश्वनिमेषभूश्चिद्घनतोन्मेषसारा चिद्घनतानिमज्जनभूमिरपि विश्वोन्मेषरूपा। यदागमः

'लेलिहाना सदा देवी सदा पूर्णा च भासते।
ऊर्मिरेषा विबोधाब्धेः शक्तिरिच्छात्मिका प्रभोः॥'

इति। श्रीमान्महेश्वरो हि स्वातन्त्र्यशक्त्या शिवमन्त्रमहेश्वरमन्त्रेश्वरमन्त्रविज्ञानाकलप्रलयाकलसकलान्तां प्रमातृभूमिकां तद्वेद्यभूमिकां च गृह्णानः पूर्वपूर्वरूपतां भित्तिभूततया स्थितामप्यन्तःस्वरूपावच्छादनक्रीडया निमेषयन्नेवोन्मेषयति उत्तरोत्तररूपतामवरोहक्रमेण, आरोहक्रमेण तूत्तरोत्तररूपतां निमेषयन्नेव ज्ञानयोगिनामुन्मेषयति पूर्वपूर्वरूपतामत एवोत्तरमुत्तरं पूर्वत्र पूर्वत्र संकोचात्मतां जहद्विकसितत्वेनासावाभासयति, पूर्वं पूर्वं तु रूपं यथोत्तरं विकसिततां निमज्जयन् सङ्कुचितत्वेन दर्शयति। एवं च सर्वं सर्वमयमेव प्रथयति, केवलं तदवभासितसंकोचमात्रत इयं भेदप्रतिपत्तिरिव यदुद्दलनायेहत्य उपदेश इत्यास्तां तावदेतत्। नीलसुखाद्याभासोन्मेषमय्यपि च संवित् प्रमात्रेकात्मकतत्स्वरूपनिमेषरूपावभात-

चरपीताद्याभासोपसंहाररूपा चेति स्वसंवेदनसिद्धामिमां युगपदेवोन्मेषनिमेषोभयरूपां प्रतिभां भगवतीं विचिन्वन्तु महाधियः संसारविच्छेदाय । अत एवोन्मेषनिमेषाभ्यामित्येतत्पदं निजवृत्तौ भट्टश्रीकल्लटेन 'सङ्कल्पमात्रेण' इत्यविभक्तमेवेच्छाशक्तिरूपतया व्याख्यायि । [1]'संग्रहकृतापि

एकचिन्ताप्रसक्तस्य यतः स्यादपरोदयः ।
उन्मेषः स तु विज्ञेयः स्वयं तमुपलक्षयेत् ॥' (३।९)

इत्यत्र प्रारब्धचिन्तासंहरणमेव परस्वरूपोदयहेतुरुन्मेष इत्यभिधास्यते। प्रवृत्तचिन्तासंहारं विना परस्वरूपोदयाभावात् । एतच्च तत्रैव वितनिष्यामः ।

'परामृतरसापायस्तस्य यः प्रत्ययोद्भवः ।
तेनास्वतन्त्रतामेति स च तन्मात्रगोचरः ॥' (३।१४)

इत्यत्राप्युदयः प्रलयपरमार्थ इति स्पष्टमेव वक्ष्यते ।

'यदा क्षोभः प्रलीयेत तदा स्यात्परमं पदम् ।' (१।९)

इत्यत्रापि क्षोभप्रलयात्मा निमेषः परपदोन्मेषरूप इत्यपि निरूपयिष्यते । तदेवमेकैवोभयरूपापि शक्तिः कदाचिदुन्मेषप्रधानतया व्यवह्रियते, कदाचिन्निमेषप्रधानतया । ततश्च यस्य सम्बन्धिन्याः स्वरूपनिमेषात्मनः कार्योन्मेषप्रधानायाः शक्तेर्हेतोर्जगतो विश्वस्य शिवादेर्धरण्यन्तस्योदयोऽभेदसारतानिमज्जनसतत्त्वो नानावैचित्र्यशाली भेदरूपः सर्गः स्वरूपोन्मेषात्मनश्च बाह्यतानिमेषप्रधानायाः शक्तेर्जगतः प्रलयोऽभेदमयतोदयात्मा विचित्रभेदरूपतासंहार इति प्रलयोऽप्युदयरूप उदयोऽपि च प्रलयरूप इति व्याख्येयम् । वस्तुतस्तु न किञ्चिदुदेति व्ययते वा, केवलं स्पन्दशक्तिरेव भगवत्यक्रमापि तथातथाभासरूपतया स्फुरन्त्युदेतीव व्ययत इव चेति दर्शयिष्यामः। स्थितिविलयानुग्रहाणां विशिष्टप्रलयोदयरूपत्वान्नाधिक्यमिति प्रलयोदयाभ्यामेव पञ्चविधं पारमेश्वर्यं कृत्यं संगृहीतम् । निर्णीतं चैवंप्रायं[2] मयैव प्रथमसूत्रमात्रविवरणे स्पन्दसंदोहे। ननु श्रीमन्महार्थदृष्ट्या सृष्ट्यादिदेवताभिरेव विचित्रा जगतः प्रलयोदयाः संपाद्यन्ते तत्कथमेतदुक्तं यस्येत्यादि, इत्याशङ्क्याह—तं शक्तिचक्रविभवप्रभवमिति। शक्तीनां सृष्टिरक्तादिमरीचिदेवीनां चक्रं द्वादशात्मा समूहस्तस्य यो विभव उद्योगावभासनचर्वणविलापनात्मा क्रीडाडम्बरस्तस्य प्रभवं हेतुम् । एता हि देव्यः श्रीमन्मन्थानभैरवं चक्रेश्वरमालिङ्ग्य सर्वदैव जगत्सर्गादिक्रीडां संपादयन्तीत्याम्नायः। अथ च कस्मात्परमेश्वरस्य जगत्सर्गसंहारादिहेतुत्वमित्याशङ्कायामेतदेवोत्तरं[3] शक्तिचक्रेति। यावद्धि किञ्चिद्विश्वं संभवति तत्प्रकाशमानत्वेन प्रकाशमयत्वात् ।

१. ग० पु० ग्रन्थकृतेति पाठः ।
२. ग० पु० एवं प्रागिति पाठः । ३. ग० पु० इदमिति पाठः ।

स्वामिनश्चात्मसंस्थस्य भावजातस्य भासनम् ।
अस्त्येव न विना तस्मादिच्छामर्शः प्रवर्तते ॥' (ई०प्र०१।५।१०)

**इति विपश्चिन्निश्चितनीत्या परमेश्वरस्यान्तःप्रकाशैकात्म्येन प्रकाशमानं स्थितं सच्छक्तिचक्रमित्युच्यते यतः परमेश्वरस्यागमेष्वनन्तशक्तित्वमुद्घोष्यते, तस्य शक्तिचक्रस्याभासपरमार्थस्य विश्वस्य यो विभवः परस्परसंयोजनावियोजनावैचित्र्यमनन्तप्रकारं तस्य प्रभवं कारणम् । स एव हि भगवान्विज्ञानदेहात्मकान्स्वात्मैकात्म्येन स्थितान्विश्वानाभासानन्योन्यं नानावैचित्र्येण संयोजयन्वियोजयंश्च विश्वोदयप्रलयहेतुः । तदुक्तं[1] श्रीभट्टकल्लटेन ।**

'विज्ञानदेहात्मकस्य शक्तिचक्रैश्वर्यस्योत्पत्तिहेतुत्वम् ।'

**इत्येतद्वृत्त्यक्षराणामत्र व्याख्याद्वयेऽप्य नुरूप्यम् । अपि च**

'शक्तयोऽस्य जगत्कृत्स्नम् ।'

**इत्यागमदृष्ट्या**

'तस्माच्छब्दार्थचिन्तासु न सावस्था न या शिवः ।' (२–४)

**इतीहत्यस्थित्या च जगदात्मनः**

'तत्खेचर्यूर्ध्वमार्गस्थं व्योम वामेशीगोचरम् ।'

**इति रहस्यनीत्या च वामेश्वरीखेचरीगोचरीदिक्चरीभूचरीरूपस्य मयैव स्पन्दसन्दोहे सम्यङ्निर्णीतस्य**

'अप्रबुद्धधियस्त्वेते स्वस्थितिस्थगनोद्यताः ।' (१।२०)

**इत्यत्रहि निर्णेष्यमाणस्यैतद् व्याख्याद्वयव्याख्यातशक्तिचक्रप्रपञ्चभूतस्य च**

'यतः करणवर्गोऽयं············।' (१।६)

**इति स्थित्येन्द्रियग्रामात्मनः**

**'तदाक्रम्य बलं मन्त्राः·······।'** (२।१)

**इति नित्यमन्त्रात्मनः**

'शब्दराशिसमुत्थस्य शक्तिवर्गस्य·······।' (३।१३)

**इति नीत्या[2] ब्राह्म्याविदेवतास्वभावस्यैवमादेरनन्तप्रकारस्यापि[3] मयैव स्पन्दसन्दोहे वितत्य निर्णीतस्य शक्तिचक्रस्य यो विभवो माहात्म्यं तत्र प्रभवतीति प्रभवं स्वतन्त्रं न तु पशुवत्परतन्त्रम् । शक्तिचक्रस्य [4]रश्मिपुञ्जस्य यो विभवोऽन्तर्मुखो विकासस्ततः प्रभव उदयोऽभिव्यक्तिर्यस्येति बहुव्रीहिणाऽन्तर्मुखतत्स्वरूपनिभालनाद्यत्नेन परमेश्वरस्वरूपप्रत्यभिज्ञानं भवतीत्यर्थः । किञ्च यस्य चिदानन्दघनस्यात्मन उन्मेषनिमेषाभ्यां स्वरूपोन्मीलननिमीलनाभ्यां 'यदन्तस्तद्बहिः' इति युक्त्या जगतः शरीररूपस्य तदनुषङ्गेण बाह्यस्यापि विश्वस्य प्रलयोदयौ**

१. ग० पु० तदेतदिति पाठः । २. ग० पु० दृष्टचेति पाठः ।
३. ग० पु० अन्येति पाठः । ४. ग० पु० स्वरश्मिचक्रस्येति पाठः ।

यथासंख्यं मज्जनोन्मज्जने भवतस्तं शक्तिचक्रविभवस्य परसंविद्देवतास्फारस्य प्रभवं भक्तिभाजामेतत्स्वरूपप्रकाशकं शङ्करं स्तुमः। तथा यस्य स्वात्मनः सम्बन्धिनो बहिर्मुखताप्रसररूपादुन्मेषाज्जगत उदयोऽन्तर्मुखतारूपाच्च निमेषात्प्रलयस्तं विश्वसर्गादिकार्युन्मेषादिस्वरूपसंविद्देवीमाहात्म्यस्य हेतुं शङ्करं स्तुम इति यथासम्भवमपि योज्यम् । देहाद्याविष्टोऽपि परमेश्वरः करणोन्मीलननिमीलनाभ्यां रूपादिपञ्चकमयस्य जगतः सर्गसंहारौ करोति । यदुक्तं रहस्यतत्त्वविदा

'तदेवं व्यवहारेऽपि प्रभुर्देहादिमाविशन् ।
भान्तमेवान्तरर्थौघमिच्छया भासयेद्बहिः ॥' (ई० प्र० १।६।७)

इति । एवंविधार्थपरिग्रहायापि 'यस्य स्वातन्त्र्यशक्त्या' इति त्यक्त्वा 'यस्योन्मेषनिमेषाभ्याम्' इति न्यरूपि गुरुणा । अत्र च शङ्करस्तुतिः समावेशरूपा प्राप्यत्वेनाभिधेया, शक्तिचक्रविभवात्प्रभवो यस्येति बहुव्रीहिणा शक्तिचक्रविकासस्तत्प्राप्तावुपाय उक्तः, शक्तिचक्रविभवस्य परसंविद्देवतास्फारस्य भक्तिभाजां प्रभवं प्रकाशकमिति तत्पुरुषेण फलमुक्तम् । यद्वक्ष्यति

'ततश्चक्रेश्वरो भवेत् ।' (३।१९)

इत्यभिधेयोपाययोरुपायोपेयभावः सम्बन्ध इत्यभिधेयोपायसम्बन्धप्रयोजनान्यनेनैव सूत्रेण सूत्रितानि ॥१॥

## TRANSLATION

Śaṃkara is one who does *śaṃ* (*śaṃ karoti iti śaṃkaraḥ*). By *śam* is meant the grace (*anugraha*) which consists in enabling the aspirant to recognize the vast expanse of His (Śiva's) Consciousness (*sva-caitanya-sphāra*) (which, in essence, is one's own consciousness) which is non-dualistic and is the Highest Bliss inasmuch as it calms the heat of all the afflictions (of the aspirant). Such Śaṃkara who is our own essential nature do we laud. Here the sense of lauding is that by considering Him as excelling the entire cosmos we enter into His being by obliterating the state of assumed agency. (*kalpita-pramātṛ-pada*) brought about by Himself (*tatklṛpta*). This treatise is going to teach that entrance in Him i.e. identification with Him is the (real) reward of liberation in life, (*jivan-mukti*). The plural in *stumaḥ* (we laud) is meant to convey the idea of our identity with all those who are worthy of His grace and who are regarded by Him with favourable glance.

The word 'tam' (Him) fully establishes His uniqueness which is suggested by the first half of the verse, viz., 'By whose mere opening of the eye-lids, etc'.

Now the great lord who is the great God of the nature of Light, has absolute Freedom (*svātantrya*), of the nature of *Parāśakti* (the Highest Power) that displays Herself in the two poles of *araṇi* (I) and *visarga* (creation or *idam* i.e. the objective world) and is always full of the flash of a compact mass of bliss and whose essence consists in Full I-consciousness which is the supreme import of the multitude of letters.[1]

Therefore the *Svātantrya Śakti* (the Power of Absolute Freedom) of the Lord is called *spanda*. This power though non-distinct from the Lord goes on presenting the entire cycle of manifestation and withdrawal on its own background like the reflection of a city in a mirror. It will be shown by apt arguments further (in the book) that though she is not anything extra (*anadhikamapi*) she goes on showing herself as if supernumerary (*adhikamiva*). This śakti of the lord who is non-moving, being of the nature of consciousness (*Citsvābhāvyād acalasyāpi bhagavataḥ*) is known as *spanda* in accordance with the rootmeaning of the word signifying slight movement (*kiñcit calattā*)[2]. Thus the essential nature of the Lord is perpetual *spanda* (creative pulsation). He is never without *spanda*. Some[3] hold that the Highest Reality is without any activity whatsoever. But in such a case the Highest Reality being devoid of activity, all this (i.e. the universe) will be without a lord or Creative Power. The great teacher has written this *śāstra* (sacred book) in order to explain the fact that our nature is identical with that of *Śaṅkara* who is full of *spanda śakti*, the essence of which consists in quivering light. Thus this *śāstra* has been appropriately named *spanda*.

This will be made clear later.

This *spanda-śakti* consists of the compact bliss of I-consciousness which holds in its bosom endless cycles of creation and dissolution, which is of the nature of the entire world of the pure and the impure, which is of the nature of exhibiting limitation and expansion of Subjects and Objects, which is worthy of adoration of all esoteric knowledge, which is simultaneously of the nature of emanation and absorption.

The same principle constitutes the stage of absorption (*nimeṣa*)[4] from the point of view of the withdrawal of the previously manifested aggregate of categories from Śiva down to the earth and from the point of view of those that are about to come into being, it is, in its aspect of manifestation, the stage of appearance or expansion (*unmeṣa*). Thus the stage of the submergence (*nimeṣa*) of the universe constitutes the emergence (*unmeṣa*) of the compactness of consciousness, so also the stage of the submergence of the compactness of consciousness constitutes the stage of the emergence of the universe. As the traditional scripture puts it.

"The goddess (i.e., the creative power) is always engaged in exercising her energy in manifestation (lit., in enjoying the taste of manifestation), and yet always appears as replete (i.e. her energy is never depleted). She is the wave of the ocean of consciousness, the volitional power of the LORD."

The glorious great Lord by His power of absolute Freedom assuming the Subjective roles of Śiva, Mantramaheśvara, Mantreśvara, Mantra, Vijñānakala, Pralayākala, and Sakala and the the role of sphere of objects appropriate for each subject, in the process of gradual descent, displays by way of the play of concealing His inner nature, the succeeding aspects by suppressing the preceding ones, though they serve as the substratum for the succeeding aspects. In the gradual process of ascent He displays the preceding aspects by eliminating the succeeding ones in the case of *Jñāna-yogīs* (the gnostic *yogīs*). Thus He shows the succeeding ones in a developed form in the preceding[6] ones by making them give up their limitation, and the preceding ones in a limited form by suppressing their higher state (in the order of descent). So He shows everything as of the nature of everything else. The usual perception of difference is due only to limitation caused to appear by Him. The teaching of this *śāstra* is meant to destroy this perception of difference. Enough of this expatiation.

The goddess Consciousness is simultaneously of the nature of display (*unmeṣa*) and suppression (*nimeṣa*). Even while she displays external perception like blue or internal perception like pleasure, she suppresses the (real) nature of her identity with the perceiver and also brings about the suppression of yellow etc. which was previously perceived. In order to put an end to transmigratory existence, let people of great intelligence closely understand the goddess Consciousness (*pratibhā*)[5] who is simultaneously of the nature of both revelation (*unmeṣa*) and concealment (*nimeṣa*) as is evident from one's own experience. That is why the exalted Kallaṭa in his gloss explained *unmeṣa* and *nimeṣa* together (not separately) by one word, viz., "by the power of mere will."

The writer[6] who prepared this conspectus also says in the following verse that the cessation of the previous idea which is the cause of the rise of the next is said to be *unmeṣa*, for without the cessation of the previous idea, the rise of the next one is impossible.

"That is to be known as *Unmeṣa* whence another thought arises in one who is already occupied with one thought. One can observe this for oneself. This will be explained at length in its proper place.

In the following verse also, the real implication of the rise of thought-constructs is the simultaneous disappearance of the bliss of immortality. This will be elucidated later. "Of the limited empirical being, the rise of the empirical thought-constructs (*pratyayodbhavaḥ*) betokens at the same time the disappearance of the bliss of Supreme immortality. By that i.e. the rise of empirical thought-constructs), the empirical being loses his independence. The rise of the empirical concepts brings about only the experience of the sphere of the *tanmātras* (i.e. of sound, form and colour, taste, smell and touch)."

In the following line also,

"When the agitation ceases, then is the highest state experienced," it will be clarified that *nimeṣa* (disappearance) in the form of the cessation of agitation implies at the same time *unmeṣa* (appearance) of the Supreme state.

Hence the same Power which is of double aspect is sometimes employed predominantly in the aspect of *unmeṣa* (appearance) and sometimes predominantly in the aspect of *nimeṣa* (disappearance).

Thus the first half of the verse should be interpreted in the following manner.

"Whose Śakti (divine power) predominant in displaying creation, *kāryonmeṣa-pradhānāyāḥ*) instinct with the concealment (*nimeṣa*) of His (*Śiva's*) essential nature, (*svarūpanimeṣātmanaḥ*) is the cause of the manifestation of the universe i.e. the manifestation from Śiva down to earth consisting of diversity which has a wealth of manifold distinctions and which submerges the essential unity (of the Divine). The same *Śakti* (divine power), predominant in submerging externality (*bāhyatānimeṣapradhānāyāḥ*) and instinct with the revelation (*unmeṣa*) of His (*Śiva*'s) essential nature brings about the dissolution of the universe which consists in the emergence of unity and submergence of multi-faceted diversity'. Thus the interpretation of the text should point out the fact that submergence (from one point of view) is also emergence (from another point of view), and similarly emergence (from one point of view) is also submergence (from another point of view). In reality, however, nothing arises and nothing subsides. We shall show that it is only the divine *spandaśakti* (the divine creative pulsation) which, though free of succession, appears in different aspects as if flashing in view and as if subsiding. *Sthiti* (maintenance of the world-process) *Vilaya* (concealment of the essential nature) and *amugraha* (grace) are not anything other than particular forms of absorption and manifestation, therefore the five -fold divine acts have been included only in *pralaya* (absorption) and *udaya* (manifestation). This point has been conclusively discussed by me in this very way in my gloss on the first *sūtra* only in Spanda-sandoha.

An objection may be raised here. "From the point of view of *Mahānaya Śāstra*[7] the different acts of absorption and manifestation of the universe are brought about by the goddesses *Sṛṣṭi* etc., then how is it that in this text it has been said (in singular number) He whose etc.? In order to clear this doubt, the verse says, "Him who is the source of the glorious powers of the group of the *śaktis*."

(*First interpretation of Śakticakra—vibhava-prabhava*)

By *śakti-cakra* is meant the aggregate of twelve[8] divinities such as *Sṛṣṭi*, *Rakta*, etc. By its *vibhava* is meant the play of that aggregate in the form of creative activity (*udyoga*), maintenance (*avabhāsana*), absorption (*carvaṇa*), and assumption of indefinable state (*anākhyā*), by *prabhava* is meant cause. So the whole phrase *Śakti-cakra-Vibhava-prabhavam* means the cause of the creative activity, etc. of the twelve divinities, such as *Sṛṣṭi*, *Rakta*, etc.

These divinities embracing the exalted Manthān-Bhairava[9] who is the lord of the aggregate (of these divinities) bring about the play of the manifestation etc. of the universe. This is what the sacred tradition (*āmnāya*) says.

A doubt may arise viz.,

Wherefore does the Lord become the cause of the manifestation, withdrawal etc. of the universe? Its solution is contained in the following(Second interpretation of *Śakti-cakra-vibhava-prabhavaṃ*)

The objective world exists only as being manifest (*prakāśamānatvena*) and being manifest means that it is of the nature of *prakāśa* or Light which is Consciousness. It has been said by the wise (Utpaladeva): "The entire gamut of entities appears (outside), because it already exists in the Lord's Self. Without its existing in Him there would be no desire for manifestation." (I.P.V I.5. 10). *Śakti-cakra* is described as the aggregate of powers, because it (already) exists as identical with the internal Light of the Supreme. It is because of this that in the revealed Scriptures it is proclaimed that the Supreme has infinite powers, *Prabhava* means cause, *Vibhava* means the infinite variety of junction and disjunction of the group of *Śaktis* whose highest *raison d'etre* consists in manifestation. So, *Śakti-cakra-vibhava-prabhavam* means the cause of the infinite variety of junction and disjunction of the aggregate of powers (*Śaktis*) Thus the Lord by mutually joining and disjoining in various ways all the objective phenomena which are of the nature of consciousness and exist in Him as identical with Him is the cause of the manifestation and absorption of the universe. The same thing has been said by exalted, Kallaṭa.

"(Who is) the cause of the appearance of the glorious powers of the aggregate of the *śaktis* which powers are of the nature of consciousness,". The two interpretations given by me are in conformity with the wording of his gloss.

*(Third interpretation of Śakti-cakra)*

Also according to the standpoint of revealed traditional scripture (*āgama dṛṣṭyā*) which avers "His powers constitute the whole world, "and also from the standpoint of this book itself (*ihatya sthityā*) which maintains that" whether in matter of word, or object or thought, there is no state which is not Śiva," the group of *śaktis* represents the world.

(*Fourth interpretation of Śakti Cakra*)

According to the esoteric teaching, viz., "The void that exists in the upper course of *khecarī* is the sphere of *Vāmeśī*," the phrase also implies the group of such *śaktis* as *Vāmeśvarī*,[10] *Khecarī*, *Gocarī*, *Dikcarī* and *Bhūcarī* which has been thoroughly explained by me in Spanda-sandoha, and which will be decisively pointed out in this book also in such a statement as, "They are intent on concealing their real nature to unawakened beings."

So as described in these two explanations, '*Śakti-cakra*' here means the group of manifold *śaktis* (*Śakti-cakra-prapañca-bhūta*).

(*Fifth interpretation of Śakti-Cakra*)

According to 'whence the group of senses', Śakti means 'the multitude of senses.'

(*Sixth interpretation*)

According to 'Relying on that strength, the *mantras*', *śakti* means 'the eternal *mantras*[11] (*nitya mantra*)'

(*Seventh interpretation*)

According to 'of the group of powers arising from the multitude of words', *śakti* stands for the 'nature of the deities like Brâhmī[12] etc.'

In these ways, I have given in detail many decisive interpretations of *Śakti cakra* in *Spanda-Sandoha*. The word *prabhava* means 'one who is Free' (in accordance with the root-meaning *prabhavati* i.e, one who prevails, one who is powerful), and not dependent on others like the animals.

(*Another interpretation of Śakti-cakra-vibhava-prabhava*):

This may be interpreted as a *Bahuvrīhi* compound, meaning 'One whose *prabhava* i.e. *udaya* or appearance or manifestation (*abhivyakti*) comes about from the *vibhava* i.e. the inner unfoldment of the mass of light i,e, the divinities of the senses (*raśmi-puñja*[13]) (i.e. *Śaṅkara* who is manifested by an inner development of the senses). The sense is that the recognition of the highest Lord is brought about effortlessly by the practice of perception of the inner nature.

(*Another interpretation of the whole verse*):

Moreover, we laud that *Śaṅkara* who is a mass of consciousness identical with the Self) *cidānandaghanasyātmanaḥ*) and by whose opening of the eye lids and closing them i.e. by whose revelation and veiling of His essential nature there ensue according to the view that what is within is also without the disappearance and appearance, in other words the sub mergence and emergence successively (*yathāsaṅkhyam*) of the world i.e. the body and through its association of the external universe also, and who to His devotee), is the revealer (*prabhava-prakāśaka*) of the nature (*etat svarūpa*) of the *Śakticakravibhava* i.e. of the glory of the greatness of the divinity in the form of the highest consciousness.

So far as possible the verse may be construed in this way also. We laud *Śaṅkara* who is the cause of the greatness of goddess Consciousness identical with *unmeṣa* and *nimeṣa* in bringing about the manifestation etc. of the universe, that *Śaṅkara* who is the Self, and by whose *unmeṣa* i.e. expansion in the form of externality there is the manifestation of the world, and by whose *nimeṣa* i.e. withdrawal in the form of internality, there is the disappearance of the world. The Highest Lord even by entering the body etc. brings about the manifestation and disappearance of the world by the opening and closing of the senses. This has been described in the following lines by Utpaladeva who knew the essence of the esoteric doctrine.

"Therefore, even in practical life, the Lord, because of His free will in the form of *Māyā Śakti* enters the body, and by His will manifests externally the multitude of objects which shine within Him." (I,P.I,6,7)

In order that people may take the sense (of the verse) in the above way, the teacher has rejected the use of "By whose power of Absolute Freedom," and adopted that of "By whose revelation and veiling."

Herein the laudation of *Śaṅkara* implies *samāveśa* or penetration in Him. As this is what is to be obtained, it is both the subject-matter and the goal. By taking the phrase *Śakti-cakra-vibhava-prabhavam* as a *Bahuvrīhi* compound and interpreting it in the sense "Whose manifestation is due to the inner unfoldment of the group of śaktis", the unfoldment of the group of *śaktis* has been said to be the means for the attainment of the goal. By taking the same phrase as a *Tatpuruṣa* compound and interpreting it as "the revealer of the glory of the goddess of the Highest Consciousness" to the devotees, the fruit has been referred to. As the author[14] (of the book) will say (later). "Then he will become the lord of the group of *śaktis*". Hence the connexion of the subject-matter (of the book) and the means (*upāya*) is that of the end (*upeya*) and means (*upāya*). Thus this *Sūtra* (*Kārikā*) gives briefly the subject-matter, the means, the connexion of the two and the fruit of the study of this subject."

## *NOTES*

1. 'Aham' which in Sanskrit is the word for 'I' consists of all the letters of the Sanskrit alphabet from 'a' to 'ha'.

2. The root-meaning of the word 'spanda' is 'having slight movement.' The Lord is *acala*, non-moving. Therefore, movement cannot be ascribed to Him. The word 'spanda' in the case of the Lord i.e. Śiva has to be taken in a figurative sense of creative pulsation, divine activity, throbbing with life, dynamism.

3. The Vedantists who maintain that Brahman is sheer calm Consciousness without any activity.

4. The teacher referred to is Vasugupta who, according to Kṣemarāja, composed the Spandakārikā.

5. 'Pratibhā' is *parā saṁvit*, the highest Divine Consciousness which holds within itself all sound, letters, etc. and the endless variety of subject and object as identical with itself.

6. This refers to Vasugupta

7. 'Mahārtha' which is also known as 'Mahānaya' system refers to the Krama school which arose in Kashmir towards the close of the 7th and beginning of the 8th century A.D.

8. These twelve divinities or *Kālīs* are a special feature of the 'Mahārtha or 'Krama' system. They are:

(i) Sṛṣṭi: when the will to create or manifest arises in *Kālī* and the would-be creation shines in outline in her, she is known as *Sṛṣṭi Kālī*. This is the conception of creative power in relation to the object (*prameya*).

(ii) *Rakta Kālī* is the conception of the power of maintenance (*sthiti*) of the objective world through the five senses.

(iii) *Sthitināśa Kālī*. This is the conception of the power of *saṃhāra* or withdrawal of the objective world i.e. when her extrovert form is terminated and she rests within herself.

(iv) *Yama Kālī* manifests herself as beyond the extrovert and the introvert aspect. She represents the *anākhyā* or indefinable power in relation to objective experience.

The first four represent the four powers (*sṛṣṭi*, *sthiti*, *saṃhāra* and *anākhyā*) in relation to object (*prameya*).

(v) *Saṃhāra Kālī*. When *Parāsaṃvid* brings about the disappearance of the externality of objects as related to *pramāṇas* or means of knowledge and grasps them within as identical with herself, she is known as *Saṃhāra kālī*. This is *sṛṣṭi* in the stage of *pramāṇa*. In the stage of *Śthitināśakālī*, the experience is "I have known the object." In the stage of *Saṃhārakālī*, the experience is, "The object is non-different from me."

(vi) *Mṛtyukālī* engulfs even the *Saṃhāra Kālī*; she swallows up even the residual traces of the idea of the withdrawal of the objective world. This is *sthiti* in the stage of *pramāṇa*.

(vii) *Bhadrakālī*. The letter *bha* in Bhadrakālī indicates *bhedana* or afflorescence of different objects and the letter *dra* indicates *drāvaṇa* or dissolving those different forms again in her essential nature. This is the aspect of *saṃhāra* in the stage of *pramāṇa*. She is also called *Rudrakālī*.

(viii) *Mārtaṇḍa Kālī*. *Mārtaṇḍa* means 'sun.' The group of twelve *indriyas* is referred to as 'sun' inasmuch as it illumines or brings to light the objects like the 'sun'. The twelve *indriyas* are the five senses of perception, the five organs of action, *manas* and *buddhi*. All the *indriyas* function only when related to *ahaṃkāra* or the 'ego feeling'. '*Mārtaṇḍa Kālī*' is so called because she brings about the dissolution of the twelve senses in the Ego-feeling. She represents the *anākhyā* power in relation to *pramāṇa*, because it brings the dissolution of the twelve senses in the ego-feeling to such an extent that they become un-namable.

The four stages 5 to 8 represent the four powers of *kālī* in relation to means of knowledge (*pramāṇa*).

The next four stages of *kālī* represent her four powers in relation to the limited Subject (*pramātā*).

(ix) Paramārkakālī. She represents her power of *sṛṣṭi* in relation to the limited subject. She brings about the emergence of the limited subject by merging *Ahaṃkāra*, the previously described ego-feeling in her creative power. It should be borne in mind that the limited subject in this context does not mean the common limited subject. This limited subject is one in whom the limitations of objects and senses have been obliterated but who still retains the limitation of *paśu* or *āṇava mala*.

(x) *Kālāgnirudrakālī*. When Parāsaṁvid brings about the identification of the limited subject with the Universal Self, she is known as *Kālāgnirudrakālī*. This *Kālī* represents the power of maintenance (*sthiti*) in relation to the limited subject as she makes the limited subject rest in the Universal Self.

She is called *Kālāgnirudrakālī*, because she dissolves the limited subject *Kālāgnirudra* in Her Universal self.

The experience at the level of *Kālāgnirudrakālī* is "I am all this". She is also known as Mahākālī, because she holds within Herself everything including Kāla or Time.

(xi) Mahākālakālī. She brings about the dissolution of the 'I' which is posited in opposition to this in the 'perfect I' which is free from all relation to objectivity. This represents the power of *saṃhāra* or withdrawal in relation to the limited subject.

(xii) *Mahābhairava-ghora-caṇḍakālī* or *Mahābhairavacaṇḍograghorakālī*.

This represents the state of *anākhyā* in relation to the limited subject. This refers to that state of *Parāsaṁvid* which transcends all description in words. Hence it is the stage of *anākhyā*. This is the *Akula* stage. In it the subject, the object, the means of knowledge and knowledge (*pramātā*, *pramāṇa* and *prameya*) are all dissolved in I-consciousness. This is also called *Parā* or the Highest, because all the previous states are Her manifestation.

As she dissolves all the states of *prameya* (object), *pramāṇa* (means of knowledge and knowledge), and *pramātā* (subject), she is called *Mahābhairava ghora-caṇḍakālī*. The word *caṇḍa* refers to the sphere of *prameya* (object), *ghora* implies *pramāṇa* (knowledge and means of knowledge), and *mahābhairava* suggests *pramātā* (subject).

9. *Manthāna Bhairava* is the ultimate resting place of all and is also called *Kuleśvara* by Maheśvarānanda.

10. *Vāmeśvarī* is the presiding deity of the whole group of these Śaktis, The word *vāma* is connected with the verb *vam* which means to spit out, emit, eject. The *Śakti* is called *Vāmeśvarī*, because she emits or projects the universe out of the Absolute. The word *vāma* also means left, reverse, contrary, opposite. This Śakti is called *Vāmeśvarī* also because while in the *Śiva*-state there is unity-consciousness, in the state of *saṃsāra*, the contrary or opposite condition happens, viz. there is difference-consciousness.

*Khecarī—Khecarī śaktis* are explained by Kṣemarāja in the following way in Spandasandoha (p. 20) *The bodhagagane caranti iti khecaryaḥ pramātṛbhūmisthitāḥ* Khecaris are those *śaktis* that move (*caranti*) in *Kha* i.e. consciousness (*bodhagagana*).

These reside in the *pramātā* or the subject, the experient. They lead those experients who have become purified to liberation, to the Divine, and bind those who are under the influence of Māyā.

*Gocarī*. The word *go* symbolizes *buddhi-ahaṃkāramanobhūmi* i.e. *antaḥkaraṇa*. *Antaḥkaraṇa* or the psychic apparatus is the sphere of *gocarī śaktis*.

*Dikcarī—Dikṣu diśāsu bāhyabhūmiṣu caranti iti dikcaryaḥ*. Those *śaktis* that function in *dik* or outer space are known as *dikcarī*. The external senses have to do with the consciousness of space. Hence they are the sphere of *dikcarī śaktis*.

*Bhūcari—Bhuḥ rūpādi pancātmakam meyapadaṃ tatra caranti iti bhūcaryah*. Those *śaktis* that have to do with the external objects, with the objective phenomena having colour, form, etc. are known as *bhūcarī*.

The empirical individual experients, their psychic apparatus. their organs of sense and action, and the objective world are the expressions of these *śaktis*.

11. *Nityamantra* or the eternal *mantra* is the *mantra* of *pūrṇāhantā*, the ever-present perfect I-consciousness of the Divine.

12. The presiding deities of the multitude of words are the following:

(1.) *Yogīśvarī* or *Mahālakṣmī* of *a-varga* i.e. of the class of vowels.

(2) *Brāhmī* of *ka-varga*, (3) *Maheśvarī* of *ca-varga*, (4) *Kaumārī* of *ṭa-varga*, (5) *Vaiṣṇavī* of *ta-varga*, (6) *vārāhī* of *pa-varga* (7) *Aindrī or Indrāṇī* of *ya-varga*, (8) *Cāmuṇḍā of śa-varga*.

13. *Raśmi-puñja*. 'Mass of light' here means the *Karaṇeśvarī devīs* i.e. the divinities of the senses. The senses when extroverted are known as *indriyas*, when introverted and resting in the self, they are known as *Karaṇeśvarī devīs*

14. This refers to Vasugupta who, according to Kṣemarāja, is the author of Spandakārikā.

## EXPOSITION

The Sanskrit words *unmeṣa* and *nimeṣa* are very rich in connotation. They cannot be expressed in one word in any other language. So they have been translated by different words in different contexts.

The first question to be considered is that this entire text of Spandakārikā is meant to prove that Śiva is changeless and one. How then two aspects of His, viz. unmeṣa and nimeṣa (appearance-disappearance, manifestation-absorption) which are mutually contradictory have been mentioned in the first verse?

The answer is that it is only Svātantrya—Freedom or Icchā Will i.e. of Śiva which brings about both manifestation and absorption. *Unmeṣa* and *nimeṣa* denote succession. Succession means Time, but Śiva is above Time. Therefore, *unmeṣa* and *nimeṣa* have not to be taken in the order of succession. They are simply two expressions of Icchā śakti of the Divine. In Spandasandoha, Kṣemarāja says that there are many names of this *Icchā Śakti* (power of will) in this system. *Spanda*, *sphurattā Ūrmi*, *Bala*, *Udyoga*, *Hṛdaya*, *sāra*, *Mālinī*, *Parā* etc. are synonyms of this *Icchā śakti*. In Spanda-nirṇaya also he says : It is only *spanda-śakti* which is simultaneously *unmeṣa* and *nimeṣa*.

Both *unmeṣa* and *nimeṣa*, i.e. manifestation and absorption simultaneously denote the *Icchā* of the Divine. They are not two mutually opposed principles. What from one point of view is *nimeṣa* is at the same time *unmeṣa* from another point of view. For instance, the disappearance (*nimeṣa*) of the world i.e. the disappearance of the idea that the world is something different *toto caelo* from *Śiva* set over against Him as another constitutes at the same time the *unmeṣa* or appearance of the essential nature of *Śiva*. Similarly, the *nimeṣa* or the concealment of the essential nature of *Śiva* is at the time the *unmeṣa* or appearance of the world as something different from *Śiva*. Kṣemarāja gives many examples in his commentary to show that what is *unmeṣa* from one point of view is simultaneously (*yugapat*) *nimeṣa* from another point of view and vice versa. He concludes by saying:

वस्तुतस्तु न किञ्चदुदेति व्ययते वा केवलं स्पन्दशक्तिरेव भगवत्यक्रमापि तथा तथा भासरूपतया स्फुरन्त्युदेतीव व्ययत इव च ।

"In reality nothing arises, and nothing subsides, only the divine *Spanda-śakti* which, though free of succession, appears in different aspects as if arising, and as if subsiding."

Kṣemarāja has pointed out that *nimeṣa* and *unmeṣa* refer to another significant concept of Śaiva philosophy. This is a philosophy of Evolution. Evolution has two aspects—the arc of descent or *avarohakrama* (*nimeṣa*) from the Divine upto the empirical individual, from Consciousness upto the matter and the arc of ascent or *āroha-krama* (*unmeṣa*) from the empirical individual upto Śiva-pramātā and from inconscient matter upto *saṁvid* or the divine consciousness. The purpose of all the scriptures including Spandakārikā is to show how the empirical individual can mount to the stage of *Śiva-pramātā*. Śiva-consciousness is the *upeya* or the goal, the methods recommended in the book are the means (*upāyas*) for reaching the goal (*upeya*).

Kṣemarāja has given many interpretations of *Śakti-cakra-vibhava-prabhava* from various points of view in his commentary which should be carefully studied.

Both Rāmakaṇṭha and Utpala Bhaṭṭa warn that *pralaya* and *udaya* are not to be taken as corresponding to *unmeṣa* and *nimeṣa* exactly in the order in which they are given in the text but rather in a different order i.e. *udaya* with *unmeṣa*, and *pralaya* with *nimeṣa*. "When there is the *unmeṣa* i.e. *aunmukhya* or inclination towards manifestation, there is the *udaya* or emergence of the world. When there is *nimeṣa* or retraction of that inclination, there is submergence of the world."

Kṣemarāja takes *pralaya* and *udaya* both ways i.e. in a different order (*bhinnakrama*) as advocated by Rāmakaṇṭha and Utpalabhaṭṭa, and also in the order as they appear in the text.

When taken in a different order, the meaning would be as given above. When taken in the order in which they appear in the text, the meaning would be as given below:

"When there is *unmeṣa* or revelation of the essential nature of the Divine, there is the *pralaya* or disappearance of the world. When there is *nimeṣa* or concealment of the essential nature of the Divine, there is the *udaya* or appearance of the world."

Both these interpretations are correct. In the first interpretation, the words *unmeṣa* and *nimeṣa* are construed with reference to *Śakti* of *Śiva*. In the second interpretation, they are construed with reference to the *svarūpa* or essential nature of *Śiva*.

The text is neither a book of poetry, nor of mere academic philosophy. It is philosophy for the practical purpose of sanctifying and divinising human nature. What then is the justification of *śaṅkaraṃ stumaḥ*—we laud Śaṅkara? All the commentators are unanimously of the view that *stumaḥ* here suggests *samāviśāmaḥ* i.e. 'we have to enter or identify ourselves with His essential nature'. As Kṣemarāja puts it beautifully *Kalpitapramātṛpada-nimajjanena samāviśāmaḥ, tatsamāveśa eva hi jīvanmuktiphala iha prakaraṇa upadeśyaḥ.* "We are united with Him by obliterating our state of assumed agency. This treatise is going to teach that identification with Him is the real reward of liberation in life."

*Introduction to the Second Verse*:

TEXT

नन्वेवंभूतशंकरस्वरूपसत्तायां किं प्रमाणं कुतश्चोपादानादिहेतुं विना जगदसौ जनयति, तस्यैवोपादानत्वे मृत्पिण्डस्येव घटेन जगता तिरोधानं क्रियेत, तिरोहिता-तिरोहिततायां च भगवतः स्वभावभेदः स्यात्, पुनरुन्मज्जने च हेतुश्चिन्त्यो, जगदुदये च द्वैतप्रसङ्ग इत्येताः शङ्का एकप्रहारेणापहर्तुमाह—

TRANSLATION

Here a doubt may be raised. What is the proof of the existence of such real nature as Śaṃkara? How can He create the world without any means such as material etc.? If He Himself is assumed to be the material cause, then His disappearance would be brought about by the world (after creation,) just as the disappearance of a lump of clay is brought about after the production of a jar.

If it be said that there can be both appearance and disappearance of the Lord, then this would give rise to difference in His nature, and also some cause has to be thought out for His re-emergence after disappearance, and on the creation of the world, there would be the contingency of duality. To remove all such doubts with one stroke, the author says:

### *Verse* 2

यत्र स्थितमिदं सर्वं कार्यं यस्माच्च निर्गतम् ।
तस्यानावृतरूपत्वान्न निरोधोऽस्ति कुत्रचित् ॥ २ ॥

Yatra sthitam idaṃ sarvaṃ kâryaṃ yasmâcca nirgataṃ/
Tasyânāvṛtarūpatvān na nirodho' sti kutracit// 2

### TRANSLATION

Inasmuch as nothing can veil His nature, there cannot be His obstruction anywhere in whom all this world rests and from whom it has come forth ?

### TEXT OF THE COMMENTARY

तस्यास्य शङ्करात्मनः प्रकाशानन्दघनस्य स्वस्वभावस्य न कुत्रचिद्देशे काल आकारे वा निरोधः प्रसरव्याघातोऽस्ति अनावृतरूपत्वादस्थगितस्वभावत्वात् । अयं भावः । इह यत्किञ्चित्प्राणपुर्यष्टकसुखनीलादिकं चित्प्रकाशस्यावरकं सम्भाव्यते तद्यदि न प्रकाशते न किञ्चित्, प्रकाशमानं तु प्रकाशात्मकशङ्करस्वरूपमेवेति किं कस्य निरोधकं को वा निरोधार्थः । एतदेव तस्येत्येतद्विशेषणेन यत्रेत्यादिनोपपादयति । यत्र यस्मिंश्चिद्रूपे स्वात्मनि इदं मातृमानमेयात्मकं सर्वं जगत्कार्यं स्थितं यत्प्रकाशेन प्रकाशमानं सत्स्थितिं लभते तस्य कथं तेन निरोधः शक्यस्तन्निरोधे हि निरोधकाभिमतमेव न 'चकास्यादित्याशयशेषः । यथोक्तम्

'तदात्मनैव तस्य स्यात्कथं प्राणेन यन्त्रणा ।' (अजडप्र० २१)

इत्यजडप्रमातृसिद्धौ । ननूत्पन्नस्य स्थित्यात्मा प्रकाशो भवति, उत्पत्तिरेव त्वस्य कुत इत्याह यस्माच्च निर्गतमिति । स्मृतिस्वप्नसङ्कल्पयोगिनिर्माणदृष्ट्या चितः

१ क० पु० किञ्चित्स्यादिति पाठः ।

स्वानुभवसिद्धं जगत्कारणत्वमुज्झित्वा अप्रमाणकमनुपपन्नं च प्रधानपरमाण्वादीनां न तत्कल्पयितुं[1] युज्यते। कार्यपदेन चेदमेव ध्वनितं कर्तुः क्रियया निष्पाद्यं हि कार्यमुच्यते न तु जडकारणानन्तरभावि जडस्य कारणत्वानुपपत्तेः ईश्वरप्रत्यभिज्ञोक्तनीत्या[2]। भविष्यति चैतत्

'अवस्थायुगलं चात्र कार्यकर्तृत्वशब्दितम्।' (१।१४)

इत्यत्र। सर्वशब्देनोपादानादिनैरपेक्ष्यं कर्तुर्ध्वनितम्। न च कार्यं घटादि कर्तुः कुम्भकारादेः कदाचित्स्वरूपं तिरोदधद्दृष्टम्। ननु निर्गतिरवस्थितस्य भवति तत्किमेतत्क्वचिदादावेव स्थितं, नान्यत्र स्थितम् अपि तु तत्रैव चिदात्मनीत्याह यत्र स्थितमिति। आवृत्त्या चैतद्योज्यम्। अयमर्थः यदि चिदात्मनि जगदहंप्रकाशाभेदेन न भवेत्तत्कथमुपादानादिनिरपेक्षं तत उदियात्। यतस्तु

'यथा न्यग्रोधबीजस्थः शक्तिरूपो महाद्रुमः।
तथा हृदयबीजस्थं जगदेतच्चराचरम्॥' (प० त्री० २४)

इत्याम्नायस्थित्या

'स्वामिनश्चात्मसंस्थस्य।' (ई० प्र० १।५।१०)

इति पूर्वोक्तयुक्त्या च तत्रैतदभेदेन स्फुरत्स्थितं ततोऽयं चिदात्मा भगवान्निजरसाश्यानतारूपं जगदुन्मज्जयतीति युज्यते। एवं च यत्र स्थितमेव सद्यस्मान्निर्गतमित्यत्र योजना जाता। च एवार्थे भिन्नक्रमः। ननु यदि तस्मात्प्रकाशवपुष इदं जगन्निर्यातं तन्न प्रथेत न हि प्रथाबाह्यं च प्रथते चेति युक्तमित्याशङ्क्य यस्मान्निर्गतमपि सद्यत्र स्थितमित्यावृत्त्या संगमनीयम्। चोऽप्यर्थे भिन्नक्रमः। एतदुक्तं भवति न प्रसेवकादिवाक्षोटादि तत्तस्मान्निर्गतमपि तु स एव भगवान्स्वस्वातन्त्र्यादनतिरिक्तामप्यतिरिक्तामिव जगद्रूपतां स्वभित्तौ दर्पणनगरवत्प्रकाशयन्स्थितः। ननु च भवत्वेवं सर्गस्थित्यवस्थयोर्जगतास्यानिरुद्धत्वं संहारावस्थया त्वभावात्मना सुषुप्तदेशीयया जगतः संबन्धिन्या कथं नैतत्तिरोधीयते, नहि ग्राह्यं जगद्विना ग्राहकश्चिदात्मा कश्चिदित्यावृत्त्यैतदेवोत्तरं यस्मान्निर्गतमपि सद्यत्रैव स्थितमुत्पन्नमपि जगत्संहारावस्थायां तदैकात्म्येनैवास्ते न त्वस्यान्यः कश्चिदुच्छेदः शून्यरूपस्तस्य वक्ष्यमाणयुक्त्या प्रकाशं भित्तिभूतं विनानुपपत्तेरित्यर्थः। यथोक्तं श्रीस्वच्छन्दशास्त्रे

'अशून्यं शून्यमित्युक्तं शून्यं चाभाव उच्यते।
देव्यभावः स विज्ञेयो यत्र भावाः क्षयं गताः॥' (४।२९२)

इति। एवं सर्वं यस्य कार्यं यत्प्रकाशेनैव प्रकाशते संहृतमपि च सद्यत्प्रकाशैकात्म्येन तिष्ठति न तस्य देशकालाकारादि किञ्चिन्निरोधकं युज्यते,—इति व्यापकं नित्यं

१ ख० पु० न तत्कल्पनमिति पाठः।
२. ख० पु० न्यायात् इति पाठः।

**विश्वशक्तिखचितं स्वप्रकाशमादिसिद्धं चैतत्तत्त्वमिति । नास्य सिद्धावज्ञातार्थ-प्रकाशरूपं प्रमाणवराकमुपपद्यत उपयुज्यते सम्भवति वा प्रत्युतैतत्तत्त्वसिद्ध्यधीना प्रमाणादिविश्ववस्तुसिद्धिः । तदुक्तमस्मद्गुरुभिस्तन्त्रालोके**

'प्रमाणान्यपि वस्तूनां जीवितं यानि तन्वते ।
तेषामपि परो जीवः स एव परमेश्वरः ॥' (त० १ आ० ५५ श्लो०)

**इति । यस्मान्निर्गतमपीदं जगद्यत्र स्थितं यत्प्रकाशेन प्रकाशमानं तथाभूतमपि यत्र स्थितं यत्प्रकाशैकरूपं । यत्प्रकाश एव; यस्य सिद्ध्यै न्यक्षेणेक्ष्यमाणं भवति न त्वन्यज्जगन्नाम किञ्चित् । अत्र यत्र स्थितमित्यावर्त्य[1] द्विर्योज्यम् । एवं च स्वानुभवसिद्धमेवास्य तत्त्वस्य सृष्टिस्थितिसंहारमेलनावभासिनोऽतिदुर्घटकारिणः सर्वदा सर्वत्रानिरुद्धत्वम् । यथोक्तं श्रीमदुत्पलदेवाचार्यैः**

'परमेश्वरता जयत्यपूर्वा तव सर्वेश यदीशितव्यशून्या ।
अपरापि तथैव ते यथेदं जगदाभाति यथा तथा न भाति ॥' (उ० स्तो० १६।३०)

**इति । अत्र हि भासमानमेव जगद्भासनैकशेषीभूतत्वाद्भासनातिरिक्तं न किञ्चिद्भातीत्यर्थः । किञ्च यत्र स्थितमित्युक्त्योपशमपदे, यस्माच्च निर्गतमिति प्रसरपदे यतोऽस्य न निरोधस्ततो निमीलनोन्मीलनसमाधिद्वयेऽपि योगिना स्वस्वभावसमावेशपरेणैव भवितव्यम् । यद्वक्ष्यते**

'यदा क्षोभः प्रलीयेत तदा स्यात्परमं पदम् ।' (१।६)

**इति । तथा**

'तस्माच्छब्दार्थचिन्तासु न सावस्था न या शिवः ।' (२।४)

**इत्यपि च । कुत्रचिदनात्मवादिनि सौगतादौ प्रमातरि कुत्रचिच्च बाधकाभिमते प्रमाणे सति न तस्य निरोधः प्रतिषेधोऽस्ति, यतो यस्तस्य प्रतिषेधको यच्च तस्य प्रतिषेधकं प्रमाणं तद्यदि न सिद्धमभित्तिकमेतच्चित्रं सिद्धिश्चास्य प्रकाशते इति [2]तत्सिद्ध्यैव भगवानादिसिद्धस्वप्रकाशमूर्तिरस्तीत्येतत्प्रतिषेधायोदितेनाप्यनक्षरमुक्तम् । भविष्यति चैतत्**

'न तु योऽन्तर्मुखो भावः ।' (१।१६)

**इत्यत्रान्तरे । एवं चानेन विश्वोत्तीर्णं विश्वमयं विश्वसर्गसंहारादिकारि शाङ्करं स्वस्वभावात्मकं तत्त्वमित्यभिदधता सर्वेषु पारमेश्वरेषु यदुपास्यं तदितः स्पन्दतत्त्वान्नाधिकं केवलमेतत्स्वातन्त्र्यवशेनैव तदुपासावैचित्र्यमाभास्यते । वस्तुतस्तु एतद्वीर्यसारमेवाशेषम् । यद्वक्ष्यत्ति**

'तदाक्रम्य बलं मन्त्राः सर्वज्ञबलशालिनः ।' (२।१)

**इत्येतदपि भङ्ग्या प्रतिपादितम् । एवं च न कश्चिदुक्तचोद्यावकाशः । एवमेता-**

१. ख० पु० आवृत्त्या इति पाठः ।
२. क० ख० पु० अनदिनि पाठः ।

दृशेषु चिन्तारत्नप्रायेषु श्रीस्पन्दसूत्रेषु यदन्यैः सर्वैर्विवृतिकृद्भिर्व्याख्यायि यच्चास्माभिः किञ्चिद्व्याक्रियते तत्रान्तरममत्सरा अनवलिप्ताश्च स्वयमेव विचिन्वन्तु सचेतसो न तु तदस्माभिरुद्घाट्य प्रतिपदं प्रदर्श्यते ग्रन्थगौरवापत्तेः ॥२॥

## Translation of the Commentary

Of that i.e. of *Śaṃkara* who is a compact mass of Light and Bliss and who is everyone's own being, there is no where i.e. in no space, time or form any obstruction i.e. any impediment in His free advance, because nothing can veil His nature. This is the purport. In this world, whatever, e.g. *prāṇa* (life-force), *puryaṣṭaka* (the subtle body)' pleasure, the blue colour, etc. that may possibly be conceived to have the capacity of veiling the Light of Consciousness is nothing if it does not come into light (*na prakāśate*) and if it does come into light (*prakāśamānaṃ tu*), then it is only the nature of *Śaṃkara* whose very form is Light (of Consciousness). Then what is that which can obstruct or what is the meaning of obstruction? The author proves this very fact by adding the qualifying clause 'in whom all this objective world rests'[1] (*yatra ityādinā*) etc. to the noun clause 'His obstruction is nowhere possible etc.' (*tasya na nirodho' sti kutracit etc.*)

*Yatra* means 'in that consciousness which is one's own Self'. *Idaṃ sarvaṃ kāryam* means 'the entire world consisting of subject or knower (*mātṛ*), means of knowledge or knowledge (*māna*). and object or the known (*meya*)'.

*Yatra sthitam idaṃ sarvaṃ kāryaṃ*, therefore, means, 'In which Consciousness this world consisting of subject, object and means of knowledge etc. rests'. By 'rests' (*sthitaṃ*) is meant by whose light, it comes into light and thus obtains stance. How can there be an obstruction of His by that world? Because by His obstruction that which is considered the obstructor itself can by no means appear. This is what is to be supplied to complete the sense. As has been said in Ajaḍapramātṛsiddhi (21). "How can there be any restraint of His by *prāṇa* (life-force) which is identical with Himself?"

(An objection). A question may be raised—"That alone can have the light of stance which is produced, but to what does it owe its very production"? In reply, it is said, 'From whom it has come forth.' Discarding the Consciousness as the cause of the world which is verified from one's own experience from the standpoint of memory, dream, ideation, creation by *yogīs*, it is not proper to suppose *pradhāna*, atom etc. to be the cause of the world, for such a cause has neither proof nor reasoning in its support.

By the word *kārya* (effect, product), this is what is implied, "That is said to be a product which is produced by the action of an agent, not that which is the outcome of another insentient cause. According to what has been said in Īśvarapratyabhijñā, causality in the case of the insentient cannot be proved. This will be made clear in the following line in this book. "The pair of states is said to be the doer and the deed. (I, 14)." The word 'all' (*sarvam*) in the verse implies that the agent is independent of material, etc. It is never witnessed that the produced product such as the jar can conceal the nature of the agent such as the potter, etc.

(Another objection). The process of coming out can occur only in the case of that which is already contained in something. Then is this world contained in something in the very beginning?

(Reply) No, it is not contained in anything else, but in the self-same Consciousness. That is why it is said in the verse, "in whom it rests". The phrase, 'in whom it rests' should be used twice by repetition This is the sense "If the world did not exist in Consciousness, undifferentiated from the light of I-ness, how could it arise from it without the need of material, etc? Since according to the sacred tradition as expressed in the following lines:

"As the great banyan tree lies only in the form of potency in the seed, even so the entire universe with all the mobile and immobile beings lies as a potency in the heart-seed[1] of the Supreme," (P. Tri 24) and according to the reasoning aforementioned in "Because it already exists in the Lord's Self." (I.P.I. 5,10), this world already rests in Him, gleaming as identical with Him. Therefore, it is perfectly valid to say that the Lord whose nature is consciousness brings about the emergence of the world in the form of congealment of His essence (i.e., He materializes His essence in the form of the world).

Thus the syntactical construction must be made differently. The particle 'ca' should be interpreted in the sense of *eva* (एव) and should be put in a different order. So now the line would stand as *Yatra sthitam eva* (*yad*) *idam sarvaṃ kāryam yasmād nirgatam*, meaning 'only as resting in Him is all this world come forth."

(A third objection) "Well, if this world has come out (i.e. separated) from that Exquisite Mass of Light, then how can it be manifest, for nothing can be manifest outside Light? It would be inconsistent to say that something is separate from Light and is yet manifest.

(Reply). To answer this question, the clause 'from whom it has come forth' should also be repeated twice and should be construed in this way, *Yasmād nirgatamapi* (*sad*) *yatra sthitam*, i.e. from whom even when it has come forth, it is still resting there. The particle 'ca' has to be taken in a different order and has to be interpreted as meaning 'even' 'This is what is meant to be said—"That (the world) has not come out from him as does a walnut from a bag. Rather the self-same Lord through His absolute Freedom manifesting, on His own background like a city in a mirror, the world as if different from Him though non-different, abides in Himself."

(Fourth objection). Well, it may be granted that there is no obstruction to Him by the world in the states of manifestation (creation) and maintenance, how can He avoid being concealed in the state of the world's dissolution which is of the nature of naught, akin to sound sleep? Without the perceptible world, the perceiver, viz., the perceiving consciousness is nothing (i.e. a subject without an object is meaningless.)

(Reply). The question can be answered by a repetition of the clause *yasmāt nirgatam api sad yatraiva sthitam* i.e. from whom even while come forth it abides in Him i.e. even the created world in the state of dissolution abides in Him as identical with Himself. There is no other annihilation of it in the form of a void. In accordance with what is said in the verse given below, the void cannot be reasonably conceived without Light serving as its support. As has been said in Svacchandaśāstra "It is (really) nonvoid (*aśūnyam*) which is said to be void (*śūnyam*), for *śūnya* only means *abhāva* or absence of objects. O goddess, that is to be known as *abhāva* (absence of objects) in which all objective existents have dissolved."

Therefore nothing whether space, time or form can be said with propriety to obstruct Him whose work is this whole world, by whose Light it is manifested, and even when dissolved it abides as identical with that Light.

Hence this principle is all-pervading, eternal, full of all powers, self-luminous, and eternally existent. In order to prove its existence, no poor means of proof which can reveal only an unknown thing can ever be appropriately applicable or possible. On the contrary, the means of proof and all other things themselves depend on the truth of this principle. This has been said by my venerable teacher in Tantrāloka:

"He the great God is the utmost life of even those proofs which constitute the life of all things." (T.I. 55)

The phrase *Yatra sthitam* (in whom it rests) should be applied twice by repetition, and so the whole thing would mean "This world even when it comes out from Him rests in Him, by whose light, it being manifest rests in Him as that light itself, with whose light it is identical, whose light alone considered in its entirety is sufficient for its (the world's) proof." The world is nothing else than this principle.

Thus there can never and nowhere be any obstruction, as is proved by one's own experience, to this Spanda principle which reveals that where manifestation, maintenance and withdrawal all meet and which brings about things most difficult to be accomplished. As has been said by Utpaladeva:

"O Ruler of all, glory to thy unprecedented rulership which has indeed nothing to be ruled (for there is nothing different from thyself over which thou couldst rule). Thy other rulership (in the form of Sadāśiva, Īśvara) is also exactly like thy own by which this world does not appear to thy devotees in the same way as it appears to others" (Utpala stotra XVI, 301). The sense of this verse is that nothing appears as different from the Light of manifestation, since the manifest world is one with the Light of manifestation.

(*Means for mystic Union*):

Moreover, since there is no obstruction to this (*spanda*)

principle whether in the state of cessation as indicated by the phrase *Yatra sthitam* (in whom resting) or in the state of expansion as indicated by the phrase *Yasmāc ca nirgatam* (from whom came forth), therefore the *yogī* should be intent on entrance in his essential nature in both *nimīlana* and *unmīlana samādhi*.[2] As will be said (in this book). "When agitation ceases, then occurs the highest state[3] '(I,9) Similarly, "Whether it is a word or object or thought, there is no state which is not Śiva.[4]" (II, 4). There cannot be an obstruction to or negation of one's real nature in any case even though there may be existing somewhere an experient like the Buddhist who maintains that there is no Self or there may be somewhere a proof which is considered to be its annulment. Because if he that is the denier of that (essential nature) is not (already) existent as a reality, then his denial becomes a picture without a canvas. Similarly, the proof which is its negation also becomes groundless without the existence of the denier. This in itself is the proof of the reality of the *spanda tattva* that it is manifest (*prakāśate iti*) in the form of that very denier. The reality of the experient (*pramātā*) which is thus proved goes to show that the Lord who is an eternally established reality (*ādi-siddha*)[5] and who is identical with the reality of one's own Self does exist. Thus the reality of the *Spanda* principle has been tacitly affirmed without using any words, even by him who had come forward to deny it. This point will be clarified later in this book in "There can be no disappearance of that inner nature." (I, 16).

Thus this book describes the fact that the principle of *Śaṅkara* which is both transcendent to and immanent in the world, which brings about manifestation, maintenance and withdrawal of the world is one's own essential nature. That which is the object of meditation in all the theistic schools is not anything different from the *spanda* principle. The diversity of meditation appears entirely owing to the absolute Freedom of this Spanda principle. In fact, the entire universe is only the manifestation of the essence of the activity of this principle. This has been explained by way of suggestion in the line. "By relying on that strength, the *mantras* become endowed with the strength of the omniscient" (II,1).

Thus there is no room for the aforesaid objection. Let intelligent people who are unprejudiced and are not haughty examine for themselves the difference between my commentary and the commentaries of others on the *Spandakārikās* which are like desire-granting gem. I have not openly shown that difference in the case of every word for fear of the increase of the volume of the book.

## NOTES

1. *Hṛdaya-bīja* (heart-seed) is also known as *Saṁhāra-bīja* symbolized by the mantra Sauḥ or *ma-ha-a*. *Sṛṣṭibīja* is *ahám*. It is also known as *piṇḍanātha-bīja*,' symbolized by the mantra 'r-kṣ-kh-eṃ.'

2. *Nimīlana* and *unmīlana samādhi*; *Nimīlana samādhi* is the inward meditative condition with closed eyes, in which the individual consciousness gets absorbed into the Universal Consciousness. *Unmīlana samādhi* is that state of the mind in which, even when the eyes are open, the external world appears as Universal Consciousness or *Śiva*.

3. This refers to the state of *nimīlana samādhi*.

4. This refers to the state of *unmīlana samādhi*.

5. *Ādi-siddha* means that it is an eternally established reality, it already stands proved before any denial or negation tries to disprove it.

## EXPOSITION

This *kārikā* expresses the fact that the world consisting of *pramātā* (subject), *prameya* (object) and *pramāṇa* (means of knowledge) exists in *Śiva* or the *spanda* principle, even as the reflection of a city may be said to exist in a mirror. It is nothing but the mirror and the various objects in the city which appear different from one another and also from the mirror are nothing but the mirror itself. Thus the world is nothing but Śiva, though it appears different from Him, even as the various objects reflected in a mirror appear different but really speaking are not anything different from the mirror.

The first point that is made out is that when we say that the world rests in *Śiva* or that it has come forth from *Śiva*, we are speaking only from the popular, empirical point of view, not from the metaphysical point of view. The world is not contained in Him as a walnut in a bag where the walnut has its own independent existence and the bag for the time being contains it. The world has no separate existence from Śiva as the walnut has from the bag. So also when we say that the world has come out from Him, it is not meant that the world has come out from Him as a walnut comes out from a bag where both the walnut and the bag are separate from each other. The world and *Śiva* are not two separate entities. *Śiva* is the world from the point of view of appearance, and the world is *Śiva* from the point of view of Reality. *Śiva* is both transcendent to and immanent in the world—both *Viśvottīrṇa* and *viśvamaya.*

The second point that is made out is that since the world owes its existence to Him, it cannot conceal Him even as a pot cannot conceal the potter, nor can it serve as an impediment in His free Self-expression and Self-expansion. That is to say He cannot be limited by space, time, figure, etc. This has another very important implication. Since the real or metaphysical Self of each individual is essentially *Śiva*, the world cannot throw a pall over it. Only the individual has to recognise his Self. As Kallaṭa puts it:

तस्य संसार्यवस्थायामपि अनाच्छादितस्वभाववत्वान्न न क्वचित् निरोधः

"Nothing can obstruct Him even in the state of the world, for the Self as Śiva has the nature which cannot be veiled."

This Kārikā has also a mystic implication. Kṣemarāja has clearly pointed that out in the following words:

निमीलनोन्मीलनसमाधिद्वयेऽपि योगिना स्वस्वभावसमावेशपरेणैव भवितव्यम् ।

"Both in introverted and extroverted state of meditation the yogī should be intent on entering his essential nature which is Śiva."

*Introduction to the third verse*:

TEXT

ननु जागरादिवशास्त्वीदृशः स्वभावो नानुभूयते यदि चायमुक्तयुक्तिभिर्न केनचिन्निरुध्यते तज् जागराद्यवस्थासु स्वयमेव निरोत्स्यते,—इति शङ्कात उक्तमप्यर्थमप्रतिपद्यमानं प्रतिबोधयन्नुपदिशति—

## TRANSLATION

An objection may be raised, "Such nature (of *Śivc*) is not experienced in the state of waking, etc. According to the arguments you have advanced, that nature is not restrained by anything or any one, but in the state of waking, etc, it is concealed by itself (because in these states such reality is not experienced)." On account of this doubt, the author explains to the uncomprehending in the following verse what has already been said.

## VERSE

जाग्रदादिविभेदेऽपि तदभिन्ने प्रसर्पति ।
निवर्तते निजान्नैव स्वभावादुपलब्धृतः ॥ ३ ॥

Jāgradādivibhede'pi tadabhinne prasarpati/
Nivartate nijānnaiva svabhāvādupalabdhṛtaḥ//3.

## TRANSLATION

Even though differing states like waking etc. occur in which, however, that *Spanda* principle remains identically the same, that *Spanda* principle never departs from its own nature as the identical Experient (in all the differing states).

## TEXT OF THE COMMENTARY

जागरापरपर्यायो जाग्रच्छब्दः शिष्टप्रयुक्तत्वात् । लोकप्रसिद्धे जाग्रत्स्वप्नसुषुप्तानां भेदे योगिप्रसिद्धेऽपि वा धारणाध्यानसमाधिरूपे प्रसर्पति—अन्यान्यरूपे प्रवहति सति अर्थात् तत्तत्त्वं निजादनपायिनः सर्वस्यात्मभूताच्चानुभवितृरूपात्स्वभावान्नैव निवर्तते । यदि हि स्वयं निवर्तेत तज्जाग्रदाद्यपि तत्प्रकाशविनाकृतं न किञ्चित्प्रकाशेत । उपलब्धृता चैतदीया जागरास्वप्नयोः सर्वस्य स्वसंवेदनसिद्धा । सौषुप्ते यद्यपि सा तथा न चेत्यते तथाप्यौत्तरकालिकस्मृत्यन्यथानुपपत्त्या सिद्धा, उपलब्धृत एव च स्वभावान्न निवर्तते, उपलभ्यं त्ववस्थादि तन्माहात्म्यान्निवर्ततां कामं कात्र क्षतिः । एवकारोऽप्यर्थे भिन्नक्रमस्तदभावेऽपि न निवर्तत इत्यर्थः । जागरादिविभेदस्य विशेषणद्वारेण हेतुस्तदभिन्ने इति, तस्माच्छिवस्वभावादभेदेन प्रकाशमानत्वात्प्रकाशरूपे इत्यर्थः । यच्च यदेकात्मकं तत्कथं तन्निवृत्ताववतिष्ठते ।

यद्वा तदिति कर्तृपदम् । अभिन्न इति तु केवलमभिन्नत्वं जागरादेः शिवापेक्षमेव । अर्थात्तत्तत्त्वं जागरादिभेदेऽपि सति प्रसर्पति प्रसरति वैचित्र्यं गृह्णाति तन्नैव स्वभावान्निवर्तत इति योज्यम् । किञ्चायं जाग्रदादिभेदः परिणामो विवर्तो वेति यत्साङ्ख्यपाञ्चरात्रशाब्दिकादयो मन्यन्ते तद्व्युदासायाप्युक्तं तदभिन्न इति । अवस्थाप्रपञ्चोऽपि यदि चिन्मात्रात्परिणामतया मनागप्यतिरिच्येत चिद्रूपं वा तत्परिणतौ मनागतिरिच्येत[1] तन्न किंचिच्चकास्यादिति तावन्न परिणामोऽस्ति । यथोक्तम्

'परिणामोऽचेतनस्य चेतनस्य न युज्यते ।'

इति श्रीकिरणे । न च भासमानोऽसावसत्यो ब्रह्मतत्त्वस्यापि तथात्वापत्तेः,—इत्यसत्यविभक्तान्यरूपोपग्राहिता विवर्त इत्यपि न सङ्गतम् । अनेन चातिदुर्घटकारित्वमेव भगवतो ध्वनितम् । यस्माज्जागरादिविभेदं च प्रकाशयति तत्रैव च स्वाभेदमिति भेदात्मना तदभेदात्मनोभयात्मना[2] च रूपेणापरापरापरापराशक्तित्रयस्वरूपेण स्फुरतीत्यनुत्तरषडर्धतत्त्वात्मतया भगवानेव स्फुरति । अतश्च जागरादिदशावस्थितोऽपि एवमिमं स्वस्वभावं परिशीलयन् यश्चिनुते स शङ्कर एवेत्युपदिष्टं भवति ॥३॥

## TRANSLATION

The word *jāgrat* is synonym of *jāgarā*, for it has been used as such by the cultured ones.[1] Though differences in the states of waking, dream, and deep sleep well-known among common people or in the corresponding states of *dhāraṇā* (concentration) *dhyāna* (meditation) and intense absorption (*samādhi*), well known among the *yogins* continue as different from one another, yet as a matter of fact, that *spanda* principle never departs from its own invariable nature as the Self of all and as the Experient of every state. If that principle were to depart, the states of waking etc. being devoid of its light would not appear at all. Its nature as Experient in the state of waking and dream, is proved from Self-experience in the case of every one. Though in the case of deep sleep, its nature as Experient is not similarly known directly, yet it is proved from subsequent memory of it (the deep sleep) which could not otherwise justifiably occur unless there was a previous experience of that deep sleep. It (the *Spanda* principle) never departs or deviates from its nature

१. क० ग० पु० रिक्तमिति पाठः ।

२. ग० पु० उभयमेलनात्मनेति पाठः ।

as the Experient. Its objects of experience, such as state of deep sleep etc. may through its greatness, deviate with pleasure. Where is the harm in this?

The word 'eva' is to be taken differently from the textual order in the sense of *api* (also). The meaning would then be 'Even in the absence of the states of waking and dream i.e. even in the state of deep sleep the *spanda* principle does not depart from its nature'.

(*First explanation of tadabhinne*):

The phrase *tadabhinne* (not separate from that) besides qualifying the phrase *jāgarādi-vibheda* (differing states of waking etc.) serves as a reason.[2] It means 'Because different states of waking etc. appear as non-different from the nature of *Śiva* (who is *prakāśa*), therefore, these are of the form of light. How can that which is identical with the other remain if the other departs? i.e. Since waking etc. are identical with *Śiva*, how can they exist, if *Śiva* or the *spanda* principle with which they are identical departs (from its nature as Experient).[3]

(Second Explanation)

Or *tat* (that) may be taken as subject of *prasarpati*, and *abhinne* (not separate) may be interpreted as the identity of waking, etc. with reference to *Śiva*. Now the construction would be *tat jāgradādi-vibhed'pi (sati) prasarpati*, and the meaning would be that "*Spanda* principle even while there are differing states like waking, etc. flows on i.e. assumes diversity. It never departs from its nature."[4]

Moreover, do the different states of walking, etc constitute *pariṇāma* (transformation or evolute) as the followers of *Sāṁkhya* and *Pañcarātra* believe or *vivarta* (illusory appearance) as grammarians, etc.[5] believe? The phrase *tadabhinne* has also been used by the author to refute their theory.

(*Rejection of the theory of pariṇāma*)

If the manifold states being transformation of consciousness were even slightly different from pure consciousness, then on their transformation, consciousness would also be slightly transformed. On the transformation of consciousness itself, nothing would appear (lit. would come to light).[6] Therefore, the theory of transformation cannot hold good. As has been said in Śrīkiraṇa.[7]

"There can be transformation only of the insentient. It cannot be rightly applied to the sentient."

(*Rejection of the theory of vivarta*):

That which is perceived cannot be unreal, for if it be unreal, there would be the predicament of the Brahman principle also becoming unreal. Therefore, the theory of *vivarta* is also inconsistent inasmuch as it connotes unreality, separation and the assumption of another form.[8]

From *tadabhinne* follows God's power of accomplishing even what is not within the range of possibility. Inasmuch as the Lord manifests the differing states of waking, etc, in the manifestation of that difference itself He manifests His identity.[1] Thus He flashes forth in difference by His power of *aparā*, in identity by His power of *parā*, in the form of identity in diversity by His power of *parāparā*. Thus it is God Himself who is manifest in the unparalleled Trika principle[10] (the principle of triad).

From the mystic point of view this verse teaches that He is Śaṃkara Himself who even when remaining in the different states of waking, etc. constantly contemplates this identical nature of himself and thus experiences himself as the (ever-present) Experient.

## NOTES

1. Strictly speaking, the noun form of the verb *jāgṛ* is *jāgarā*, but 'jāgrat' has also been used as a noun even by well-cultured writers. Hence the use of 'jāgrat' in place of jāgarā' is justified.

2. This is known as *hetugarbha viśeṣaṇa* i.e. an adjective which does not only qualify the noun but contains implicitly a reason also. The reason which is implicit in this adjective clause is that 'because the states of waking, dream, etc are non-different from (i.e. identical with) the nature of Śiva which is light, therefore, they are also of the form of light'.

3. The idea is that since waking, etc. are identical with the *spanda* principle, they cannot remain i.e. they cannot appear or be manifest if the *spanda* principle as Experient departs. In the absence of the Experient, they will also vanish.

4. The nature of *Śiva* is not only permanent experiencing principle, but while remaining permanent experient, He assumes various kinds of differing forms

5. Et cetera refers to the Vedantins.

6. Just as when milk is transformed into curd, the milk has disappeared. It is no longer milk. It is now curd. Even so if consciousness is transformed into the manifold states, it can no longer remain consciousness. On the disappearance of consciousness, the manifold states will also vanish, for there can be no experience without the experient.

7. Śrīkīraṇa is the title of a book on *tantra* which is not available now.

8. There are three characteristics of *vivarta*, viz.

(1) it connotes illusory appearance (2) separation and (3) assumption of a different form. Since the world is not unreal, nor separate from, nor of a form different from *Śiva* or Consciousness, the theory of *Vivarta* cannot be accepted.

9. Without the Experient's continuing as identical in the different states, their differences themselves cannot be experienced. Therefore the experience of difference itself reveals the non-different i.e. the identical nature of the Experient.

10. *Ṣaḍardha* or half of six means three. This refers to the Trika philosophy of Kashmir which maintains that in manifestation there are three *śaktis* (powers) of *Śiva* that function, viz (1) *parā* the highest stage in which difference from *Śiva* has not yet started, (2) *parā-parā*, the intermediate stage in which in spite of difference the sense of identity persists, (3) *aparā* in which there is complete difference.

## EXPOSITION

Two important points have been made out in this *kārikā*. Firstly, states of experience may differ, but the Experient does not deviate from his nature as Experient. He remains identical. As Kallaṭa puts it:

यस्माद् उपलब्धृ-रूपत्वं त्रिष्वपि पदेषु साधारणम्, न तस्य स्वरूपान्यथाभावः, यथा विषस्याङ्कुरादिपु च पञ्चसु स्कन्धेषु ।

"Since the Experient remains the same in all the three states of waking, dream, and deep sleep, there is no deviation in his nature, just as the lotus remains the same in all its five parts. The following verse quoted by Utpala Bhaṭṭa beautifully expresses the same idea:

अवस्थास्वेव भेदोऽयं नावस्थातुः कदाचन ।
यथा विषस्याङ्कुरादौ तच्छक्तेर्न तु भिन्नता ।

"This difference is of the states not of the Experient who holds them i.e. who experiences those states just as there is difference in the sprouts etc. of the lotus. but not in the *śakti* (power) of the lotus."

The differences themselves point to one common identical Reality which acts as *anusandhātā* i.e. which joins those differing states into the unity of the experience of one individual in the form 'I who was awake, had a dream in sleep and then enjoyed sound sleep.'

Secondly, the different states of experience are nothing but an expression of Consciousness itself. They are not different from Consciousness.

These differing states can neither be explained as *pariṇāma* or transformation of consciousness nor as *vivarta* or illusory appearance. They are simply a display of the *Svātantrya* (absolute freedom) of *Śiva*.

There is a practical aspect of this philosophical truth in *Sādhanā*. One who contemplates zealously over the identity of the Experient in the midst of the changing states of experience becomes identified with *Śiva*.

*Introduction to the 4th verse*:

## TEXT

अथ ये 'एकमेवेदं संविद्रूपं हर्षविषादाद्यनेकाकारविवर्तं[1] पश्याम' इत्युक्त्या ज्ञानसन्तान एव तत्त्वमिति सौगता मन्यन्ते; ये चाहंप्रतीतिप्रत्येयः सदैव सुखाद्युपाधितिरस्कृत आत्मेति मीमांसकाः प्रतिपन्नास्तानेकेनैव श्लोकेनापवदति

१ ख० पु० विश्रान्तमिति पाठ. ।

## TRANSLATION

The followers of Buddha say that we see that joy, depression, etc, are only different altered forms of one single consciousness. On the strength of this argument they hold that the continuum of *jñāna* or knowledge alone is Reality. (i.e. there is no *jñātā*-knower or experient apart from *jñāna* or knowledge). The *Mīmāṃsakas* hold that, that which is known in the consciousness of 'I' eclipsed by the conditions of pleasure etc is the Self. Both are refuted by a single verse (which follows)

## TEXT OF THE VERSE

अहं सुखी च दुःखी च रक्तश्चेत्यादिसंविदः ।
सुखाद्यवस्थानुस्यूते वर्तन्तेऽन्यत्र ताः स्फुटम् ॥ ४ ॥

Ahaṃ sukhī ca duḥkhī ca raktaśca ityādisamvidaḥ/
sukhādyavasthānusyūte vartante 'nyatra tāḥ sphuṭaṃ//4.

## TRANSLATION

I am happy, I am miserable, I am attached—these and other cognitions have their being evidently in another in which the states of happiness, misery etc. are strung together-4.

## TEXT OF THE COMMENTARY

य एवाहं सुखी स एव दुःखी सुखानुशायिना रागेण युक्तत्वाद्रक्तो दुःखानुशायिना द्वेषेण सम्बन्धाद्द्विष्ट[1]श्चेत्यादयः संविदो ज्ञानानि ता अन्यत्रेति अवस्थातर्यात्मतत्त्वे वर्तन्ते तत्रैवान्तर्मुखे विश्राम्यन्ति स्फुटं स्वसाक्षिकं कृत्वा । अन्यथा क्षणिकज्ञानानां स्वात्ममात्रक्षीणत्वात्तत्संस्कारजन्मनामपि विकल्पानामनुभवागोचरे प्रवृत्त्यभावादनुसन्धानमिदं न घटेत । चकारास्तुल्ययोगितापरा अनुसन्धानं द्योतयन्ति । कीदृशेऽन्यत्र, सुखाद्यवस्था उदयप्रलयिन्योऽनुस्यूता—दृब्धा यस्मिंस्तस्मिन् सुखाद्यवस्थानुस्यूतेऽन्तःस्रक्सूत्रकल्पतया स्थिते । ता इत्यनेनानुसन्धीयमानावस्थानां स्मर्यमाणतामभिदधत्क्षणिकज्ञानवादिमतेऽनुभवसंस्कारोत्पन्नत्वादर्थाकारारूपितत्वेऽपि स्मृतेः काममनुभवसदृशत्वं भवतु, न त्वनुभवानुभूतातीतकालार्थव्यवस्थापकत्वं घटते, सर्वसंविदन्तर्मुखे तु प्रमातरि सति सर्वं युज्यत इति सूचितवान्,—

१. क० ख० पु० द्वेष्टेति पाठः ।

इत्यलं सुकुमारहृदयोपदेश्यजनवैरस्यदायिनीभिराभिः कथाभिः । एतदर्थिभिः प्रत्यभिज्ञा परीक्ष्या । ग्रन्थकृतैव तु यत इह युक्तिरासूत्रिता ततोऽस्माभिः किञ्चिदुद्घाटितमिति सचेतोभिर्नास्मभ्यमसूययितव्यम् । मीमांसकपरिहाराय तु एतदित्थं व्याख्यातव्यम् । अहं सुखीत्यादिसंविदो यास्ता अन्यत्रेति पुर्यष्टकस्वरूपे प्रमातरि सुखाद्यवस्थाभिरनुस्यूते श्रोतप्रोतरूपे स्फुटं लोकप्रतीतिसाक्षिकं वर्तन्ते तिष्ठन्ति, न त्वस्मदभ्युपगतेऽस्मिश्चिदानन्दघने शङ्करात्मनि स्वस्वभावे,—इति न सर्वदा सुखाद्युपाधितिरस्कृतोऽयमात्मापि तु चिन्मयः । यदा तु निजाशुद्ध्या वक्ष्यमाणयायं स्वस्वरूपं गूहयित्वा तिष्ठति तदा पुर्यष्टकाद्यवस्थायां सुखित्वादिरूपतास्य तत्रापि न निरोधस्तैः सुखादिभिरस्येत्युक्तमेवेति न तत्तिरस्कृतोऽयं कदाचिदपि । अहं कृशोऽहं स्थूल इत्यादिप्रतीतिपरिहारेण अहं सुखी दुःखीत्यादि वदतोऽयमाशयः—सुखित्वादिप्रतीतिसम्भिन्नां पुर्यष्टकभूमिमन्तर्मुखे पदे निमज्जयंस्तदनुषङ्गेण बाह्यस्यापि देहघटादेर्गलनात्प्रत्यभिजानात्येव स्वं शिवस्वभावत्वमिति सर्वथा पुर्यष्टकशमनायैव यत्न आस्थेय इति ॥४॥

## TRANSLATION OF THE COMMENTARY

The same I who am happy, am miserable, am attached, being connected with affection which rests in pleasure, am full of hatred, being connected with dislike which is associated with pain—these cognitions or experiences abide in another which is the possessor of these states (*avasthātari*), which, in other words, is the permanent principle of Self. They rest inwardly in that evidently i.e. with one's Self as witness. Otherwise the inter-connection (*anusandhāna*) of the ephemeral cognitions and the ideas born of their residual traces will not be possible, for those cognitions disappear as soon as they arise and cannot leave behind any traces. Thus the *vikalpas* (ideas) supposed to arise out of them cannot actually arise. Not being perceived in experience, they cannot lead to any activity.[1]

The particles 'ca' used with equal fitness (with all the three) express their inter-connexion. *Anyatra* means in another. Of what kind is this other ? *Sukhādyavasthānusyūta* qualifies *anyatra* (the other) and means that other in which states of pleasure, pain, etc. which arise and subside are interwoven i.e. are strung together i.e. that in which pleasure, pain, etc. stay inwardly as flowers are strung together in the form of a wreath in a string.

१. ग० पु० एतदिति पाठः ।

*Tāḥ* i.e. the previously experienced states when set in a congruous connection refer to their recollection. According to the view of the philosophers who believe in the momentariness of cognitions, memory is born of the residual traces of the previous experience, and is, as such, only a form tinged with the previous experience. Thus it can only be similar to the previous experience. It cannot bring back to consciousness the thing as it was actually experienced in the past.[2] (Let such philosophers please themselves with such a view of memory. It cannot be accepted by others).

The author suggests that when there is a permanent experient who abides inwardly in the consciousness of all, every thing is set aright. Enough of these subtleties which will only prove to be unpleasant to students of tender heart. Seekers after such subtleties may look into *Pratyabhijñā*.[3] Since the author has referred to this reasoning, I have tried to explain it briefly. Let intelligent people not blame me for this brevity.

*(Second explanation of the text)*

In order to refute the *Mīmāṃsaka*, this (i.e. the word *Ātman* or Self) should be interpreted in this way.

Those experiences such as 'I am happy.' I am miserable exist *anyatra* i.e. in another. 'In another' in this case should be interpreted as 'in the *puryaṣṭaka* Experient'. So the experiences of pleasure, pain, etc. exist in the *puryaṣṭaka* experient who is suffused with these experiences. *Sphuṭam* or 'evidently' means 'to which popular belief bears witness.' *Anyatra* in their case does not mean 'in *Śaṃkara*' who is compact mass of light and bliss and who is our own essential nature as is accepted by us. Therefore, this Self is not always tarnished by the conditions of pleasure, pain, etc, but is rather of the nature of consciousness. When He by His own impurity to be described later conceals his essential nature and appears in that state, then He is in the *Puryaṣṭaka* state, and has the experience of happiness, etc. It has already been said that even in that state, pleasure etc. cannot obstruct His real nature. He is never concealed by pleasure, etc.

The real purport in saying 'I am happy; I am miserable' etc. by abandoning such beliefs as I am thin; I am fat etc is this.

One recognises one's essential nature as *Śiva* by submerging his *Puryṣṭaka* state which is full of experiences like pleasure, etc. in the inner essential Self and also by dissolving along with it the external aspect consisting of the body, jar, etc. Thus one should always make an earnest effort for allaying the *Puryaṣṭaka*.

## NOTES

1. The idea is that when *jñāna* (perception or cognition) disappears as soon as it arises, it cannot leave behind any traces. Thus on this theory of the momentariness of perception, memory, will not be possible.

2. This means to say that similarity of the past experience which is all that the Buddhists can maintain on the basis of their theory of the momentariness of cognitions cannot lead to the belief that it is the same thing which was actually experienced in the past. Similarity is not sameness. Without the belief in the sameness of the past experience, memory is not possible. And without an identical *pramātā* or experient who can connect the past experience with the present, there cannot be any sameness of experience. Thus without an identical *pramātā* or experient, memory would be impossible.

3. This refers to *Īśvara-pratyabhijñā* of Utpaladeva.

## EXPOSITION

The first point to be borne in mind is the significance of the use of plural in *saṃvid*. *Saṃvid* in plural (*saṃvidaḥ*) means perception, cognitions, experiences. They are not the same *saṃvid* which is one identical, uniform consciousness underlying all other *saṃvids*. As Rāmakaṇṭha puts it:

"एकैव संविद् उपलब्धृरूपा अहमिति स्फुरन्ती पारमार्थिकी, मायाशक्तिजनित-तथाविधस्वभावपरामर्शाभावबलात् सुखाद्यनित्यवस्तुवेदकत्वेन अहं सुखी दुःखी च—इत्यादिना बुद्ध्याद्यवस्थासामानाधिकरण्यम् उपगता सती, संविद इति बहुवचनेन निर्दिष्टा" ।

"*Saṃvit* or Consciousness in its highest sense is really one, the Experient of all, flashing forth as 'I'. On account of the absence of that awareness brought about by *māyā-śakti*, it becomes the cognizer of such impermanent incidental experience as 'I am happy,

I am miserable, etc., Really speaking these are the states of *buddhi* (inner determinative consciousness which assumes the role of the self or the Experient, and the real Experient on account of its co-relation with *buddhi* etc. misconceives these states as his own. It is because of this that the word *saṃvid* has been used in plural. They really belong to the pseudo-experient *buddhi*, not to the underlying *Saṃvit*, the Self, the unchanging, identical Experient.

The other important point to be borne in mind is that though these states are not of the Self, though they do not belong to the essential nature of the Self, they are held together into the unity of one experience by that unchanging identical Experient that runs like a thread through them all. This is what is meant by saying सुखाद्यवस्थानुस्यूते वर्तन्ते ताः "Those states have their *ratio essendio* in another Experient that runs like a thread through them all. Rāmakaṇṭha explains the status of this experient beautifully in the following words:

म च पूर्वापरावस्थाव्यापकत्वेन समस्तप्रमातृप्रसिद्धः
सकलव्यवहारहेतोः अनुसन्धानम्य कर्ता, नित्य
उपलब्धृमात्ररूपत्वाद् एक एव प्रकाशते ॥

"He (the Experient) pervades all the preceding and the succeeding states throughout which is well-known even to all empirical selves:he provides that synthetic unity which serves as the foundation of all pragmatic life. which being unchanging. permanent Experient ever shines as one and the same."

It is this important truth which the great German philosopher Kant expressed after nearly one thousand years, in his famous concept of the 'synthetic unity of apperception'.

Lastly, this philosophic truth must lead to *yogic* practice which Kṣemarāja describes in the last section of his commentary.

Knowing that changing states like pleasure, pain belong to the *puryaṣṭaka* i,e, the psychological or the empirical self. one should establish oneself in his essential Self which is the real Experient, which is the nature of *Śiva*.

*Introduction to the 5th Verse*:

TEXT

उक्तोपपत्तिसिद्धां समस्तवादानामनुपपन्नतामनुवदन्नुपपत्तिसिद्धं स्पन्दतत्त्वमेवास्तीति प्रतिजानाति युक्त्यनुभवागमज्ञो रहस्यगुरुप्रवरः

## TRANSLATION

After re-asserting the untenability of all other theories by means of the aforesaid reasoning, the best[1] of the teachers of the secret doctrine, who knew the revealed traditional teaching, the reasoning on which the truth was based and who had also personal experience, firmly declares that the *spanda* principle established by reasoning is decidedly the truth.

## TEXT OF THE VERSE

न दुःखं न सुखं यत्र न ग्राह्यं ग्राहकं न च ।
न चास्ति मूढभावोऽपि तदस्ति परमार्थतः ॥ ५ ॥

Na duḥkhaṃ na sukhaṃ yatra na grāhyaṃ grāhakaṃ na ca/
Na cāsti mūḍhabhāvo' pi tadasti paramārthataḥ// 5

## TRANSLATION

Wherein neither pain, nor pleasure, nor object, nor subject, exists, nor wherein does even insentiency exist—that, in the highest sense, is that *Spanda* principle-5.

## COMMENTARY

इह यत्किञ्चिद्दुःखसुखाद्यान्तरं नीलपीतादिकं बाह्यं ग्राह्यं यच्चैतद्ग्राहकं पुर्यष्टकशरीरेन्द्रियादि तत्तावत्सौषुप्तवदसञ्चेत्यमानं स्फुटमेव नास्तीति वक्तुं शक्यम् । यदापि तु सञ्चेत्यते तदा सञ्चेत्यमानस्याप्यस्य चैतन्यमयत्वाच्चैतन्यमेवास्तीत्यायातम् । यदाहुः

'प्रकाशात्मा प्रकाश्योऽर्थो नाप्रकाशश्च सिध्यति ।' (ई० प्र० १।५।३)

इति रहस्यतत्त्वविदोऽस्मत्परमेष्ठिनः श्रीमदुत्पलदेवपादाः श्रीमदीश्वरप्रत्यभिज्ञायाम् । इहापि वक्ष्यते—

'तत्संवेदनरूपेण तादात्म्यप्रतिपत्तितः' (२।३)

इत्यतो दुःखसुखादि नीलादि तद्ग्राहकं च यत्र नास्ति तत्प्रकाशैकघनं तत्त्वमस्ति । नन्वेवं सर्वग्राह्यग्राहकोच्छेदे शून्यात्मैव तत्त्वमित्यायातं, नेत्याह न चास्ति मूढभावोऽपि इति । मूढभावो मूढत्वं शून्यरूपतापि यत्र नास्ति सोऽपि हि न प्रथते कथमस्ति, प्रथते चेर्त्तार्हि प्रथात्मकत्वान्नासौ कश्चित्प्रथैवास्ति, न च प्रथायाः कदाचिदभावो भवति तदभावे प्रथाभावस्याप्यसिद्धेः । भविष्यति चैतत्

'न तु योऽन्तर्मुखो भावः' । (१।१६)

**इत्यत्र । अपि मूढभाव ऐश्वर्यात्मकविमर्शशून्यप्रकाशमात्रतत्त्वो ब्रह्मरूपोऽपि यत्र नास्ति यच्छ्रुत्यन्तविदः प्रतिपन्नाः 'विज्ञानं ब्रह्म' इति, तस्यापि स्वातन्त्र्यात्मकस्पन्दशक्तिं विना जडत्वात् । यथोक्तं प्रत्यभिज्ञायाम्**

'स्वभावमवभासस्य विमर्शं विदुरन्यथा ।
प्रकाशोऽर्थोपरक्तोऽपि स्फटिकादिजडोपमः ॥' (ई० प्र० १।५।११)

**इति । भट्टनायकस्तोत्रेऽपि**

'नपुंसकमिदं नाथ परं ब्रह्म फलेत्कियत् ।
त्वत्पौरुषी नियोक्त्री चेन्न स्यात्त्वच्छक्तिसुन्दरी ॥'

**इति । एवं च 'यत्र स्थितम्' इत्यतः प्रभृति यत्तत्त्वं विचारितं तदेवास्ति, तच्चास्त्येव परमार्थतो युक्त्यनुभवागमसिद्धेन रूपेण, परमार्थत एव चाकल्पितेन पूर्णेन रूपेणास्ति न तु नीलादिवत्कल्पितेन । यथोक्तं महागुरुभिः**

'एवमात्मन्यसत्कल्पाः प्रकाशस्यैव सन्त्यमी ।
जडाः प्रकाश एवास्ति स्वात्मनः स्वपरात्मभिः ॥' (अजडप्र० १३)

**इति । तत्रभवद्भर्तृहरिणापि**

'यदादौ च यदन्ते च यन्मध्ये तस्य सत्यता ।
न यदाभासते तस्य सत्यत्वं तावदेव हि ॥'

**इति । सावधारणत्वात्सर्ववाक्यानामेवकारोऽत्र नियोज्यः । एवमनेन सूत्रेण सुखाद्याकारसंवित्सन्तानवादिनां सुखादिकलुषितप्रमातृतत्त्ववादिनां ग्राह्यग्राहकनानात्ववादिनां सर्वेषामभाववादिनां निष्परामर्शप्रकाशब्रह्मवादिनां[1] च मतमनुपपन्नत्वादसत्त्वेनानूद्य पारमार्थिकं स्पन्दशक्तिरूपमेव तत्त्वमस्तीति प्रतिज्ञातम् । अथ च यस्मिन्नस्मिन् सोपदेशसावधानमहानुभावपरिशील्ये स्फुरत्तासारे स्पन्दतत्त्वे स्फुरति दुःखसुखग्राह्यग्राहकतदभावादिकमिदं सदपि न किञ्चिदेव सर्वस्यैतच्चमत्कारैकसारत्वात्तदेवैतदस्तीत्युपदिष्टम् । यन्महागुरवः**

'दुःखान्यपि सुखायन्ते विषमप्यमृतायते ।
मोक्षायते च संसारो यत्र मार्गः स शाङ्करः ॥' उ० स्तो० २०।१२)

**इति । शाङ्करो मार्गः—'शङ्करात्मस्वभावप्राप्तिहेतुः पराशक्तिरूपः प्रसरः'** ॥५॥

## TRANSLATION

It can be said that here whatever inner object there is like pain, pleasure, etc., or whatever external object there is like blue or yellow and whatever subject there is like the *puryaṣṭaka*, body and senses have evidently no existence like the stage of

१ ख० पु० ब्रह्मतत्त्ववादिनामिति पाठः ।

deep sleep as long as they are not experienced. When they are experienced, then being experienced, they are of the nature of consciousness. They are simply consciousness, this is what it comes to. As has been said in Īśvarapratyabhijñā by my great grand teacher, revered Utpaladeva who knew the essence of the secret doctrine.

"The object that is made manifest is of the nature of the light of consciousness. What is not light cannot be said to exist." (I.pr.I,5,3). In this book also, it will be said

"Because of being of the form of His cognition, and owing to the acquisition of identity with Him." (II,3).

Thus that is the real principle of the compact mass of light in which there is neither an object like pain, pleasure, blue etc. nor their experient.

(*objection*)

Well, if all subjects and objects are disposed of as non-existent, Reality is then mere Void. This is what it comes to.

(*Reply*)

No, there is also not mere insentiency. This means that there is not mere vacuity also. Insentiency is either manifest or non-manifest. If it is non-manifest, how can it be said to exist at all. If it is manifest, then because of its being manifest, it is nothing else but light. There can never be absence of light. In its absence, even the absence of light cannot be proved. This will find its place in 'not that internal nature', (I,16) in this book.

(Another explanation of *mūḍha-bhāva*).

Further, in these where is no insentiency, insentiency as understood by the vedāntists, viz. as 'Brahman', i.e. mere light devoid of the supreme power of *vimarśa* is also not there. The Vedāntists say 'Knowledge is Brahman', but such Brahman without the power of *Spanda* in the form of absolute Freedom would be mere lifeless, insentient, inert matter. As has been said in Īśvara-pratyabhijñā.

"People know *vimarśa* as the very nature of the light of consciousness, Otherwise light even if reflecting things would be insentient like a crystal". (I.pr.I.5.11).

In the following verse of Bhaṭṭa Nāyaka also, it is said:

"O Lord, how much fruit can this great Brahman being

enuch bear if thy beautiful *Śakti* were not there to stimulate thy masculine power ?"

Thus that principle alone has real existence which has been discussed in 'where all this rests' (verse 2) and further on. That and that alone exists in the highest sense as is proved by reasoning, experience, and revealed traditional scripture. That exists in the natural, perfect form, not in the artificial form like blue, etc. As has been said by the great teacher:[1]

"The insentient things are in themselves as good as non-existent. They have their existence only when connected with light. The light of oneself alone exists both in one's own form and in the form of others i.e. both as Subject (*pramātā*) and object (*prameya*) (Ajaḍa pr,13)

Revered Bhartṛhari[2] also says:

"That which exists in the beginning, in the end, and also in the middle alone has reality. That which simply appears has no reality, it is real only as long as it appears."

As the sentences of the text convey a determinate, limited sense in each case, the word *eva* should be joined thrice[3]. Thus by this *kārikā* the author has declared that ultimate Reality is only of the form of *Spanda-Śakti* by repeatedly pointing out the nonreality, on account of untenability of the views of the *Bauddhas* who maintain that Reality is a continuum of consciousness in the form of pleasure, etc., of the *Cārvākas* who maintain that reality is only the subject affected by pleasure, etc., of the followers of *Sāṃkhya* who maintain the plurality of the subject and the object, of the nihilists who maintain the absence of everything, of the *Vedantists* who maintain that *Brahman* is only *prakāśa* (light) without any activity.

Moreover, when in that noble person who attentively pursues the teaching, the *Spanda* principle, whose quintessence is flashing. throbbing consciousness, becomes manifest, then even when experiences of pain, pleasure, object, subject or their absence occur, they are considered by him as naught, because to him everything appears only as the quintessence of the delight of *Spanda*.

It has been taught that this is what is *spanda*. The venerable teacher refers to this truth in the following verse.

"That is the path pertaining to *Śaṅkara* in which pains become pleasure, poison becomes nectar, and the world that binds the soul becomes liberation."( U. Stotra 20,12).

The path pertaining to *Śaṅkara* means the preeminent expansion of the Highest *Śakti* who becomes a means to the attainment of the nature of *Śaṅkara*.

## NOTES

1. This refers to Utpaladeva.
2. This refers to the grammarian Bhartṛhari who wrote the philosophy of Grammar known as *Vākyapadīya*.
3. Kṣemarāja means that with the addition of *eva* the sentence would read as follows:

"यदादौ च तस्य एव सत्यता, यदन्ते च तस्य एव सत्यता, यन्मध्ये च तस्य एव सत्यता" ।

4. This again refers to Utpaladeva.

## EXPOSITION

The main point that has been stressed in this verse is that neither the experience of internal states like pleasure and pain, nor of external states like blue and yellow are the highest reality. Even the subject who experiences these states is not the highest reality. What the author means to say is that neither the psychological experiences, nor the psychological subject is the Highest Reality.

Kallaṭa, in his *vṛtti*, expresses the nature of the Highest Reality in the following words:

"तस्य चायं स्वभावो-यत्र सुखदुःखग्राह्यग्राहकमूढतादिभावैरस्पृष्टः स एव परमार्थतोऽस्ति नित्यत्वात् सुखादयः पुनः सङ्कल्पोत्थाः क्षणभंगुरा आत्मबाह्याः शब्दादिविपयतुल्याः" ।

This is the nature of Śiva (or the Spand principle) that He is untouched, unaffected by the experiences of pleasure, pain, etc; for Śiva or the Essential Self is the eternal experient. Pleasure, pain cannot be His nature, for two reasons. Firstly, they are passing phases of experience, perishing in an instant (*kṣaṇabhaṅgurā*). The Self is eternal. Therefore, they are external to the nature of the Self like sound, form and other objects (*ātmasvarūpā bāhyāḥ śabdādi-viṣayatulyāḥ*). Secondly, they arise from thought constructs (*saṅkalpotthāḥ*), whereas the Self is *nirvikalpa* i.e. it transcends the sphere of thought-constructs. For this reason also, pleasure, pain etc. cannot constitute the nature of Self.

Why are pleasure, pain etc. rejected as not forming a part of the nature of the Self? Rāmakaṇṭha answers the question in the following words in his *vivṛti*.

"By the rejection of pleasure, etc, it is the objectivity of Self that is rejected". The Self can never be reduced to an object, it is the eternal Subject.

A pertinent question that arises here is this:

In verse three, it has been said, "He (Śiva) never departs from His nature as the Experient." In verse five, it is said, "He is neither the subject i.e. experient nor the object." Are these two statements not inconsistent? How can they be reconciled?

Rāmakaṇṭha anticipates this objection and answers it in the following way:

ग्राहकोऽपि मायीयः प्रमाता अत्र विवक्षितः, न तात्त्विक उपलब्धृमात्रस्वरूपः, तस्य एवं नित्यसत्त्वेन प्रतिपाद्यमानत्वात् । एवं मायीयो देहाद्यहंकारमयो ग्राहको-ऽपि यत्र नास्ति ।'

"By subject here, what is intended to be said is the *māyīya pramātā* i.e. the empirical subject, not the real, metempirical Self, for he has been explained only as the Eternal Experient. Thus the psychosomatic subject is not that Reality."

Finally, another question that arises is this. If he has nothing to do with the subject or object, if he is neither object, nor subject, then is he mere negation, mere void, insentient like a stone?

Kṣemarāja has in his commentary controverted all these views with merciless logic, and concludes by saying

तत्र पारमार्थिकं स्पन्दशक्तिरूपमेव तत्त्वमस्ति

"It is metempirical reality whose essential form is *Spanda-śakti.*"

Rāmakaṇṭha also says:

तत् वस्तु परमार्थतः अस्ति, सततम् अविलुप्तोपलब्धृमात्रलक्षणस्वभावत्वात् ।
(p.34) "He is the highest Reality whose nature it is to be an eternal Subject (never an object)."

The mystic application of this teaching consists in the fact that he who realizes this truth is never affected by the misfortunes of life.

*Introduction to the sixth and seventh verse*

TEXT

एवमुपपत्तिपरिघटिततत्त्वप्रत्यभिज्ञानाय साभिज्ञानमुपायं निरूपयति—

TRANSLATION

Now the author describes the means with hint for the recognition of that principle which has been logically demonstrated.

VERSES 6 and 7

TEXT

यतः करणवर्गोऽयं विमूढोऽमूढवत्स्वयम् ।
सहान्तरेण चक्रेण प्रवृत्तिस्थितिसंहृतीः ॥ ६ ॥
लभते तत्प्रयत्नेन परीक्ष्यं तत्त्वमादरात् ।
यतः स्वतन्त्रता तस्य सर्वत्रेयमकृत्रिमा ॥ ७ ॥

Yataḥ karaṇa-vargo 'yaṁ vimūḍho 'mūḍhavat svayam/
Sahāntareṇa cakreṇa pravṛtti-sthiti-saṃhṛtīḥ//6
Labhate tatprayatnena parīkṣyaṁ tattvam ādarāt/
Yataḥ svatantratā tasya sarvatreyam akṛtrimā//7

TRANSLATION

That principle should be examined with great care and reverence by which this group of senses, though insentient, acts as a sentient force by itself, and along with the inner group of senses, goes towards objects, takes pleasure in their maintenance, and withdraws into itself, because this natural freedom of it prevails everywhere. 6 and 7.

COMMENTARY

TEXT

तन्निर्णीतं तत्त्वमादरात् श्रद्धया प्रयत्नेन च
'उद्यमो भैरवः' (१।५)

**इति शिवसूत्रप्रतिपादितेन सर्वभेदोपसंहारात्मना निजौजोवृत्तिस्फारणरूपेण परिपूर्णान्तर्मुखस्वरूपसेवनात्मना भैरवरूपेणोद्यमेन परीक्ष्यम् । यत इयमिति सर्वस्य स्वसंविदिता तस्य शङ्करात्मनः स्वस्वभावस्याकृत्रिमा सहजा-स्पन्दतत्त्वरूपा स्वतन्त्रता सर्वत्र-जडाजडविषये स्फुरन्ती स्थितेति शेषः । किं तत्तत्त्वमित्याह–यत इत्यादि लभत इत्यन्तम् । अयमिति लोकप्रसिद्धो गोलकादिरूपो न तु शास्त्रतस्तस्य नित्यपरोक्षत्वेनायमिति निर्देशाभावात्, करणवर्गस्त्रयोदशेन्द्रियाणि विशेषेण मूढो मायावशाज्जडाभासीभूतोऽणोर्मूढादप्यधिकं मूढत्वं प्राप्तोऽमूढवच्चेतनवत्स्वयं प्रवृत्ति-स्थितिसंहृतीर्लभते विषयोन्मुखीभवति तत्र रज्यते ततश्च निवर्तत इत्यर्थः । कथं सहान्तरेण चक्रेण, इहान्तरं चक्रं करणेश्वर्यो नान्तःकरणानि तेषां वर्गशब्देन स्वीकारात्, न वक्ष्यमाणं पुर्यष्टकं तत्स्थस्यान्तःकरणत्रयस्य वर्गशब्देनैव गृहीतत्वात्, तन्मात्राणां च वासनामात्ररूपाणामुपदेश्यमयोगिनं प्रति साक्षात्प्रवृत्त्यादिकर्तृत्वे-नासिद्धेः, योगिनस्तु साक्षात्कृततन्मात्रस्य स्वयमेव परतत्त्वपरिशीलनावहितस्योप-देश्यत्वाभावात्; तस्मादेतदेकीयमतमसत् । विमूढोऽमूढवदित्यनेन करणवर्ग एव सम्बन्ध्यो, न त्वान्तरमपि करणेश्वरीचक्रं, तस्य चिच्चमत्काररूपत्वात् । एवमभिद-धानस्यायमाशयः, यदयं शङ्करात्मा स्वस्वभावोऽतिदुर्घटकारिणः स्वातन्त्र्याद्युगपदेव संवित्तिसारं च करणेश्वरीचक्रं जडाभासरूपं च करणवर्गमैक्यतयैव निर्भासयन् प्रवृत्तिस्थितिसंहृतीः कारयति येन भगवत्यः करणेश्वर्यो यथा तत्तद्भावसृष्ट्यादि विदधति तथा करणवर्गो जडोऽपि तत्कारीव लक्ष्यते । यद्यपि रहस्यदृष्टौ न कश्चि-ज्जडः करणवर्गोऽस्ति अपितु विज्ञानदेहाः करणेश्वर्य एव विजृम्भन्ते तथापीह सुप्रसिद्धप्रतीत्यनुसारेणोपदेश्यः क्रमेण रहस्यार्थोपदेशेऽनुप्रवेश्य इत्येवमुक्तम् । एवं च गोलकादिरूपकरणवर्गप्रवृत्त्यादिक्रमेण तदधिष्ठातृरूपं निजमरीचिचक्रं चिन्वानेनैव तदुभयप्रचोदकं श्रीमच्छङ्करात्मकं स्वस्वरूपं परीक्षणीयं, यतस्तत्प्राप्तौ तदीयाकृत्रिमा स्वतन्त्रतास्य[1] योगिनः स्यादित्यनेनैवोक्तं भवति । तदेतदेव परीक्षणार्हं परमोपादेयत्वादेतदेव च परीक्षितुं शक्यमुक्तयुक्त्या सुखोपायत्वात्, अत एवादरेणाभिलषितविषयोपभोगानिरोधात्मना बहुमानेन । अत्र परीक्षण-स्येहत्योपदेशानुसारेण प्राप्तकालता । यथोक्तं रहस्यगुरुभिः**

'निजनिजेषु पदेषु पतन्त्विमाः करणवृत्तय उल्लसिता मम ।
क्षणमपीश मनागपि मैव भूत्त्वद्विभेदरसक्षतिसाहसम् ॥' (उ० स्तो० ८।७)

**इति । परीक्ष्यमित्यर्हे शक्ये प्राप्तकालतायां प्रैषादौ च कृत्यः । अथ च जडः करण-वर्गो यद्बलादमूढवत्प्रवृत्त्यादि लभते इति सर्वस्यानुभवसाक्षिकमभिदधदिन्द्रियादि-चैतन्यवादिचार्वाकमतमप्यनेन व्युदस्तवान् ॥७॥**

१. ख० पु० स्वतन्त्रा सर्वत्रास्येति पाठः ।

## *Translation of the Commentary*

That principle which has been finally ascertained with the exposition of 'Udyamo Bhairavaḥ' given in Śiva-sūtras (5,6) should be examined with great care and reverence. That principle should be examined as the cessation of all differences[1] (in the state of dissolution), as the expansion of one's own power (in the state of manifestation) as cherishing of the perfect inner nature (in the state of maintenance) and in the form of the emergence of the nature of Bhairava.

That innate Freedom in the form of Spanda principle known to every one through Self-experience being one's own essential nature, identical with *Śiva* is manifest everywhere both with reference to the sentient and the insentient.[2]

*Sphurantī sthitā* i.e. 'abides flashing' is to be supplied to complete the sense.

What is that principle? The author describes it from 'Yataḥ upto the end of 'labhate.'

*Ayaṁ karaṇavargaḥ* means 'this group of senses.' This group of senses refers to the sense-organs well known to people, not to *karaṇeśvarī-varga* (the group of the divinities of the senses) which is described in the *śāstras*, for being always imperceptible, it cannot be referred to as 'this'. By group of senses is meant the thirteen senses (5 organs of sense+5 organs of action +*manas, buddhi* and *ahaṃkāra* i.e. the ego-sense). The adjective *vimūḍha* (insentient) applied to 'the group of senses' means 'distinctly insentient' i.e. appearing as insentient owing to the influence of Māyā.' This group of senses, though insentient to a great degree in a limited empirical being, acquires, like the non-insentient i. e. the sentient, the power of going forth, staying, and withdrawing (*pravṛtti* (*sthiti-saṃhṛtiḥ*). *Pravṛtti* means going forth i.e. being directed towards the objects of sense[1]; *sthiti* means 'feeling attached to them' and '*saṁhṛti*' means 'withdrawing from them'.

How do they go forth? They do so along with the inner group. One view is that here the inner group means the *karaṇeśvarīs*[3], (the sense-divinities), and not *antaḥ-karaṇa* i.e. the inner senses, for the inner senses are already included in *karaṇa-varga* (the group of senses). Nor does the *antara-cakra* i.e. the inner group of *śaktis* refer to *puryaṣṭaka* (the group of eight i.e. the five *tanmātrās*, and *manas*, *buddhi* and *ahaṃkāra*) to be described later, for the triad of the inner senses (i.e. *manas*, *buddhi* and *ahaṁkāra*) residing in *puryaṣṭaka* is already included in *karaṇa varga* (the group of the senses).

The triad of *manas*, *buddhi* and *ahaṁkāra* may not be included in (*antara cakra*, what about the five *tanmātras*? Kṣemarāja takes up the question of the *tanmātras* now).

The five *tanmātras* are also not to be included in the *antara cakra*, for they are like mere seminal impressions and are not known as directly functioning in *pravṛtti*, etc. in the case of beginners who are mere pupils and are not *yogis*. So far as *yogī* is concerned, he has directly experienced the *tanmātras*, and is himself intent on realizing the supreme principle. So he needs no instruction. Therefore, this partisan view is wrong.[4]

*Vimūḍho amūḍhavat*—Though insentient like a sentient being—'this phrase also refers to the group of senses,' not to the inner group of sense-divinities, for that (i.e., the group of sense-divinities) is of the nature of Consciousness-bliss.

The sense of what is said in the first four lines is this:

"This *Śaṅkara* who is one's own essential nature through His Freedom which accomplishes impossible things manifests simultaneously as one the group of sense-divinities (*Karaṇeśvarī-cakra*) which is the quintessence of consciousness and the group of senses (*karaṇavarga*) which is apparently insentient and makes them perform such acts as moving towards objects, staying there (for a short while) and then withdrawing. Thus whatever the sense-divinities do, as for instance, bringing about the manifestation of different objects etc. that the group of senses, though insentient, also appears to be doing.

Though from the esoteric point of view there is no such thing as insentient group of senses—rather it is the sense-divinities which are of the nature of consciousness that expand in that way, still in this world a pupil has to be taught at first according to well-known beliefs and then gradually he has to be led to the teaching of esoteric matters.

Thus one should, by watching carefully the group of one's own sense divinities, presiding over the functions of forth-going etc. of the sense-organs, etc. carefully examine one's essential Self identical with *Śaṅkara* who impels both the group of senses and the group of sense-divinities. This is also implied by the above teaching that the *yogin*, in acquiring his essential nature, will also acquire its natural Freedom.[5]

Hence, this being the highest aim is worthy of being examined. This alone can be examined, because by the aforseaid reasoning, it is easy means (for the attainment of the aim). Therefore, it should be examined with respect and great consideration, for it leads to the unhindered enjoyment of one's desired object. Such an examination according to the teaching contained in this book is done at the fit time. As has been said by the teacher who[6] knew the secret doctrine:

"These sense-activities of mine may, in their joy, have full play in their objects. But, O Lord, grant that I may not have the temerity of losing even for a moment and even slightly the enjoyment of the bliss of identity with thee" (U.Sto.VIII,5).

The *kṛtya* suffix in *parīkṣyam* ('should be examined') denotes *arhā* or worthiness, *śakyatā* or practicability, *prāptakālatā* or timeliness, *praiṣa* or command, etc.[7]

By maintaining that the insentient group of senses acquires its power from the *Spanda* principle and acts like a sentient being in moving towards the objects, etc. a fact to which the self-experience of every one bears witness, the author has incidentally refuted the view of *Cārvākas* who attribute consciousness to the senses.[8]

## NOTES

1. *Sarvabhedopasaṁhāra* indicates the power of dissolution (*saṃhāra*), *nijauja-vṛtti-sphāraṇa-rūpeṇa* indicates the power of manifestation (*sṛṣṭi*); *paripūrṇāntarmukhasvarūpa-sevanātmanā* indicates the power of maintenance (*sthiti*).

2. *Jaḍa* (insentient) refers to *karaṇa-varga* or the group of senses, and *ajaḍa* (sentient) refers to *Karaṇeśvarī-varga*, the inner senses-divinities.

3. *Karaṇeśvarīs* means the group of the inner divinities that preside over the senses and make them function properly.

4. The view that *antara-cakra* refers to the inner *karaṇeśvarīs* the inner sense-divinities, and not to *antaḥ-karaṇa*, the inner group of senses (*manas*, *buddhi* and *ahaṁkāra*) is, according to Kṣemarāja, wrong.

5. This *svatantratā* or Freedom is called *akṛtrimā* i.e. natural or innate, because as Rāmakaṇṭha puts it, it is *akṛtrimā sahajaiva, na tu upādāna-sahakāryādi-kāraṇātarāpekṣiṇī svecchāmātrādhīna-sakala-kārya-kartṛtvarūpā* (p. 33) i.e. it is not dependent on any material cause or any other auxiliary cause (in achieving its object), because it is self-sufficient to accomplish every thing by its mere Will.

6. This refers to Utpaladeva.

7. There is *kṛtya* suffix in *parīkṣyam*. According to Pāṇini, *kṛtya* suffix denotes *arhā* or worthiness. *śakyatā* or practicability, *prāptakālatā* or fitness of time, *praiṣa* or command. All these apply to *parīkṣyam*. One's essential nature or *Spanda* principle should be examined, because nothing can be so worthy of examination as one's own essential nature. This is *arhatā* or worthiness of examination. It can be examined. It is practicable, it is not impossible. This shows *śakyatā* or practicability of examination. When the senses are functioning and are engaged in their objects, that is the exact time when one should examine the power behind the senses that makes them function in that way. This shows *prāptakālatā* or fitness of time for the examination.

Finally, *parīkṣyam* i.e. 'should be examined' denotes *praiṣa* or command of the teacher who knows the secret doctrine.

8. Cārvākas believe that the senses have consciousness. By showing that the senses do not have consciousness *per se* but derive it from the *spanda* principle, the author has refuted the theory of the *Cārvākas*.

## EXPOSITION

People in general and the materialists in particular think that it is the senses which carry out the function of *pravṛtti*, *sthiti* and *saṃhṛti* i.e. it is the senses which actively go out towards the objects of perception (*pravṛtti*) maintain them in perception for a while (*sthiti*) and finally return to themselves (*saṃhṛti*).

This verse teaches that the senses do not have the power of these functions in themselves; they derive this power from something else. That something else should be reverentially examined. That is the *Spanda* principle, that is Śiva; that is one's own essential Self.

It is because this Self is not perceptible as an object, therefore we are unaware of it. This has to be known inwardly as the Seer of all the seen. Utpala Bhaṭṭa in his *Spanda-pradīpikā* quotes a beautiful verse to re-enforce this truth:

अदृश्यं नेत्रवद् ब्रह्म द्रष्टृत्वं चास्ति नेत्रवत् ।
स्वात्मन्येवोपलम्भोऽस्य दर्शनं घटवन्न तु ॥

"Like the eye, Brahma is not the seen, like the eye, it is only the seer. Its ascertainment is only within One's own Self; it is not an object of sight like a jar."

*Introduction to the 8th Sūtra.*

## TEXT

अथ कथमुक्तं ततस्तत्त्वाच्चेतनतामिवासाद्येन्द्रियाणि स्वयं प्रवृत्त्यादि लभन्त इति, यावतायमेव ग्राहक इच्छया दात्रादीनीव करणानि प्रेरयति । यदप्युक्तं तत्तत्त्वं प्रयत्नेन परीक्ष्यम् इति तदपि कथं, यतोऽस्माकमिच्छा बहिरेवानुधावति न तु तत्त्वपरीक्षायां प्रवर्तितुमुत्सहत इत्याशङ्क्याह—

## TRANSLATION

Now, how is it said that the senses having obtained consciousness from that Spanda-principle move towards objects, etc. when it is known that the experient himself, by his own will dirccts the senses like scythe, etc? How is this also said that that principle should be examined with great care, because our desire moves only towards outside and does not exert itself in marching towards the examination of that reality. In reply to this objection, the author says:

## TEXT OF THE VERSE

न ह्रीच्छानोदनस्यायं प्रेरकत्वेन वर्तते ।
अपि त्वात्मबलस्पर्शात्पुरुषस्तत्समो भवेत् ॥ ८ ॥

Na hīcchānodanasyāyam prerakatvena vartate/
Api tvātmabalasparśāt puruṣastatsamo bhavet//8.

## TRANSLATION

The empirical individual cannot drive the goad of desire. But by coming in contact with the power of the Self, he becomes equal to that principle.8

### Text of the Commentary

अयं लौकिकः पुरुष इच्छैव नोदनं प्रतोदस्तस्य प्रेरकत्वेन करणप्रवर्तनार्थंव्यापारणाय यस्मान्न प्रवर्तते, अपि तु आत्मनश्चिद्रूपस्य यद्बलं स्पन्दतत्त्वात्मकं तत्स्पर्शात्तत्कृतात्कियन्मात्रादावेशात्तत्समो भवेत्, अहन्तारसविप्रुडभिषेकादचेतनोऽपि चेतनतामासादयत्येव । ततस्तत्तत्त्वं न केवलं करणानि यावत्तत्प्रेरकत्वेन शङ्कितं कल्पितमपि प्रमातारं चेतनीकृत्य स्वयं प्रवृत्त्यादिपात्रं करोति येनास्यायमभिमानोऽहं करणानि प्रेरयामीति । स्पन्दतत्त्वानुवेधं विनापि तु स एव न किञ्चिदिति करणानां ग्राहकस्य च स्वरश्मिचक्रप्रसरानुवेधेन चेतनीभावापादकं तत्त्वं परीक्ष्यमिति युक्तमेव । यदि पुनरिच्छाख्येन प्रतोदरूपेण करणान्तरेण करणानि प्रेरयेत् तदपीच्छाख्यं करणं प्रेर्यत्वात्करणान्तरं स्वप्रेरणायापेक्षेत तदप्यन्यदित्यनवस्था स्यात् । यत्तूक्तम् 'अस्माकमिच्छा न तत्र प्रवर्तितुमुत्सहते' इति तत्राप्याद्यं श्लोकार्धमभ्युपगमेन, परं तूत्तरतया योज्यम् । सत्यं, नायं पुरुषस्तत्त्वपरीक्षार्थमिच्छां प्रवर्तयितुं शक्नोति नेच्छया तत्त्वं विषयीकर्तुं क्षमस्तस्याविकल्प्यत्वादपि तु विषयाननुधावन्तीमिच्छां तदुपभोगपुरःसरं प्रशमय्य यदा त्वन्तर्मुखमात्मबलं स्पन्दतत्त्वं स्वकरणानां च चेतनावहं स्पृशति तदा तत्समो भवेत् तत्समावेशात्तद्वत्सर्वत्र स्वतन्त्रतामासादयत्येव, यस्मादेवं तस्मात्तत्त्वं परीक्ष्यमित्यर्थः । शक्तिभूमेः स्पर्शप्रधानत्वादात्मबलस्पर्शादित्युक्तम् ॥८॥

### Translation of the commentary

*Ayaṃ* means this empirical individual. *Icchaiva nodanaṃ pratodaḥ tasya* means 'of the goad of desire'. The whole of the first line of the verse means 'he does not set out to move the senses (towards their objects)'.

But he becomes equal to it (*tatsamo bhavet*) by the contact i.e. by the entrance into him, to some extent, of the power of the Self which is Consciousness and which is of the nature of *Spanda*. The sense is that the sense-group, even though insentient acquires sentiency by the consecration of the drops of blissful sap of I-consciousness. Thence that Spanda principle not only moves the senses but rather by infusing consciousness into the supposed experient makes him capable of effecting the movement, etc. of the senses by virtue of which he is full of the erroneous conception, "I am directing the senses". He himself is nothing without the infusion of the Spanda principle into him. Therefore, it is perfectly right to say that one should examine that principle which provides consciousness to both the senses and the perceiver by the impenetration of the forth-going rays of its own light.

If it is maintained that one directs the senses by an internal sense which uses a goad called desire, then that sense called desire being itself of the nature of the directed would require another sense for setting it in motion, and that in its turn would require another and so on. Thus there would be *regressus ad infinitum.*

As regards the objection that is raised, viz., 'Our desire does not exert itself in moving towards that' in that case also, the first half of the verse should be used as an admission of this position, and the latter half as a reply.

True this empirical individual cannot move his desire to examine the Spanda-principle, nor is he capable of experiencing that reality by desire, because it is beyond the range of thought, even then when, calming down his desire which is in pursuit of objects of pleasure by at first allowing it to have its enjoyment, he contacts the Spanda-principle which is the power of the inner Self and which endows his senses with consciousness, then he becomes equal to that Spanda-principle i.e. by being immersed in that reality, he acquires freedom everywhere like that. Since such is the case, that principle should be examined. This is the sense. The expression 'by the touch of the power of Self' has been used, because the quality of touch is predominant in the stage of Śakti.

## EXPOSITION

The gist of the verse is that man falsely imagines that he moves his senses to perform their respective functions by the power of his will or desire. His so-called desire has no power of its own. It derives its power of both knowing and doing from *Śiva* or *Spanda*-principle whose very nature is knowledge and activity. One has, therefore, to acquire the power of *Spanda* which is our own essential Self, neither by weaving intellectual cobwebs, nor by maiming desire, but by surrendering all desires, the entire personal will to the Divine. As Tennyson puts it:

"Our wills are ours, we know not how to make them thine."

When the personal *citta* or mind completely empties itself, then is it truly filled.

Kṣemarāja brings out in his commentary a very important principle of this system. It believes that while Śakti, the Divine Creative Power rejects all the perceptual qualities like *rūpa*, *rasa*, *gandha*, etc. she retains *sparśa* or touch. How is that Reality to be touched? Kṣemarāja says: "Tatsamāveśāt" 'i.e. by penetration, by diving mentally into its innermost depth. This is the mystic union.

*Introduction to the ninth verse*

TEXT

ननु चायं क्षेत्री परमेश्वरमयोऽपि किं न सदा पारिपूर्ण्येन स्फुरति, कस्मादन्तर्मुखात्मबलस्पर्शमपेक्षत इत्याशङ्क्याह—

TRANSLATION

A question arises here "Why does this embodied Self not shine in all its perfection, even though it is of the nature of the greatest lord? why does it require the touch of the force of the inner Self, the Experient *par excellence*? In reply to this question, the author says:

Text of the verse

निजाशुद्ध्यासमर्थस्य कर्तव्येष्वभिलाषिणः ।
यदा क्षोभः प्रलीयेत तदा स्यात्परमं पदम् ॥ ९ ॥

Nijāśuddhyāsamarthasya kartavyeṣv abhilāṣiṇaḥ/
Yadā kṣobhaḥ pralīyeta tadā syāt paramaṃ padam//9

## TRANSLATION

When the perturbation of that empirical individual who is incapacitated by his own impurity and is attached to actions disappears, then the highest state appears.

## COMMENTARY

## TEXT

निजा स्वात्मीया स्वस्वातन्त्र्योल्लासिता येयं स्वरूपाविमर्शस्वभावा इच्छाशक्तिः संकुचिता सत्यपूर्णम्मन्यतारूपा अशुद्धिराणवं मलं, तन्मलोत्थितकञ्चुकपञ्चकाबिलत्वात्, ज्ञानशक्तिः क्रमेण भेदे सर्वज्ञत्वकिञ्चिज्ज्ञत्वान्तःकरणबुद्धीन्द्रियतापत्तिपूर्वमत्यन्तं सङ्कोचग्रहणेन भिन्नवेद्यप्रथारूपं मायीयं मलमशुद्धिरेव। क्रियाशक्तिः क्रमेण भेदे सर्वकर्तृत्वकिञ्चित्कर्तृत्वकर्मेन्द्रियरूपसङ्कोचग्रहणपूर्वमत्यन्तं परिमिततां प्राप्ता शुभाशुभानुष्ठानमयं कार्मं मलमप्यशुद्धिः। तयासमर्थस्य पूर्णज्ञत्वकर्तृत्वविकलस्य तत एव कर्तव्येषु लौकिकशास्त्रीयानुष्ठानेष्वभिलाषिणोऽभीष्टानवाप्तेर्नित्यमभिलाषव्याकुलस्य तत एव क्षणमप्यलब्धस्वरूपविश्रान्तेः। यदा उक्तवक्ष्यमाणोपपत्त्यनुभवावष्टम्भतोऽभिलाषविवशग्राहकाभिमानात्मा क्षोभः प्रलीयेत अनात्मन्यात्माभिमाननिवृत्तिपुरःसरमात्मन्यनात्माभिमानोपशान्तिपर्यन्तेन प्रकर्षेण लीयेत तदा परमं स्पन्दतत्त्वात्मकं पदं स्यादस्य प्रत्यभिज्ञाविषयतां यायादित्यर्थः। न तु तदैव भवति तस्य नित्यत्वात्। उक्तं च विज्ञानभैरवे इति।

'मानसं चेतना शक्तिरात्मा चेति चतुष्टयम्।
यदा प्रिये परिक्षीणं तदा तद्भैरवं वपुः॥' (श्लो० १३८)

निजाशुद्धिशब्देन मलं नाम द्रव्यं पृथग्भूतमस्तीति ये प्रतिपन्नास्ते दूष्यत्वेन कटाक्षिताः॥९॥

## TRANSLATION

*Nija* means one's own. (Now *aśuddhi* or impurity is explained). First of all there is the *mala*[1] or limitation pertaining to the *aṇu* or *jīva*, the empirical being which consists in the consciousness of imperfection. This *āṇava mala* is the first *aśuddhi*. This occurs when *Icchā-śakti* (Will power of *Śiva*) becomes limited owing to non-contemplation of His essential nature which is brought into play by the absolute Freedom of *Śiva* Himself.

*Jñānaśakti* (the power of knowledge) being polluted by the five *kañcukas* or coverings (of Māyā) arisen from that (*āṇava-mala*) gradually acquires limitation in the sphere of difference so that its omniscience becomes reduced to limited knowledge and at last it acquires utmost limitation in the formation of the psychic apparatus (*antaḥkaraṇa*) and the organs of sense (*buddhīndriya*). This is *māyīya* limitation (i.e. limitation brought about by Māyā) which brings about consciousness of difference among objects. This *māyīya mala* is the second *aśuddhi*.

*Kriyā śakti* (the power of activity) gets limited gradually in the sphere of difference when omnipotence is reduced to limited activity till at last by the formation of the organs of action, the empirical individual gets limited to the utmost extent. He thus performs good and bad acts. This is the *Kārma mala* or limitation due to action. This is the third kind of impurity.[2]

Thus by such impurity, the individual becomes devoid of omniscience and omnipotence.

(Now Kṣemarāja explains the phrase *Kartavyeṣu abhilāṣiṇaḥ* of the text.)

Being thus incapacitated he is attached to all kinds of actions—worldly and those prescribed by the scriptures. On account of the non-attainment of all his desired objects, he is distracted by his desires and is unable to find rest in his essential nature even for a moment.

(Now Kṣemarāja explains the remaining half of the verse from *Yadā* . . . upto *padam*).

When by a firm support of the reasoning already mentioned and also to be mentioned later on and of self-experience, his perturbation[3] appearing in the form of an experient who is helplessly dominated by desires, thoroughly dissolves (*pralīyeta* = *prakarṣeṇa līyeta*) through the vanishing of the misconception of the not-Self as the Self and of the Self as the not-self, then the highest state, viz. the *spanda*-principle will emerge i.e. will come within the range of recognition of that experient. Not that the *Spanda*-principle is something that comes into existence only at that time, for it is eternal (i.e. the Spanda-principle is always there; only its recognition is new).

It has been rightly said in Vijñānabhairava: "O dear one, when the ideating mind (*manas*), the ascertaining intellect (*buddhi*), the vital energy (*prāṇa śakti*) and the limited experient, I—this set of four dissolves, then the previously described (*tat*) state of Bhairava appears". (verse, 138).

Those who by the phrase 'one's own impurity' think that there is a separate substance called *mala* (dross) have been indirectly criticized in the above commentary.

## NOTES

1 *Aśuddhi* or impurity simply means *mala*. *Mala* does not mean an impure substance but only limiting condition.

2. The experient becomes limited by three kinds of *mala-āṇava*, *Māyīya* and *Kārma*. *Āṇava mala* is the primal limiting condition which reduces the universal consciousness to an *aṇu*, a small, limited entity. It is owing to this that the *jīva* (individual soul) considers himself *apūrṇa*, imperfect, cut off from the universal consciousness. In this condition, the individual forgets his essential divine nature.

*māyīya mala* is the limiting condition brought about by *māyā* that gives to the soul its gross and subtle body. It is *bhinna vedya prathā*—that which brings about the consciousness of difference owing to the differing limiting adjuncts of the bodies.

*Kārmamala* arises on account of the limitation of the organs of action and is due to the residual impressions of good and bad actions.

*Āṇava mala* is the innate ignorance of one's essential nature. *Māyīya mala* arises on account of the limitation of *jñāna-śakti* (the power of knowledge), and *Kārma mala* arises on account of the limitation of *Kriyāśakti*.

3. *Kṣobha* or perturbation is due to primal ignorance owing to which the limited individual considers the not-Self, as Self and the Self as the not-Self.

## EXPOSITION

If man is really divine, why is he so imperfect and stands in need of the power of the inner Self? The ninth verse contains the answer to this question.

The divine plan of evolution contains two movements. There is first of all gradual descent of the Self in inconscient matter. Two things happen in this process of descent. The empirical being forgets his essential divine nature. This is *āṇava mala*. Secondly, he gets confined to subtle and gross bodies. This is *māyīya mala*. As he is engaged in all sorts of good and bad acts, these leave behind their impressions in his mind which act as a a strong force dragging him down to material existence of further experiences. This is *Kārma mala*. These limiting conditions are called *aśuddhi* (impurity, limitation) in the verse.

It is only at the human level that ascent to the divine status can start. The main obstacle in his ascent is his pseudo-self that arrogates to itself the status of the main actor in the drama. This pseudo-self has been called *kṣobha* in the verse, for it is this that is responsible for all the fret and fever of life. When this is dissolved, then Self-forgetfulness is replaced by Self-recollection and man's evolution is complete.

*Introduction to the tenth verse*

TEXT

ननु च ग्राहकाहंभावात्मनि क्षोभे क्षीणे निस्तरङ्गजलधिप्रख्यमस्पन्दमेव तत्त्वं प्रसक्तमित्याशङ्कां शमयति

TRANSLATION

Well, if the perturbation in the form of I-consciousness of the limited, empirical individual is dissolved, then reality will be devoid of activity and will become like a waveless ocean. To allay this doubt, the author says:

*Text of the 10th Verse*

तदास्याकृत्रिमो धर्मो ज्ञत्वकर्तृत्वलक्षणः ।
यतस्तदेप्सितं सर्वं जानाति च करोति च ॥ १० ॥

Tadāsyākṛtrimo dharmo jñatvakartṛtvalakṣaṇaḥ/
Yatas tadepsitaṃ sarvaṃ jānāti ca karoti ca//10

TRANSLATION

Then will flash forth his innate nature characterized by cognition and activity, by which he (the experient) then knows and does all that is desired (by him). 10

## COMMENTARY

### TEXT

तदेत्युपदेश्यापेक्षया अकृत्रिमः सहजो धर्मः प्राङ्निर्दिष्टस्वतन्त्रतारूपः परमेश्वरस्वभावो ज्ञत्वकर्तृत्वे सामरस्यावस्थितप्रकाशानन्दात्मनी ज्ञानक्रिये लक्षणमव्यभिचारिस्वरूपं यस्य तादृक् तदा क्षोभोपशमेऽस्य पुरुषस्य स्यादभिव्यज्यत इत्यर्थः । कुत एतदभिव्यज्यत इत्याह, यतस्तदा परमपदप्रवेशसमये सर्वमीप्सितमिति यद्यज्जिज्ञासितं चिकीर्षितं वास्य तत्प्रविविक्षायामभूत् तत्तज्जानाति च करोति च । चकारावत्र यौगपद्यमाहतुः, न तु यथैके चकाराभ्यां ज्ञानक्रिययोरैकात्म्यं सूचयतीति, तद्धि ज्ञत्वकर्तृत्वलक्षण इत्यनेनैवैकधर्मविशेषणेन सम्बन्धिनिर्देशेन वास्तवस्वरूपाभिधायिनोक्तम् ॥१०॥

### TRANSLATION

The word *tadā* meaning 'then' is used with reference to the pupil who is to be instructed. *Akṛtrimo dharmaḥ* means innate nature, which has been previously explained as Freedom, which is the nature of the highest Lord. *Jñatva* and *Kartṛtva* mean 'cognition' 'activity' of the nature of light and bliss blended harmoniously. *Lakṣaṇa* means everpresent characteristic. The whole compound word *Jñatva-kartṛtva-lakṣaṇa*, therefore, means that whose ever present characteristic is *Jñāna* (knowledge) and *kriyā* (activity) of the nature of light and bliss which are harmoniously blended. *Tadā* means that this characteristic becomes manifest in the limited empirical individual at the time of the cessation of perturbation.

Wherefore does it become manifest in him ? The author answers this query in the following way.

At the time of entrance in the supreme state, all that he (the limited experient) desired to know or to do at the time of the desire to enter that state, he is able to know and do.

The particle *ca* repeated twice (attached to *jānāti* and *karoti*) suggests simultaneity, not as some think, identity of knowledge and activity. It (i.e. the identity of knowledge and activity) is already implied by the adjectival phrase 'characterized by knowledge and activity' qualifying *dharma* or nature, and by pointing out that with which it is connected, it becomes descriptive of its real nature.

## EXPOSITION

The knowledge and activity of the empirical individual are *kṛtrima* (artificial) because firstly they are limited, secondly they are borrowed, i.e. derived from another source, viz., the *Spanda*-principle or the higher Self.

When the limited ego of the individual is dissolved and his perturbation ceases, then he does not become inert like stone; then he requires the real, innate nature of *jñāna* and *kriyā* which is characteristic of the existential Self. Then his inability to know and do whatever he wants to know and do ceases and he is now able to know and do whatever he desires to know or do.

Rāmakaṇṭha adds "वस्तुत एकैव ईश्वरस्य स्वभावप्रत्यवमर्शरूपा शक्तिः, सा संवेदनरूपत्वाज् ज्ञानशब्देन उच्यते, तावन्मात्रसंरम्भरूपत्वात् क्रियाशब्देन च उद्घोष्यते"। (p. 42)

"Really speaking there is one *śakti* of the Divine, viz. the consciousness of his essential nature as I. The same *Śakti* in the form of perceiving or feeling, is known as jñāna or knowledge; in the form of its volitional activity, it is known as *kriyā* or activity."

*Introduction to the eleventh Kārikā*

## TEXT

अथ यतः करणेति निजाशुद्धीति सूत्रप्रतिपादितोन्मेषक्रमसमाधानसाक्षात्कृतस्य स्पन्दतत्त्वस्यं दृढावष्टम्भाद्व्युत्थानमपि समाध्येकरसं कुर्वतो भवोच्छेदो भवतीत्याह-

## TRANSLATION

Now the author is going to explain that the world of life and death ceases to him who makes even the normal consciousness after trance (*vyutthāna*) similar to (*samādhi*) (meditation) by a firm grip of the *Spanda*-principle which is realized by *unmeṣa samādhi* which is explained in the verses 6-7 (*yataḥ karaṇa*, etc) and 9 (*nijāśudhyā*, etc).

Text of the 11th verse

तमधिष्ठातृभावेन स्वभावमवलोकयन्।
स्मयमान इवास्ते यस्तस्येयं कुसृतिः कुतः ॥ ११ ॥

Tam adhiṣṭhātṛbhāvena svabhāvam avalokayan/
Smayamāna ivāste yastasyeyaṃ kusṛtiḥ kutaḥ// 11

## TRANSLATION

How can this accursed way of life and death be his (any longer) who stands struck with amazement as he observes that nature (viz. *Spanda*) which presides over all the activities of of life (as I) ?

## COMMENTARY

### TEXT

**उक्तोपपत्त्युपलब्ध्यनुशीलनप्रत्यभिज्ञातं तं स्पन्दतत्त्वात्मकं स्वभावमात्मीयमधिष्ठातृभावेन व्युत्थानदशायामपि व्याप्नुवन्तमवलोकयंश्चिन्वानः**

'न व्रजेन्न विशेच्छक्तिर्मरुद्रूपा विकासिते ।
निर्विकल्पतया मध्ये तथा भैरवरूपधृक् ॥' (वि० भै० २६)

**इति, तथा**

'सर्वाः शक्तीश्चेतसा दर्शनाद्याः
स्वे स्वे वेद्ये यौगपद्येन विष्वक् ।
क्षिप्त्वा मध्ये हाटकस्तम्भभूत-
स्तिष्ठन्विश्वाकार एकोऽवभासि[1] ॥'

**इति श्रीविज्ञानभैरवकक्ष्यास्तोत्रनिर्दिष्टसंप्रदाययुक्त्या निमीलनोन्मीलनसमाधिना युगपद्व्यापकमध्यभूम्यवष्टम्भादध्यासितैतदुभयविसर्गारणिविगलितसकलविकल्पोऽक्रमस्फारितकरणचक्रः**

'अन्तर्लक्ष्यो बहिर्दृष्टिर्निमेषोन्मेषवर्जितः ।
इयं सा भैरवी मुद्रा सर्वतन्त्रेषु गोपिता ॥'

**इत्याम्नातभगवद्भैरवमुद्रानुप्रविष्टो मुकुरान्तर्निमज्जदुन्मज्जन्नानाप्रतिबिम्बकदम्बकल्पमनल्पं भावराशिं चिदाकाश एवोदितमपि तत्रैव विलीयमानं पश्यन् जन्मसहस्रापूर्वपरमानन्दघनलोकोत्तरस्वस्वरूपप्रत्यभिज्ञानाज् झटिति त्रुटितसकलवृत्तिः स्मयमानो विस्मयमुद्रानुप्रविष्ट इव महाविकासासादनाच्च सहसैव समुदितसमुचिततात्त्विकस्वभावो यो योगीन्द्र आस्ते तिष्ठति न त्ववष्टम्भाच्छिथिलीभवति, तस्येयमिति सकलजगत्कम्पकारिणी कुत्सिता जननमरणादिप्रबन्धरूपा सृतिः प्रवृत्तिः कुतो निजाशुद्धिलक्षणस्य तद्धेतोरभावान्नैव भवतीत्यर्थः । यथोक्तं श्रीपूर्वशास्त्रे**

---

१ ख० पु० विभातीति पाठः ।

'तत्त्वे निश्चलचित्तस्तु भुञ्जानो विषयानपि ।
नैव संस्पृश्यते दोषैः पद्मपत्रमिवाम्भसा ॥
विषापहारिमन्त्रादिसन्नद्धो भक्षयन्नपि ।
विषं न मुह्यते तेन तद्वद्योगी महामतिः ॥' (मा० वि० १८।१२०)
इति ॥११॥

## TRANSLATION

A *Yogī* who closely observes his own (inmost) nature which is the *Spanda*-principle recognized by means of the reasoning (already) mentioned, apprehends knowledge and activity as the presiding principle[1] of life as the 'I' pervading the normal consciousness even after meditation has ceased. His middle state (*madhya daśā*) develops as described in Vijñānabhairava in the following words :

"When the middle state develops by means of the dissolution of all dichotomising thought-constructs (*nirvikalpatayā*), the *prāṇa śakti* in the form of exhalation (*prāṇa*) does not go out from the centre (of the body) to *dvādaśānta*[2], nor does that *śakti* in the form of inhalation (*apāna*) enter into the centre from *dvādaśānta*. In this way, by means of Bhairavī who expresses herself in the form of the cessation of *prāṇa* (exhalation) and *apāna* (inhalation), one acquires the form of Bhairava. "(V. B. verse 26), or as described in Kakṣyāstotra in the following words :

"Throwing by will all the powers like seeing, etc. simultaneously on all sides into their respective objects and remaining (unmoved) in the middle like a gold pillar, you (O *Śiva*) alone appear as the form of the entire cosmos."

Thus all his thought-constructs vanish (*vigalita-sakalavikalpo*) by means of the traditional teaching, by *nimīlana* and *unmīlana samādhi* by the firm hold of the middle state[3] which pervades simultaneously both *nimīlana* (*Visarga*) and *unmīlana samādhi* (*araṇi*). As taught in the sacred tradition, he enters the *Bhairavamudrā* in which all his senses are widely open simultaneously but the attention is turned within as described in the following verse :

"Attention should be turned inwards; the gaze should be

turned outwards, without the twinkling of the eyes. This is the *mudrā*[4] pertaining to Bhairava, kept secret in all the Tantras."

He sees the totality of objects appearing and disappearing in the ether of his consciousness like a series of reflections appearing and disappearing in a mirror. Instantly all his thought-constructs are split asunder by the recognition, after a thousand lives, of his essential nature surpassing common experience and full of unprecedented bliss. He is struck with amazement, as though entering the *mudrā* of amazement.[5] As he obtains the experience of vast expansion, suddenly his proper, essential nature comes to the fore.

The word *āste* in the verse denotes the idea that he does not relax his firm hold (of the *Spanda*-principle).

*Iyaṃ kusṛtiḥ* means this wandering (*sṛtiḥ*) consisting in the wretched succession of life and death which causes tremor in all people of the world does not occur in his case, because of the absence of its cause consisting in innate impurity. As has been said in Śrī Pūrva Śāstra :[6]

'One' whose mind is fixed on reality, even though enjoying sense-objects, cannot be touched by vice, even as a lotus-leaf cannot be touched by water.

As one who is equipped with *mantra,* etc. that removes the effect of poison, does not, even after devouring poison, become unconscious under its influence, similarly a *yogī* of great wisdom (is not affected by the enjoyment of sense-objects)" (M. V. XVIII, 120).

## NOTES

1. Presiding principle means the principle that is the permanent Experient of all experiences.
2. *Dvādaśānta*—a distance of twelve fingers from the tip of the nose.
3. The middle state is *cidānanda*-consciousness-bliss.
4. *Mudrā* means the disposition and control of certain organs of the body as help in concentration.
5. This refers to *vismaya-mudrā* in which the mouth is wide open, and the tongue lolls out.
6. Pūrva-śāstra is another name of Mālinī-vijaya-tantra.

## EXPOSITION

When the yogī realizes the *spanda* principle, then he knows that this is his essential Self, and not the empirical, psycho-somatic creature whom he had so long considered to be his Self. He has now broken his shackles and is truly free.

### Introduction to the 12th and 13th Verse

### TEXT

अथ ये श्रुत्यन्तविदक्षपादमाध्यमिकादयः क्षोभप्रलये विश्वोच्छेदरूपमभावात्मकमेव तत्त्वमवशिष्यत इत्युपादिक्षन् तान्प्रतिबोधयितुं तदुपगततत्त्वप्रातिपक्ष्येण लोकोत्तरतां प्रकरणशरीरस्य स्पन्दतत्त्वस्य निरूपयति

### TRANSLATION

The Vedāntists, the Naiyāyikas the Mādhyamikas have taught that after the dissolution of agitation, there remains only the principle of naught i. e. universal destruction. In order to awaken them (from their ignorance), the author, in opposition to the reality as understood by them, elucidates the extra-ordinary characteristic of the *spanda*-principle which is the subject-matter of this treatise.

### Verses 12 and 13

### TEXT

नाभावो भाव्यतामेति न च तत्रास्त्यमूढता ।
यतोऽभियोगसंस्पर्शात्तदासीदिति निश्चयः ॥ १२ ॥
अतस्तत्कृत्रिमं ज्ञेयं सौषुप्तपदवत्सदा ।
न त्वेवं स्मर्यमाणत्वं तत्तत्त्वं प्रतिपद्यते ॥ १३ ॥

Nābhāvo bhāvyatāmeti na ca tatrāsty amūḍhatā/
Yato 'bhiyoga-saṃsparśāt tadāsid iti niścayaḥ// 12
Atastatkṛtrimaṃ jñeyaṃ sauṣupta-padavat sadā/
Na tvevaṃ smaryamāṇatvaṃ tat tattvaṃ pratipadyate// 13.

## TRANSLATION

Mere non-existence cannot be an object of contemplation, nor can it be said there is no stupefaction in that state, because on account of the application of backward reference, it is certain that it (i.e. the experience of stupefaction) was there (in that state).

Hence that artificial object of knowledge is always like sound sleep. It is not in this manner i.e. as a state of recollection that the *Spanda*-principle is known.

## COMMENTARY

### TEXT

'असदेवेदमग्र आसीत् ।' (छा० ३।१९।१)

**इत्याद्युक्त्या श्रुत्यन्तविदाद्यभिमतोऽभावो भाव्यतां नैति भावनाया भाव्यवस्तु-विषयत्वादभावस्य न किञ्चित्त्वाद्भाव्यमानतायां वा किञ्चित्त्वे सत्यभावत्वाभावात् । किञ्च भावकस्यापि यत्राभावः स विश्वोच्छेदः कथं भावनीयः भावकाभ्युपगमे तु न विश्वोच्छेदो भावकस्यावशिष्यमाणत्वादिति न विश्वाभाव एव तत्त्वम् । अथ कल्पितोऽयं भावको विश्वोच्छेदं विकल्पयमानं भावयन् भावनापरिनिष्पत्तौ भाव्यतादात्म्यादभावरूपः सम्पद्यत इति पक्षः । तत्रोच्यते, तत्राभावभावनायां नामूढता न च तत्रास्त्यमूढता अपि तु मोह एवास्ति**

'तस्माद्भूतमभूतं वा यद्यदेवातिभाव्यते ।
भावनापरिनिष्पत्तौ तत्स्फुटं कल्पधीफलम्' ।।

**इति न्यायाद्विश्वोच्छेदात्मन्यभावे भाव्यमाने न कदाचित्परमार्थाप्तिर्भवति । अथोच्यते**

'सर्वालम्बनधर्मैश्च सर्वतत्त्वैरशेषतः ।
सर्वक्लेशाशयैः शून्यं न शून्यं परमार्थतः ।।'

**इति नागार्जुनोक्तमीदृशं तच्छून्यमिति । सत्यं, यदि चिदानन्दघना स्वतन्त्रा पारमार्थिकी भित्तिभूता भूरभ्युपेयते यथा विज्ञानभैरवादौ पारमेश्वरी**

'दिक्कालकलनातीता' । (वि० भै० १४)

**इत्यादिना पारमार्थिकीं भित्तिभूतां चिद्भूमिमवस्थाप्य शून्यभावनोक्ता । अन्यथा न शून्यमिति शून्यैवेयमुक्तिः 'यद्यदेवातिभाव्यते' इति प्रतिपादितत्वात् । यत्तु**

'सावस्था काप्यविज्ञेया मादृशां शून्यतोच्यते ।
न पुनर्लोकरूढ्येव नास्तिक्यार्थानुपातिनी' ।।

इत्यालोकमालायामुक्तं तत्तु सत्यं, त्वादृशामविज्ञेया अविज्ञेयत्वाद्वक्तुमशक्येत्युच्यतां, शून्यतेति तु कुतः, शून्यतापि च यावद्भाव्यते तावद्विकल्पोल्लिखितत्वादसौ विज्ञैव। यदि च त्वादृशां सा ज्ञातुमशक्या तत् तत्पदसाक्षात्काराभिज्ञसद्गुरुसपर्या कार्या, न तु शून्यतेति स्वमनीषिकयैव व्यवहृत्यात्मा परश्चागाधे महामोहे निक्षेप्तव्य इत्यलम् । अथ कुतो ज्ञातं तत्र मूढतास्तीत्यत्रानेनोत्तरमाह यत इति । अभियोगः समाधानोत्थितस्य कीदृगहमासमिति तदवस्थाभिमुखविमर्शात्माभिलापस्ततत्सं-स्पर्शात् तद्वशाद्धेतोस्तदासीदिति यतो निश्चयः 'गाढमूढोऽहमासम्' इति यतोऽस्ति प्रतिपत्तिः अतो मोहावस्थैव सा कल्पिता तथा स्मर्यमाणत्वात्, सा चानुभूयमान-त्वादनुभवितुः प्रमातुरवस्थातृरूपस्य प्रत्युत सत्तामावेदयते न त्वभावमिति । विश्वा-भावावस्थायां चिद्रूपस्याखण्डितमेव रूपं तिष्टतीति नामुष्याभावो जातुचिद्वक्तुं शक्यत इत्युक्तं भवति । ननु दृष्टं निश्चितं नीलादि स्मर्यते न च शून्यभूतस्य न्यग्भूतबुद्धिवृत्तेर्निश्चयोऽस्ति तत्कथमुक्तं तदासीदित्यौत्तरकालिकान्निश्चयान्मूढता सेति । उच्यते वेद्यस्यैषा गतिः, यस्मात्तदिदन्तासारमिदन्तया यावत्प्रमात्रा स्वात्मोपारोहेण न निश्चितं तावन्न स्मर्यते, वेदकस्तु कल्पितशून्याद्यवस्थासु सङ्कुचितोऽप्यसांकेतिकाहन्तापरमार्थ एवेति न तस्य स्वात्मनि पृथक्तास्तीति तन्निश्चायको विकल्पः,—इत्यहंविमृश्यमेव तदा स्वसंवेदनेनैव सिद्धं, शून्यप्रमातृ-रूपं विश्वप्रतियोगित्वाच्च संकोचसारं संदुत्तरकालं स्मर्यत इति न काचिदनुपपत्तिर्य-स्मादेवमतस्तच्छून्यात्मकं पदं कृत्रिमम्

'तस्माद्भूतमभूतं वा यद्यदेवातिभाव्यते' ।

इति [1]तदुक्तयैव नीत्या अभूतभावनयैवोत्थापितं परमेश्वरेणैव ज्ञानगोपनायै मूढा-नामुपेयतया तथा भासितमित्यर्थः । ज्ञेयं ज्ञातव्यं ज्ञेयरूपं च सदा सुषुप्तवदिति दृष्टान्तः । अयं भावः—सदा सुषुप्तं मोहरूपमप्रयाससिद्धं सर्वस्यास्त्येव तत्किमनेन समाधिप्रयत्नोपार्जितेनान्येन शून्येन कृत्यं, द्वयस्याप्यवस्तुत्वाविशेषादिति । प्राय-श्चास्मिन् शून्ये दुरुत्तरे महामोहार्णव एव वेदान्तविदक्षपादसांख्यसौगतादिप्राया बह्वोऽनुप्रविष्टाः । स्पन्दतत्त्वसमाविविक्षूणामपि च शिथिलीभूतप्रयत्नानां शून्यमेतद्विघ्नभूतम् । यद्वक्ष्यति

'तदा तस्मिन्महाव्योम्नि' । (१।२५)

इत्यारभ्य

'सौपुप्तपदवन्मूढः·······।' (१।२५)

इति । अत एतदुच्छेदे ग्रन्थकारस्य महान् संरम्भो लक्ष्यते । तथा चेह हेयतयैव तन्निर्णीयापि पुनरपि निर्णेष्यते

'कार्योन्मुखः प्रयत्नो यः···' (१।१५)

---

१ क० ख० पु० एतदिति पाठः ।

इत्यत्र । ततोऽस्माभिरेतद्दूषणारम्भः कृत इति न नः कोपः कार्योऽत्रभवद्भिरुपदेशनिभालन[1]दत्तकर्णैः । सौगतेषु दूषितेषु श्रुत्यन्तवादादयो दूषिता एव तुल्यन्यायत्वादिति नाभ्यधिकमुक्तम् । तदिदानीं प्रकृतमेव ब्रूमहे तत्तु स्पन्दाख्यं तत्त्वमेवमिति शून्यवन्न स्मर्यमाणत्वं प्रतिपद्यते, तस्य सर्वदानुस्यूतोपलब्धृैकरूपस्य कदाचिदप्यनुपलभ्यत्वायोगात् । तथा चाहुः

'विज्ञातारमरे केन विजानीयात्' । (बृ० आ० उ० ४।५।१५)

इति । यद्यपि च समावेशदशा व्युत्थितेन प्राणादिसंस्कारवशात्स्मर्यते तथापि न तावदेव स्पन्दतत्त्वम् । अपि तु सर्वानुस्यूतानवच्छिन्नप्रकाशानन्दसारपरप्रमातृरूपमेव तत् । यद्वक्ष्यति

'तस्माच्छब्दार्थचिन्तासु न सावस्था न या शिवः' । (२।४)

इति । अतोऽस्यानवच्छिन्नचमत्काररूपस्य न जातुचित्स्मर्यमाणत्वं मूढत्वं वा । यस्तु तत्तत्त्वमितीह तच्छब्देनास्य निर्देशः कृतः स

'स्वातन्त्र्यामुक्तमात्मानं……' । (ई० प्र० १।५।१६)

इति श्रीप्रत्यभिज्ञाकारिकोक्तनीत्या कल्पितस्यैवापारमार्थिकस्वरूपस्य न तु तत्त्वतः पारमार्थिकस्य । न प्रतिपद्यते इत्यनेनेदमाह—अस्य तत्त्वस्य स्मर्यमाणत्वेन प्रतीतिरेव नास्तीति ॥१२-१३॥

## TRANSLATION

Non-existence as understood by the Vedāntist according to the statement, 'Verily, in the beginning, all this was not' cannot be an object of contemplation, for contemplation is (always) of an object that can be existent. *Abhāva* or non-existence is simply nothing.

If the existential conception be ascribed to it, it will have to be treated as something, and thus there will be the negation of non-existence. (i.e. in that case there will be the non-existence of non-existence itself, for something implies existence).

Moreover, how can that universal extinction be conceived or contemplated where the conceiver or contemplator himself disappears? If the conceiver or contemplator is accepted (as existing), then universal extinction is an impossible conception, for in that case the conceiver remains (as the witness of the extinction, and even if one conceiver is there, then the adjective

---

१. ख० पु० निफालनेति पाठः ।

'universal' will not apply to extinction). Hence universal extinction or negation does not constitute Reality.

*(Elucidation of the position of the Mādhyamika)*

This is the position of the Mâdhyamika (*iti pakṣaḥ*),

The so-called (imaginary) conceiver or the contemplator contemplating universal negation by imagination becomes, on the perfection of contemplation, himself non-existent, being identified with his object of contemplation which is *abhāva* or non-existence.

*(The author's reply)*:

It is said in reply—For the contemplation of total negation or void, there is no non-insentiency, but rather there is insentiency or stupefaction.

"Therefore whether existent or non-existent, whatever is imagined later, on the perfection of the contemplation. is evidently only a product of imagination."

According to the above principle, by the contemplation of negation in the form of universal extinction there can never be the attainment of the highest Reality, the ultimate object of life.

If it is said that *śūnya* or void is like this as stated by Nāgārjuna in the following lines:

"That which is devoid of all supports (whether external or internal), that which is devoid of all *tattvas* (constitutive principles), that which is devoid of the residual traces of all the *kleśas*, that is *Śūnya* or void. In the highest sense, it is not *śūnya* or void as such," then our reply is, "True, if the absolutely free, and ultimate state consisting of Consciousness-bliss be admitted as the substratum (of all), as has been described in Vijñānabhairava, that contemplation of the void should be made by making the divine, supreme reality of consciousness as the substratum, as declared in the verse "The Highest is that which is free of all notions pertaining to direction (*dik*), time (*kāla*) etc. (V. Bh. Verse 14), otherwise, the statement, "there is no void as such" would be devoid of all sense, as has been explained in the verse *Yad yad eva atibhāvyate* above.

The statement that is made in Ālokamālā, viz., "That state is called void which is something unknown to people like ourselves, not that which, according to the popular belief, is the sense assigned to it by the atheists."

This is true, but if it is unknown to people like yourselves, it should be said that on account of its unknowability, it is impossible to express it. Why call it void? But even void, so long as it is conceived, is verily knowable, because of its being delineated in thought.

If people like you are unable to realize that state, then you should serve reverentially the real spiritual guide who is proficient in the realization of that state, and not, by using a term like void, according to your own judgement, throw yourself and others, in the unfathomable abyss of immense delusion. Enough of this.

How is it known that there is insentiency in that state? In reply to this, it is said, "Because etc." *Abhiyoga* means declaration of the nature of reflection concerning that state made by the person who has risen from *samādhi* or trance in the form, "In what condition was I?" Because of the experience, *Tadāsīt iti niścayaḥ* i.e. "I was exceedingly in an insentient state." Hence that state of insentiency is artificial i.e. imagined one because of its being recollected in that way. On the contrary, that state (i.e. the state of insentiency) being experienced only declares the existence of the experient, the knower who had that experience, not non-existence or void. In the state of so-called universal negation, the undivided state of *cit* or consciousness that is the knower decidedly abides. It is never possible to speak of its non-existence. This is what is meant to be said.

(*Another objection*):

Well, memory is possible only of that which has been already observed and determined, as for instance, blue etc. There can be no determination of that which is void, in which the function of the *buddhi* (determinative faculty) is suppressed. Then how is it said, 'on the basis of subsequent ascertainment in the form 'it was' that this denotes insentieney ?

(*Reply*)

In reply, it is said that such is the condition only of the known or the object. So long as, through the impression retained in the Self, the known or the object is not determined by thisness, it cannot be remembered. Though limited in the imaginary states of void, etc, the knower or the subject, however, abides as the real (lit. unconventional), ultimate Reality. He cannot be separate from himself. Therefore, there is a thought determinative of him only. Thus in that state there is a knower as I. This is evident from self-experience. It is this experiencer of the void who is recollected subsequently in memory as exceedingly limited in opposition to the universe.

Hence there is no inconsistency here. As this is the exact position, therefore the state of the void is only artificial. In accordance with the declaration made in the line "therefore, when whether existent or non-existent, if it is only contemplated afterwards, it is only a product of imagination," the state of void is brought into being only by an imaginary conception of the non-existent. The Supreme Lord himself, in order to conceal the real knowledge, shows to the fools void as a reality so that they may accept it as the goal to be achieved.

The word *jñeyam* (knowable) in the verse, which means the form of the knowable is used as an example to show that it is always like sound sleep.

(*Summary*)

This is the sense. Every one without any effort has the experience of sleep which is like insentiency. Then what is the use of another void which can be acquired only by the effort of meditation. Both are similar in point of unreality. Many philosophers like the Vedāntists, the Naiyāyikas, the followers of Sāṁkhya and Buddhists and others have fallen into this great uncrossable ocean of immense insentiency in the form of the void. *Śūnya* has proved to be an obstacle even to those who were desirous of entering the *Spanda* principle when their efforts slackened. This will be described in the verse, beginning with, "Then, in that great ether," and ending with, "insentient like sound sleep" (I, 25). Therefore, the author's great effort is noticed in demolishing this theory. Even though he has definitely established here that it is a position to be abandoned, he will further establish it in "The effort directed towards action" (I, 15) Hence I have made an effort to expose its defects. The worthy students, who have lent their ears to this teaching for practising it, should, therefore, not be annoyed with me.

When the defects of the Buddhists have been exposed, the defects of the Vedāntists also stand exposed, for their reasoning is similar. Therefore, nothing further is said.

Now let us turn to the subject under discussion. The *Spanda*-principle cannot be recollected like the void. That can never be said, with propriety, to be absent, for it is involved uniformally as the Experient in all the experiences. It has been rightly said, "Ah, by what means can one know the knower?" (B. A. U. IV, 5, 15).

Though the state of entry into Reality is remembered on account of the impression of *prāṇa*, etc., when one comes back to normal consciousness after meditation, the *Spanda*-principle is not similarly remembered. It is rather the highest Experient, the quintessence of uninterrupted light and bliss involved in all experiences.

As the author will say later, "Whether it is word, or thought, or object, there is no state which is not *Śiva*." (II,4). Hence this principle which is uninterrupted bliss of consciousness can never be an object of memory or a state of insentiency.

Regarding the question that this principle has been referred to by the word 'that', it must be understood that according to the statement made in Īśvarapratyabhijñā, viz., "The Self not deprived of Freedom," the word 'that' refers to the so-called experient who is not the ultimate Reality, not to the Experient who is the Absolute, Ultimate Reality. By the phrase *na pratipadyate*, it is said that that principle cannot be known as an object of memory.

## EXPOSITION

These two verses are very important. The Mādhyamikas maintained that the Ultimate Reality is *Śūnya* or void in which there is neither knower, nor knowledge, nor known, i.e. neither subject nor object nor the means of knowing. That state cannot be characterized by any other term than void. How is it known that the ultimate state is only void? The Mādhyamika says, "We have an experience of it in *samādhi* in which there is neither consciousness of 'I' nor of this, nor of any link between the two." How is it known that there was such a state? The only reply that can be given to this question is that after the *samādhi*, in subsequent memory we know that there was such a state.

Three important points have been made against the Mādhyamika by the author.

Firstly, the experience of *abhāva* or *śūnya* or total absence of objectivity is *mūḍhatā* i.e. insentiency or stupefaction like sleep. How is this known? This is known by *abhiyoga*, i.e. by a backward reference in memory. But firstly, like sleep this is only a particular state of the *manas*. It is only a passing phase, not something eternal. It cannot be the characteristic of Reality or the *Spanda*-principle as such.

Secondly, since this experience is a matter of memory, therefore, also, it cannot be a characteristic of Reality or the *Spanda*-principle or *Śiva* or the Experient, the *Ātmā* or the Essential Self whichever way one may like to put it. For memory is a matter of recollection, and recollection is not possible without a recollector. The *Spanda*-principle is the recollector, not something recollected. This is what the 13th verse says

The *Spanda* principle is not an object to be recollected."

As Kallaṭa puts it in his *vṛtti*

"सा शून्यावस्था अतीता मम इति स्मर्यंते, न च आत्मस्वभाव एषः, यस्मान्न त्वेवं चिद्रूपत्वं मूढावस्थावत् स्मर्यंते, तस्य सर्वकालमनुभवितृत्वेनानुभवो नित्योदितत्वात् ।"

"That state of void is remembered after *samādhi* (trance or absorbing meditation) as a past experience. This cannot be the characteristic of the *Ātmā* or the *Spanda*-principle, for firstly *Ātmā* or *Spanda* is of the nature of consciousness, and to say that consciousness is remembered as insentiency would be contradiction in terms. Secondly, it is always the experient, the knower, the cogniser."

Thirdly, the main point at issue, however, is not that the Mādhyamika maintains that there is an experience of void: that even the follower of Trika philosophy admits, for he believes there is a *śūnya pramātā*, the experient of the void. The crucial point is that the Mādhyamika maintains that *śūnya* or void is the characteristic of Reality, that there is no such thing even as a *pramātā* or the Experient.

Against this, the author of the spandakārikā has been at pains to prove two things. Firstly that the Experient is the ever-present subject; it can never be reduced to an object. It is always the *vedaka* (subject), not *vedya* (object). Secondly, that it runs like a thread through all experience; even the experience of void would not be possible without that experient. The denier even in the very denial affirms it. In the words of Śaṃkara, "The denier simply affirms the existence of 'Ātmā'.

The Experient never takes a holiday, for without Him, no experience is possible. In the words of Kaṭhopaniṣad "It is the light that makes all appearance possible."

### *Introduction to the* 14*th*, 15*th*, *and* 16*th Verse*

### TEXT

ननु यत्र स्थितमित्यादौ चिद्रूपस्यैव विश्वकार्यरूपताग्राहित्वमुक्तं तद्बानोत्थापितं कृत्रिममभावात्मकं रूपं तेनैव गृहीतमिति कथमस्यानवच्छिन्नचमत्काररूपममूढत्वमित्याशङ्कायामाह

### TRANSLATION

The objector says, "You yourself have said in verse 2 that all this universe, all this objectivity remains in it and comes forth from it which means that consciousness itself assumes the form of universal objectivity. In other words, consciousness has itself, by relinquishing its nature, assumed an artificial form of negation or void. In the face of this, how do you maintain that it is uninterrupted bliss and is never insentient?

In reply to this the author says:

### *Verses* 14, 15, 16

अवस्थायुगलं चात्र कार्यकर्तृत्वशब्दितम् ।
कार्यता क्षयिणी तत्र कर्तृत्वं पुनरक्षयम् ॥ १४ ॥

कार्योन्मुखः प्रयत्नो यः केवलं सोऽत्र लुप्यते ।
तस्मिँल्लुप्ते विलुप्तोऽस्मीत्यबुधः प्रतिपद्यते ॥ १५ ॥

न तु योऽन्तर्मुखो भावः सर्वज्ञत्वगुणास्पदम् ।
तस्य लोपः कदाचित्स्यादन्यस्यानुपलम्भनात् ॥ १६ ॥

Avasthāyugalaṃ cātra kāryakartṛtva-śabditam/
Kāryatā kṣayiṇī tatra kartṛtvam punarakṣayaṃ//14

Kāryonmukhaḥ prayatno yaḥ kevalaṃ so'tra lupyate/
Tasmin lupte vilupto'smityabudhaḥ pratipadyate//15

Na tu yo'antarmukho bhāvaḥ sarvajñatva-guṇāspadam/
Tasya lopaḥ kadācitsyād anyasyānupalambhanāt//16

## TRANSLATION

Of this Spanda principle, two states are spoken about, viz., of the doer or the subject and the deed or the object. Of these two, the deed or the object is subject to decay but the doer or the subject is imperishable. 14

In the samādhi of void, only the effort which is directed towards objectivity disappears. It is only a fool who, on the disappearance of that effort, thinks 'I have ceased to be'. 15

There can never be the disappearance of that inner nature which is the abode of the attribute of omniscience in the event of the non-perception of anything objective. 16

## COMMENTARY

### TEXT

अत्र स्पन्दतत्त्वे कार्यत्वं कर्तृत्वमिति च शब्दितं—शब्दव्यवहारमात्रेण भेदितमवस्थायुगलमस्ति, वस्तुतो हि तदेकमेव स्वतन्त्रप्रकाशघनशङ्कररूपं तत्त्वं कर्तृसत्त्वाव्यतिरिक्तया प्रकाशात्मना क्रियया व्याप्तं, तदभेदेन प्रकाशमानं तत्त्वभुवनशरीरतदभावादिरूपत्वं स्वीकुर्वत्कार्यमित्युच्यते तदन्यस्य कस्यापि कारणत्वायोगात् । यथोक्तं श्रीप्रत्यभिज्ञायाम्

'जडस्य तु न सा शक्तिः सत्ता यदसतः सतः ।
कर्तृकर्मत्वतत्त्वैव कार्यकारणता ततः ॥' (ई० प्र० २।४।२)

इति । तस्य चेदमेव कार्यत्वं यदयं विचित्रदेशकालाद्याभाससंयोजनवियोजनक्रमेणानन्तान् देहनीलाद्याभासांश्चिदात्मनः स्वरूपादनतिरिक्तानपि मुकुरप्रतिबिम्ब-

---

१. ख० पु० बुद्धयते इति पाठः ।

बदतिरिक्तानिवाभासयति, यावच्च किञ्चिदाभासयति तत्सर्वमाभास्यमानत्वादेव बहिर्मुखेन रूपेण क्षयधर्मकं, क्षयश्चास्येदन्ताभासनिमज्जनेनाहन्तारूपतयावस्थानम्, अत एव देहादेर्ग्राहकस्य यो वेद्यांशः स एव भगवता सृज्यते संह्रियते च न त्वहन्ताप्रकाशात्मकं कर्तृ रूपं तस्य देहाद्यावेशेऽपि भगवदेकरूपत्वात्; अतस्तत्र तयोः कार्यकर्तृत्वयोर्मध्यात्कार्यता क्षयिणी कर्तृत्वं चित्स्वातन्त्र्यरूपं पुनरक्षयं, जगदुदयापाययोरपि तस्य स्वभावादचलनात् । चलने तु जगदुदयापायावपि न कौचिच्चकास्यातामिति मूढाद्यवस्थायामप्यखण्डितचमत्कारसारममूढमेवैतत् । नन्वभावसमाधाननिष्पत्तौ सुषुप्तादौ चास्य कर्तृत्वं नोपलभामहे, क्वचिदपि प्रवृत्त्यदर्शनात् । सत्यं, कार्योन्मुखइन्द्रियादिप्रेरणात्मकव्यापारप्रवणो यः प्रयत्नः संरम्भः सोऽत्र कार्यक्षयपदे लुप्यते विच्छिद्यते, तस्मिंल्लुप्ते सति अबुधोऽभावसमाध्यपहारितात्मरूपो मूढो विलुप्तोऽस्मीति मन्यते । यः पुनरन्तर्मुखोऽहन्ताप्रकाशरूपः स्वभावोऽत एव सर्वज्ञत्वगुणस्यास्पदम् उपलक्षणं चैतत्सर्वकर्तृत्वादेरपि, तस्य लोपो न कदाचित्स्याद्भवतीति न कदाचिदपि सम्भावनीयोऽन्यस्य तल्लोपमुपलब्धुः कस्याप्यनुपलम्भात्, यदि स कश्चिदुपलभ्यते स एवासावन्तर्मुखश्चिद्रूपो, न चेदुपलभ्यते तर्हि सा लोपदशास्तीति कुतो निश्चयः । अथ चान्यः कश्चित्तल्लोपं नोपलभतेऽपितु स एव प्रकाशात्मा तत्कथं तस्याभावः । एवं चान्यस्यानुपलम्भनादित्यत्रान्यकर्तृकस्योपलम्भस्याभावादित्यर्थः । अथ च घटाभावो यथा घटविविक्तभूतलाद्युपलम्भनान्निश्चीयते तथैवात्माभावोऽप्यात्मविविक्तस्य कस्यचिदुपलम्भान्निश्चीयेत तदुपलम्भकसत्तावश्यंभाविनीति तदुपलम्भकस्वात्मनास्तिता न सिध्यति । यदि च कार्योन्मुखप्रयत्नलोपे स लुप्येत तदोत्तरकालमन्यस्य कस्याप्युपलम्भो न भवेद् अन्योपलम्भाभावः प्रसज्येतेत्यर्थः । अपि चान्यस्य बहिर्मुखस्य प्रयत्नस्य सौषुप्तादावनुपलम्भात् कथमन्तर्मुखस्य तत्त्वस्य वालिशैर्लोप आशङ्कितो, यतोऽन्यस्य लोपेऽन्यस्य किं वृत्तम् । अथ चान्यस्य कार्योन्मुखप्रयत्नस्यानुपलम्भादनुपलम्भप्रकाशनान्न कदाचित्प्रकाशात्मनोऽन्तर्मुखस्य तस्योपलब्धुर्लोपः, यतोऽसावन्तर्मुखोभावः सर्वज्ञत्वगुणस्यास्पदं तामप्यभावदशां वेत्त्येव अन्यथा सैव न सिध्येदिति । अन्यस्येति कर्तरि कर्मणि च षष्ठी । अन्तर्मुखे कार्यत्वप्रतियोगितामिव कर्तृत्वस्य सम्भाव्यावस्थात्वमुक्तं वस्तुतस्तु उक्तयुक्त्या तस्यावस्थातृत्वमेव । अन्तर्मुख इति अन्तःपूर्णाहन्तात्मकं मुखं प्रधानं यस्येति योज्यम् ।।१६।।

## TRANSLATION

*Atra* in *avasthāyugalaṃ cātra* means *spanda*-principle *Kāryatvaṃ kartṛtvaṃ ca śabditam* spoken of as the doer and the deed implies that the two states are differentiated only by the use of words i.e. only in speech. In reality, the two states are but one, viz. the principle of Śiva who is absolutely free and mass of light. This principle which is not in any way different from the existence of the subject or the agent being pervaded by activity or *spanda* in the form of light, and appearing as identical with it., assuming the form of *tattva* (constitutive principles), *bhuvana* (world) and body or their absence, etc. is called the object, because any other principle than that cannot have causality. As has been said in Īśvarapratyabhijñā:

"It is not in the power of the insentient (e.g. the seed) to bring forth anything into existence (e.g. the sprout) whether it (the sprout) be considered to be already existent in the cause or not existent in it. Therefore, the causal relation (i.e. the relation between cause and effect) is really the relation between the doer or creator and the deed or the object of creation"[1] (I. Pr. II, 4,2).

The creativity of the creator consists in the fact that by the process of uniting and separating various manifestations such as space, time, etc. he manifests innumerable things like body, blue, etc. which, though non-different from the essential nature of consciousness appear as different like reflections in a mirror (which though non-different from the mirror appear as different).

All that which He manifests is perishable as regards its external form. Its perishableness is, however, nothing else than its submergence of thisness (i.e. objectivity) and abiding as the I. Therefore, it is only the objective aspect of the subject such as the body, etc. which is manifested and withdrawn by the Lord, not the Subjective aspect which is identical with the light of the Supreme I, for even though the subject (the individual Self) has entered the body, it is identical with the Lord. Hence of the two, viz. of the objective and the subjective, the objective is perishable, the doer or the Subject who is identical with the Freedom of Consciousness is, however, imperishable, for even at the manifestation and withdrawal of the world, he does not deviate from his nature of the imperishable Subject and Creator. If he were to do so, even the manifestation and withdrawal of the world would not be perceptible. Hence, even in the state of insentiency; the Spanda principle is only Sentiency with the essence of uninterrupted bliss.

(*An objection*)

On the consummation of meditation on the void and in deep sleep, we do not notice its creativity, for its activity is nowhere seen in that state (How is it then that it is said to be the eternal actor or creator?) (Commentary on the author's reply contained in the 15th and 16th verse).

True, on the cessation of all work of the nature of objective perception, only the effort consisting in directing the senses, etc. towards the objects disappears. On its disappearance, only a fool, whose sense of Self or Subject is eclipsed owing to meditation on the void, thinks "I have ceased to be".

The cessation, however, of him can never be possible whose nature consists in the inner light of I-consciousness and who is, therefore, the abode of omniscience. Omniscience also implies omnipotence. No one can be found as the perceiver of the cessation of that inward nature. If any such person is found, it is just he who is the inner consciousness (that was supposed to have ceased). If no such person is found, how then can it be decided that there was ever such a state of cessation?

(*Commentary on the last line of the* 16*th Verse*) :

Moreover, nobody else feels the cessation of the subject, excepting he himself, whose nature is the light of consciousness. Then how can his cessation be asserted? Thus the phrase 'on account of the non-perception' means 'on account of the absence of the perception of another subject.'

Further, it may be said that just as the absence of jar is ascertained from the observation of the ground without the jar, even so the absence of Self may be ascertained from the observation of some one without the Self. But the existence of the perceiver of the absence of Self is unavoidable in this case. Therefore the non-existence of the perceiver of the absence of the Self cannot be established.

If on account of the cessation of the effort directed towards some object or action, the agent or director himself were to cease, then at the subsequent time there will be no perception of any body. Hence there would arise the contingency of the non-perception of any being.

Further, on account of the non-perception of another i.e. external effort during deep sleep, etc., how can the cessation of the internal principle be suspected even by blockheads, for how can the disappearance of one thing affect another. Therefore from the non-perception of another, viz., of the effect towards an object, there can never be the disappearance of the inner perceiver who is of the nature of light i.e. consciousness, for this inner nature[2] which is the abode of omniscience knows that state of absence also, otherwise the very state of absence cannot be proved.

The genitive case 'of another' used here conveys the sense of the nominative and the accusative.[3]

By the use of the expression 'in the inner,' the possible state of the subject in opposition to the object has been mentioned. In fact by the afore-said reasoning, the state of the knowership of the Subject has been stated. The expression *antarmukha* should be construed thus :

'*Antaḥ*=perfect I-ness, and *mukhaṃ*=chief, the whole phrase meaning, *Spanda-tattva*, the main characteristic of which is perfect I-ness.'

## NOTES

1. *Kārya-kāraṇabhāva* or causality in this system actually means the *kartṛ-karmatva-bhāva* i.e. the relation between the creator and his object of creation, for in the final analysis, all the so-called causes derive their power from the Ultimate Agent, the Divine.

2. Rāmakaṇṭha clarifies the *antarmukha-bhāva* or the inner nature of the self in the following words :

"आत्मनो ज्ञानक्रियाभेदेन द्विविधा या शक्तिः सा सौषुप्ताद्यवस्थायाम् अन्तः-करणबहिष्करणव्यापारोपरमे सति, केवलस्वात्ममात्राभिमुख-ज्ञशक्तिमात्रत्वे-नावशिष्यते; तेन अन्तर्मुखो भाव इत्युक्तम् ।

"The Self has two main powers, viz. of knowledge and activity. When during deep sleep, etc., the activity of the inner and outer senses ceases, only the knowledge aspect which is turned towards the Self is prominent. That is why the expression *antarmukhabhāva* has been used."

3. The nominative case would stand as 'There is no other seer.' The accusative case would stand as 'अन्यं न उपलभते' "There is nothing other to be seen."

## EXPOSITION

Two main arguments have been brought out in these three verses. Firstly, the *Spanda*-principle or the Divine appears in two aspects, viz. the subject and the object. The object is subject to decay and change; the subject is never subject to these. The Mādhyamika avers that it is not only the object that in the ultimate analysis disappears but the subject also. It is maintained by the author that the subject can never be absent, for by nature he is not subject to decay or change.

Secondly, in the meditation on the void, it is only the effort towards external objectivity that has ceased to be and therefore, it is only the object that has ceased to be. That does not prove that the subject also has ceased to be. As Rāmakaṇṭha puts it :

"अभावसमाध्यवस्थासु कार्याभावात् करणव्यापारविरतिमात्रेणात्माभाव-भ्रान्तिरिति"

"In the meditation on the void, since there is the absence of objectivity, to conclude, on account of the cessation of the activities of the instruments (inner and outer) that there is the cessation of the Self is sheer delusion."

*Introduction to the 17th verse*

## TEXT

एवमप्रबुद्धो बहिर्मुखव्यापारनिरोधे ग्राहकस्याप्यात्मनोऽनुपपन्नमप्यभावं निश्चिनुत इति प्रतिपाद्य सुप्रबुद्धाप्रबुद्धयोर्यादृगात्मोपलम्भस्तं निरूपयति

## TRANSLATION

Having discussed how on the cessation of external activities the unenlightened decides about the unjustifiable cessation of the experient or the self, the author now describes how the fully enlightened and the partially enlightened consider the Self.

*Text of the 17th Verse*

**तस्योपलब्धिः सततं त्रिपदाव्यभिचारिणी ।**
**नित्यं स्यात्सुप्रबुद्धस्य तदाद्यन्ते परस्य तु ॥ १७ ॥**

Tasyopalabdhiḥ satataṃ tripadâvyabhicāriṇī/
Nityaṃ syât suprabuddhasya tadâdyante parasya tu//17

## TRANSLATION

The fully enlightened has, always and incessantly, the undeviating knowledge of the Self in all the three states; the other one (viz. the partially enlightened) has it only at the beginning and end of each state.

## COMMENTARY

## TEXT

**तस्य प्राकरणिकस्वभावस्य योपलब्धिः अनवच्छिन्नः प्रकाशः, सा कथितयुक्त्यवष्टम्भात्सुष्ठु प्रबुद्धस्याप्रबुद्धतासंस्कारेणापि शून्यस्य, सततं त्रिष्वपि जागरस्वप्नसौषुप्तपदेषु नित्यमिति आदौ मध्येऽन्ते चाव्यभिचारिणी-अनपायिनी स्याद्भवत्येव-सदासौ शङ्करात्मकस्वस्वभावतया स्फुरतीत्यर्थः । परस्याप्रबुद्धस्य पुनस्तासां दशानां स्वोचितसंविद्रूपाणां प्रत्येकमादावुद्बुभूषायामन्ते च विश्रान्त्यात्मकान्तर्मुखत्वे न तु स्वोचितार्थावभासावस्थितिरूपे मध्यपदे । यदुक्तं श्रीशिवदृष्टौ**

यावत्समग्रज्ञानाग्रज्ञातृस्पर्शदशास्वपि ।
स्थितैव लक्ष्यते सा तु तद्विश्रान्त्याथवा फले ॥' (शि० दृ० २।५)

**इति । भट्टलोल्लटेनापि तदाद्यन्त इत्येवमेव व्याख्यायि स्ववृत्तौ । भट्टश्रीकल्लटवृत्त्यक्षराण्यपेक्ष्य वयमपि तद्वृत्त्यक्षरानुरोधेन सौत्रमर्थमतिविमलमपि क्लिष्टकल्पनया व्याकर्तुमशिक्षिताः यत एवासुप्रबुद्धस्य तदाद्यन्तेऽस्ति तदुपलब्धिः अत एवायमिहाधिकारी स्पन्दोपदेशैः सुप्रबुद्धीक्रियते ।**

**यद्वक्ष्यति**

'अतः सततमुद्युक्तः स्पन्दतत्त्वविविक्तये ।
जाग्रत्·····················॥' (१।२१)

**इत्यादि**

'सौषुप्तपदवन्मूढः प्रबुद्धः स्यादनावृतः ।' (१।२५)

**इति**

तथा स्वप्नेऽपि (३।२)

**इत्यादि**

'प्रबुद्धः सर्वदा तिष्ठेत् ।' (३।१२)

**इत्यादि च । अत्र हि जागरादित्रिषु पदेषु आद्यन्तकोटिवन्मध्यमप्यर्थावसायात्मकं पदं तुर्याभोगमयं कर्तुं प्रबुद्धस्य सुप्रबुद्धतापादनायोपदेशः प्रवृत्तः, एतच्च निर्णेष्यामः । तथा च शिवसूत्रम्**

'जाग्रत्स्वप्नसुषुप्तभेदे तुर्याभोगसम्भवः ।' (शि० सू० १।७)

**इति । तथा**

'त्रिषु चतुर्थं तैलवदासेच्यम् ।' (शि० सू० ३।२०)

**इति**

त्रितयभोक्ता वीरेशः ।' (शि० सू० १।११)

**इति ॥१७॥**

## TRANSLATION

*Tasya* means 'of the real nature which is the topic of this treatise; *upalabdhi* means 'uninterrupted knowledge.' The fully enlightened has, by the firm grip of the process, described that awareness in all the three states of waking, dream, and deep sleep. The fully enlightened is one who is completely free from even the residual traces of unenlightenment. *Nityaṃ* (always) means "at the beginning, in the middle, and at the end."

*Avyabhicāriṇī* means invariable, undeviating, unfailing. The meaning is "The fully enlightened is one whose inner nature always shines as identical with Śiva."

Of the three states characterized by specific knowledge appropriate to them, the partially awakened one has awareness (of *Spanda*) only at the beginning or at the end of each state. At the beginning means 'just when that state is about to start;' 'at the end' means 'at its cessation when the perceiver's mind is withdrawn within.' He does not have this awareness in the middle of each of these states which is characterised by specific knowledge appropriate to itself. It has been rightly said in Śivadṛṣṭi[2] "The awareness of Śivatā or real state of the Experient is observed at the beginning of all knowledge, or it is observed at the end because of the cessation of that knowledge (when the mind is withdrawn within)."

Bhaṭṭa Lollaṭa[3] has also similarly explained in his commentary that that awareness exists only at the beginning and the end of each state of waking, dream, and deep sleep in the case of the partially awakened. We have not been taught to give far-fetched explanation of the clear meaning of these *kārikās* (verses) in accordance with the wording of the gloss of Bhaṭṭa Śrī Kallaṭa.[4]

Since the partially awakened has this awareness (of the *Spanda* principle) at the beginning and at the end of each state, therefore, he is fit to be fully awakened by the instruction, regarding *Spanda*. The author will speak about it in the verse, beginning with "Therefore, one should be on the alert for the discernment of the *Spanda* principle while waking (I, 21) and in "The un-enlightened one remained stupefied as one is (stupefied) in deep sleep while he who is not enveloped by (spiritual) darkness abides as the enlightened one" (I,25), similarly in the passage, beginning with, 'even in dream,' and also in 'one should always remain awakened.'

Here, for the purpose of enlightening fully the partially enlightened *yogī*, the instruction is given to fill even the middle state consisting of the determination of objects, with the rapturous experience of the fourth state, just as he fills with that bliss the initial and the final phases of the three states of waking, etc. This will be explained later on.

A similar view is expressed in the following in the *Śiva-sūtra* also :

"Even during the three different states of consciousness in waking, dreaming and profound sleep, the rapturous experience of the I-consciousness of the fourth state abides". (I, 7)

"The fourth state of *Ātmic* consciousness should be poured like (uninterrupted flow of) oil in the three states" (III, 20) "Being an enjoyer of the rapture of I-consciousness in the three states, he is verily the master of his senses." (I,7).

## NOTES

1. The specific knowledge appropriate to waking is the knowledge of each object (pot, flower, etc.) which is common *to all people*, the knowledge dream is *specific or particular only to the particular dreamer*; *the specific characteristic* of deep sleep is only the *residual traces* (*saṃskāra*) of every one's experiences.

2. *Śiva-dṛṣṭi* is written by Somānanda who was the great grand teacher of Abhinavagupta.

3. Bhaṭṭa Lollaṭa was a poet, a critic and a philosopher. He was a younger contemporary of Bhaṭṭa Kallaṭa. He lived in the second and third quarter of the 9th century A.D. His gloss on *Spandakārikā* referred to as *Vivṛti* by Kṣemarāja is not available.

4. Kallaṭa was a pupil of Vasugupta and flourished in 855 A.D. He wrote a gloss on Spandakārikā, called *Vṛtti,* which is published in the Kashmir Series of Text and Studies.

## EXPOSITION

There are three categories of experients in the world: (1) the common empirical individual of the world who is completely ignorant of spiritual Reality, referred to as *aprabuddha*, the unawakened. He has absolutely no interest in *yoga* and is not yet qualified to appreciate its teaching. (2) The partially enlightened *yogī* who has some experience of the essential Self or *Spanda tattva*. He has an awareness of it in the beginning and end of waking, dreaming and profound sleep but not in the middle of any of these states; the experience of *Spanda* or the divine state is not perpetually present in his case. He is called *prabuddha* or partially enlightened. In comparison to *Suprabuddha*, he is also referred to as *aprabuddha*. He is the fit candidate for *yoga*, and the teachings are given for his improvement.

(3) *Suprabuddha*, sometimes referred to simply as *prabuddha* is the experient who has an integral awareness of *spanda* i.e. he has an uninterrupted awareness of it in all the three states, viz., waking, dreaming, and profound sleep. He needs no teaching of *yoga*. He has, in the evolutionary scheme, already attained the highest experience that is open to man.

The 17th verse gives a description of the second and third categories of *yogīs*.

### *Introduction to the* 18*th Kārikā*

## TEXT

सुप्रबुद्धस्य त्रिषु पदेषु यादृश्युपलब्धिस्तां विभागेन दर्शयति—

## TRANSLATION

The author now shows separately what kind of experience the fully enlightened one has in each of the three states.

*Text of the 18th verse*

ज्ञानज्ञेयस्वरूपिण्या शक्त्या परमया युतः ।
पदद्वये विभुर्भाति तदन्यत्र तु चिन्मयः ।। १८ ।।

Jñānajñeya-svarūpiṇyā śaktyā paramayā yutaḥ/
padadvaye vibhurbhāti tadanyatra tu cinmayaḥ// 18

## TRANSLATION

The all-pervading lord, possessed of the supreme power in the form of knowledge and knowable (object of knowledge), appears in the two states of waking and dream as knowledge and objects of knowledge, and in the other than these two only as consciousness.

*Text of the Commentary*

सुप्रबुद्धस्य भूम्ना ज्ञानज्ञेयस्वरूपया मध्यमे पदे ज्ञानाग्रपर्यन्तयोस्तु स्वस्वरूपयैव स्पन्दतत्त्वात्मना पराशक्त्या युक्तो विभुः शङ्करात्मा स्वभावो जागरास्वप्नरूपे पदद्वये भाति । तत्र हि विश्वमसौ सदाशिवेश्वरवत्स्वाङ्गवत्पश्यति, तदन्यत्र तु-सुषुप्ते न तु यथांन्ये सुषुप्ततुर्ययोरिति, 'त्रिपदाव्यभिचारिणी' इति प्रक्रान्ते तुर्यस्याप्रस्तुतत्वात् तदुपलब्धेरेव च तुर्यरूपत्वात्, असौ विभुश्चिन्मय एवास्य भाति अशेषवेद्योपशमात् । इत्येतत्सुप्रबुद्धाभिप्रायमेव न तु वस्तुवृत्तानुसारेण 'तदन्यत्र तु चिन्मयः' इत्यस्यानुपपन्नत्वापत्तेः, लोके सौषुप्तस्य मोहमयत्वात्, शिवापेक्षया तु जाग्रत्स्वप्नयोरपि चिन्मयत्वात् । एवमपि च प्रकृतानुपयुक्तत्वात् । इतः प्रभृति प्रथमनिःष्यन्दान्तो ग्रन्थः प्रबुद्धस्य सुप्रबुद्धतायै स्थितो यथा टीकाकारैर्न चेतितस्तथा परीक्ष्यतां स्वयमेव, कियत्प्रतिपदं लिखामः ॥१८॥

## TRANSLATION

The all-pervading *Saṃkara* who is one's own essential nature, possessed of the supreme powe r, appears predominantly to the fully enlightened in the two states of waking and dreaming in the form of knowledge and knowable in the middle of these two states and in his own essential form of *Spanda* principle at the initial and final stages of the knowledge. Therein (i.e. in the middle of the waking and dream states) he sees the universe, like Sadāśiva and Īśvara, as his own body. In the other than these two, i.e. in sound sleep, this all-pervading principle (i.e. *spanda*) appears to him only as consciousness on account of the cessation of the entire gamut of objects. 'In the other than these two' (*tadanyatra*) refers only to sound sleep (*suṣupti*), not to both sound sleep and the fourth state, as others have interpreted, because the previously mentioned phrase 'unfailing in the three states' (in verse 17) makes the fourth state irrelevant, and also because the realization of that (*spanda* principle) is itself the fourth state.

The above state relates only to the fully enlightened *yogī*. It has not been mentioned with reference to the actual state of the common people, for in this case, the statement 'in the state other than the two, it is only pure consciousness' would get involved in inconsistency, because the deep sleep of the common folk is only of the nature of stupefaction and with reference to Śiva even waking and dream states are pure consciousness. Besides, it is out of point so far as the topic under discussion is concerned.

Henceforward upto the end of the first section, the book has to do only with the perfect enlightenment of the partially enlightened. Other commentators have not understood this fact. Readers may examine this for themselves. How far can I go on pointing this out with regard to every word?

## EXPOSITION

This verse is important inasmuch as it throws brilliant light on the realization of the fully enlightened *yogī*.

In his case, the *Spanda* principle appears as knowledge (*jñāna*) and objects of knowledge (*jñeya*) in the middle of the two states of waking and dream. Even here, the knowledge and the objects of knowledge do not appear as completely external from him but as his own body, fully integrated to his I-consciousness, just as they appear to Sadāśiva and Īśvara.

Then again, at the initial and final stages of *jñāna* in these two stages also, it is in its own essential nature that the *Spanda*-principle appears. In the deep sleep state, since there is complete absence of all knowables or objects, it appears, only as sheer consciousness (*cinmaya*).

*Introduction to the 19th verse*

TEXT

यथेयं जागराविमध्यदशापि प्रबुद्धं न प्रतिबध्नाति तथोपपादयति—

TRANSLATION

Now the author proves how even the middle state of waking and dream does not hamper the perfect realization of the fully enlightened.

*Text of the 19th Verse*

गुणादिस्पन्दनिष्यन्दाः सामान्यस्पन्दसंश्रयात् ।
लब्धात्मलाभाः सततं स्युर्ज्ञस्यापरिपन्थिनः ॥ १९ ॥

Guṇādispandaniṣyandāḥ sāmānyaspandasaṃśrayāt/
Labdhātmalābhāḥ satataṃ syur jñasyāparipanthinaḥ//[19]

TRANSLATION

The particular emanations of *Spanda* which begin with the *guṇas* and which acquire their existence by having recourse to generic *Spanda* can never stand in the way of the one who has realized his essential nature.

COMMENTARY

TEXT

गुणाः सत्त्वरजस्तमांसि येषां प्रकृतितत्त्वं विभवभूः ते मायातत्त्वावस्थिता इहाभिप्रेताः । यथोक्तं श्रीस्वच्छन्दे मायामसूरकविन्यासे

'अधश्छादनमूर्ध्वं च रक्तं शुक्लं विचिन्तयेत् ।
मध्ये तमो विजानीयाद्गुणास्त्वेते व्यवस्थिताः ॥' (स्व० सं० २।६५)

इति । त आदयो येषां कलादीनां क्षित्यन्तानां स्पन्दानां विशेषप्रसराणां तेषां ये

निःष्यन्दास्तनुकरणभुवनप्रसरा नीलसुखादिसंविदश्च तथा योग्यपेक्षया बिन्दु-नादादयस्ते सततं ज्ञस्य सुप्रबुद्धस्य कस्यचिदेवापश्चिमजन्मनोऽपरिपन्थिनः-स्वस्वभावाच्छादका न भवन्तीति निश्चयः, यतस्ते सामान्यस्पन्दमुक्तरूपमाश्रित्य 'यत्र स्थितमिति' अत्र निर्णीतदृशा लब्धात्मलाभास्तत एवोत्पन्नास्तन्मयाश्चेत्यर्थः। तथाहि

'स्वाङ्गरूपेषु भावेषु पत्युर्ज्ञानं क्रिया च या।
मायातृतीये त एव पशोः सत्त्वं रजस्तमः ॥' (ई० प्र० ३।३।४)

इति श्रीप्रत्यभिज्ञोक्तदृशा चितिशक्तिरेव पारमेश्वरी ज्ञानक्रियामायाशक्तित्रितयतया श्रीसदाशिवादिपदे स्फुरित्वा सङ्कोचप्रकर्षात्सत्त्वरजस्तमोरूपं क्रीडाशरीरं श्रयति, यतो निजचिच्छक्तिस्फारमयत्वात्तदधिष्ठितमेव सर्वदा सर्वं जानन्सुप्रबुद्धो गुणादिविशेषस्पन्दाननुच्छिन्दन्नपि स्पन्दतत्त्वावेशमय एव ॥१९॥

## TRANSLATION

*Guṇas*[1] i.e. *sattva* (harmony), *rajas* (motion) and *tamas* (inertia) which are the outcome of *Prakṛti* are here to be understood as having their abode in Māyā. As has been said in Svacchanda-tantra regarding the arrangement of the pillow of Māyā. "One should consider its (i.e. the pillow's) lower cover as red (symbolic of *rajas*), the upper cover as white (symbolic of *sattva*), and the middle one i.e. the pillow itself as black (symbolic of *tamas*). These *guṇas* are thus arranged." (Sv-T. II, 65). They begin with *kalā* and end with earth which are particular ramifications of *Spanda*, and their proliferations are bodies, senses and worlds and experiences like blue, pleasure etc. or in the case of *yogīs*, they may be considered to be *bindu* (light) and *nāda* (sound), etc. These can never stand in the way of the fully enlightened *Yogī* who has no future birth i.e. it is certain that they can never veil his essential nature. Because these acquire their own existence by resorting to the aforesaid generic *spanda* in accordance with the ascertained principle of *Spanda* described in the words "in which abide all objects and from which they come forth." (Sp. K. Verse 2) i.e. because they are born out of and are identical with *Spanda*.

As has been described in Īśvarapratyabhijñā[2] "Those powers which are *jñāna*, *krīyā*, and *māyā* as the third in the case of the

Lord (*Śiva*) in respect of the objective realities which are His own limbs appear in the case of the limited, empirical individual as *sattva*, *rajas* and *tamas*."

According to this, it is the Divine Consciousness-power itself which displaying itself in the triad of powers, viz., *jñāna*, *kriyā* and *māyā* in the stages of *Sadāśiva*,[3] *Īśvara*, etc. appears owing to excess of limitation, as the body of the Lord's sport in the form of *sattva*, *rajas* and *tamas*. Because of this, the fully enlightened *yogī*, always knowing all the states of waking, dream and deep sleep as presided over by the *cit-śakti* which is identical with the diffusion of his own Consciousness-power, never puts himself in opposition to the particular *Spanda*-forms such as the *guṇas*, etc. and only feels himself immersed in the generic *Spanda*-principle.

## NOTES

1. *Guṇas* are constitutive principles. They are *sattva* *rajas* and *tamas*. *Sattva* is the aspect of harmony, goodness, enlightenment and sukha or pleasure. *Rajas* is the aspect of movement, activity and *duḥkha* or commotion. *Tamas* is the aspect of inertia and *moha* or dulness.

2. *Īśvarapratyabhijñā* was written by Utpaladeva, the great grand teacher of Kṣemarāja.

3. According to this statement, *jñāna* is the predominant śakti of Sadāśiva, *kriyā* of Īśvara and *māyā* of Śuddha or Sahaja Vidyā. In Pratyabhijñāhṛdayam, Kṣemarāja has mentioned *ichhā* as the predominant *śakti* of Sadāśiva, *jñāna* of Īśvara and *kriyā* of Śuddha Vidyā.

## EXPOSITION

There are two aspects of *Spanda* viz., *sāmānya*, and *viśeṣa*. *Sāmānya* is the general principle or power of *cit* or Consciousness; *Viśeṣa* is the manifestation of *Spanda* in particular constitutive aspects like *sattva*, *rajas*, *tamas* etc. or objective experiences like blue, pleasure, etc.

Ordinary people considering these particular manifestations of *Spanda* as something entirely different from Consciousness get entangled in them, but the fully enlightened *yogī* or *Suprabuddha*, considering them only as forms of *Spanda*, the ultimate

Consciousness-Power is not befuddled.

*Introduction to the 20th verse*

TEXT

यथा त्वप्रबुद्धान्बध्नन्त्येते तत्प्रतिपादयति

TRANSLATION

Now the author describes how the particular forms of *spanda* prove a shackle for the unawakened ones.

*Verse*

अप्रबुद्धधियस्त्वेते स्वस्थितिस्थगनोद्यताः ।
पातयन्ति दुरुत्तारे घोरे संसारवर्त्मनि ॥ २० ॥

Aprabudhadhiyas tvete svasthitisthaganodyatāḥ/
Pātayanti duruttāre ghore saṃsāra-vartmani//20

TRANSLATION

These (the *guṇas* etc), however, intent on veiling their real nature push the people of unawakened intellect into the terrible ocean of transmigratory existence from which it is difficult to pull them out.

COMMENTARY

TEXT

अप्रबुद्धधियः प्रायः सर्वानप्रत्यभिज्ञातपारमेश्वरीशक्त्यात्मकनिजस्पन्दतत्त्वान्देहात्ममानिनो लौकिकान्प्राणाद्यात्माभिमानिनश्च मितयोगिनस्त्वेते पूर्वोक्ता गुणादिस्पन्दनिःष्यन्दाः स्वस्याः स्पन्दतत्त्वात्मनः स्थितेः स्थगनायोद्यता नित्यं तदुद्यमैकसाराः, दुःखेनोत्तार्यन्तेऽस्मादृशिकैर्जन्तुचक्रमिति दुरुत्तारे-लङ्घयितुमशक्ये घोरे-दुःखमये संसरणमार्गे पातयन्ति । यथोक्तं श्रीमालिनीविजये

'विषयेष्वेव संलीनानधोऽधः पातयन्त्यणून् ।
रुद्राणून्याः समालिङ्ग्य घोरतर्योऽपराः स्मृताः ॥' (मा० वि० ३।३१।)

इति । तथा हि पूर्वं प्रतिपादिता येयं स्पन्दतत्त्वात्मा परा शक्तिः सैव विश्वस्यान्तर्बहिश्च वमनात्संसारवामाचारत्वाच्च वामेश्वरी शक्तिः । तदुत्थापितानि तु खेचरी-

गोचरीदिक्चरीभूचरीरूपाणि चत्वारि देवताचक्राणि-सुप्रबुद्धस्य परभूमिसञ्चारीणि अप्रबुद्धानां तु अधराधरसरणिप्रेरकाणि । तथा हि या एव सुप्रबुद्धस्य खे बोधगगने चरन्त्यः खेचर्योऽकालकलितत्वाभेदसर्वकर्तृत्वसर्वज्ञत्वपूर्णत्वव्यापकत्वप्रथाहेतवस्ता एवाप्रबुद्धस्य शून्यप्रमातृपदचारिण्यः कञ्चुकरूपतया स्थिताः कालकलितत्व-किञ्चित्कर्तृताकिञ्चिज्ज्ञताभिष्वङ्गनियमहेतवः । गौर्वाक् तदुपलक्षितासु संजल्प-मयीषु बुद्धयहंकारमनोभूमिषु चरन्त्यो गोचर्यः सुप्रबुद्धस्य स्वात्माभेदमयाध्य-वसायाभिमानसंकल्पाञ्जनयन्ति, मूढानां तु भेदैकसारान् । दिक्षु दशसु बाह्येन्द्रिय-भूमिषु चरन्त्यो दिक्चर्यः सुप्रबुद्धस्याद्वयप्रथासाराः अन्येषां द्वयप्रथाहेतवः । भूः रूपादिपञ्चकात्मकं मेयपदं तत्र चरन्त्यो भूचर्यस्तदाभोगमय्या आश्यानीभावतया तन्मयत्वमापन्नाः भूचर्यः सुप्रबुद्धस्य चित्प्रकाशशरीरतयात्मानं दर्शयन्त्य इतरेषां सर्वतोप्यवच्छिन्नतां प्रथयन्त्यः स्थिताः,—इत्येवं प्रमात्रन्तःकरणबहिष्करणप्रमेय-रूपतयैव तानि चत्वारि चक्राणि गुणादिस्पन्दमयान्यप्रबुद्धबुद्धींल्लौकिकांस्तथा-बिन्दुनादादिप्रथामात्रसन्तुष्टान् योगिनस्तत्तत्त्वप्रसररूपे संसारे पातयन्ति ॥२०॥

## TRANSLATION

*Aprabuddadhiyaḥ* means all those worldly people who have not recognised their *spanda* principle which is divine *śakti* (power), and who consider their bodies as the Self and also all those partially awakened *yogīs* who consider *prāṇa*, etc. as their Self.

The word 'etc' i.e. 'these' of the verse refers to the particular emanations of *Spanda* beginning with *guṇas*' (of the previous verse).

*Svasthitisthagaṇodyatāḥ* means always intent on veiling their real nature which is *spanda* principle. *Duruttāre ghore saṃsāra-vartmani pātayanti*'[1] means they push the whole lot of creatures into the miserable transmigratory existence from which it is difficult for their directors to pull them out.

As has been said in Śrī Mālinī Vijaya Tantra:

"The non supreme ones (*aparāḥ*) are called *ghoratarī śaktis* who while they embrace the *Rudra* souls, push down and down those *jīvas* (empirical souls) who cling to objects of sense." (M.V. III, 31).

Thus that very supreme power (*parā-śakti*) which has been previously described as of the nature of *Spanda* is called *Vāmeśvarī*[2] *śakti* because she manifests both internally and externally and because she has to do with the contrary course of the world.[3] By her are brought into being four groups of divinities known as *Khecarī*, *Gocarī*, *Dikcarī*, and *Bhūcarī* who lead the fully awakened soul to the highest stage, but drive the unawakened ones to lower and lower paths.

Thus those very *Khecarī śaktis*, moving in the ether of knowledge become, in the case of the fully enlightened ones, means of non-difference, omnipotence, omniscience, perfection and all-pervasiveness because of their being beyond the influence of time, while in the case of the unawakened ones, they make them move in the stage of the experient of the void and remaining there as cloaks become the means of the limitation of time, limited efficacy, limited knowledge, attachment, and limitation in respect of space and cause (i. e. *niyama* or *niyati*). So far as *Gocarī* is concerned, the word 'go' means speech. This implies those stages which make use of speech, viz., *buddhi*, the determinative faculty, *ahaṁkāra*, the ego-sense, and *manas*, the ideating faculty. They move in these stages (*caranti*), and bring about in the case of the fully enlightened ones, such determination, ego sense and ideation as bring about the sense of non-difference with the essential Self, while in the case of the unawakened ones, they bring about determination, etc. only of difference. *Dikcarī* are those *śaktis* which move about in the sphere of the ten external senses. In the case of the fully enlightened ones, they are sources of the manifestation of non-duality, while in the case of the unenlightened ones, they are the causes of duality.

The word *bhū* denotes the stage of knowables (objects), viz. the pentad of form, etc. Moving about in this sphere, and being their fully developed forms, they became congealed and thus identical with them. They reveal themselves to the fully enlightened in the form of the light of consciousness, while in the case of others, they appear in the form of limitedness all round.

Thus these four groups of *Śaktis*, viz., *Khecarī* in the form of experients, *Gocarī* in the form of the psychic apparatus, *Dikcarī* in the form of the external senses, and *Bhūcarī* in the form of objects which are full of particular forms of *Spanda* in the form of *guṇas*, etc. throw the worldly people of unenlightened intellect and the partially enlightened *yogīs* who are satisfied only with the experience of light (*bindu*), and sound (*nāda*) into the world which is only an expansion of those particular elements.

## NOTES

1. *Mālinī Vijaya Tantra* mentions three *śaktis* that operate in individual souls: (1) *ghoratarī* who help the Rudra souls who are not attached to objects of sense, and push down and down those souls that are attached to objects of sense. They are known as *aparā* (non-supreme), (2) *ghorā* those who bring about attachment to fruits of *karma* and are thus an obstacle in the path of liberation. They are known as *parāparā*, (3) *Aghorā*- who lead to the state of *Śiva*. They are known as *parā* (supreme).

2. Internally she brings about the sense of *abheda* or non-difference; externally, she brings about the sense of *bheda* or difference.

3. *Vāmeśvarī*. There are two explanations of the word *Vāmeśvarī*. The word *vāma* means (1) left, reverse, contrary and (2) beautiful. According to the first meaning, she is called *Vāmeśvarī*, because she has to do with the contrary course of *saṃsāra* which is full of *bheda* or difference. According to the second meaning, she is called *Vāmeśvarī*, because she manifests the world which is beautiful expression of Śiva.

In *Spandasandoha*, *Kṣemarāja* gives the following explanation of *Vāmeśvarī*:

यत्र वमन्ति विश्वं भेदाभेदमय भेदसारं च, गृणन्ति उच्चैर्गिरन्ति च भेदसारं, भेदाभेदमयं च अभेदसारम् आपादयन्ति इति संसारवामाचाराः वामाः शक्तयः तासाम् ईश्वरी स्वामिनी ।

*Khecarī*, *Dikcarī*, etc. are *Vāmā Śaktis* pertaining to the world, because they project the world full of difference and identity in differences, declare it as full of difference, and in the case of *yogīs* bring about this world full of both difference and identity to a state of pure identity. The presiding deity of these *Vāmā śaktis* is called *Vāmeśvarī*.

## EXPOSITION

The particular forms of *Spanda* attract those people who are not awakened to their divine source. There are various *śaktis* (powers) who preside as divinities over the particular forms of *Spanda*. They push down those who deny any divine origin of life and obstinately cling to sensuous pleasure, while they help those in their spiritual journey in whom a higher sense of values has dawned.

The *Śaktis* push them down to mundane existence, because they always think of their Self as some thing material and not as pure Consciousness. So material existence is their proper place.

*Introduction to the* 21*st verse*

TEXT

यत एवम्

TRANSLATION

Since, it is thus

*Text of the* 21*st verse*

**अतः सततमुद्युक्तः स्पन्दतत्त्वविविक्तये ।**
**जाग्रदेव निजं भावमचिरेणाधिगच्छति ॥ २१ ॥**

Ataḥ satatam udyuktaḥ spanda-tattva-viviktaye/
Jāgradeva nijaṃ bhāvam acireṇādhigacchati// 21

TRANSLATION

Therefore, one should be always on the alert for the discernment of the *Spanda* principle. Such a person attains his essential state (as *spanda*) even in the waking condition in short time.

COMMENTARY

TEXT

उक्तवक्ष्यमाणरूपस्य स्पन्दतत्त्वस्य विविक्तये-विमर्शनाय सततमुद्युक्तः
'मय्यावेश्य मनो ये मां नित्ययुक्ता उपासते ।' (भ० गी० १२।२)
इति गीतोक्तदृशा सततमेवान्तर्मुखस्वरूपनिभालनप्रवणो यः स जाग्रदेव जागरावस्थास्थित एव निजमात्मीयं शङ्करात्मकं स्वस्वभावमचिरेणाधिगच्छति, तथा अस्य शंकरात्मा आन्तरः स्वभावः स्वयमेवोन्मज्जति येन प्रबुद्धो नित्योदितसमावेशासादनात्सुप्रबुद्धो जीवन्मुक्तो भवतीत्यर्थः ॥२१॥

## TRANSLATION

He, who is always on the alert for the discernment of the *Spanda* principle which has been already described and which will be described further, attains, in short time, his essential nature which is the same as *Śaṃkara* even in the state of waking,[1] if, as has been said in the Gītā, "Those who merging their mind in me, always united with me, wait upon me" (Bh. Gītā, XII, 2), he is always intent on the close observation of the inner (divine) nature.[2]

Thus his inner nature, which is *Śaṃkara*, itself emerges before him by which the awakened one, by the attainment of ever-present absorption in it, becomes fully enlightened (*suprabuddha*), and becomes liberated while living.

## NOTES

1. Not only in the state of meditation but also when he is actively engaged in the hum-drum routine of life in the waking condition.

2. This means the constant awareness of the divine.

## EXPOSITION

The mind of those who have constant awareness of the Divine is transformed by the mysterious alchemic force present within and thus they acquire Integral Divine Consciousness. Utpalabhaṭṭa adds that the discernment referred to should be practised in the following way:

अहं शुद्धबोधैकरूपो जगच्चेदं मत्स्फार एव ।

"I am only pure Consciousness: this world is only a glorious manifestation of myself".

### *Introduction to the 22nd Verse*

## TEXT

यथास्योद्युक्तस्य बलवदालम्बनवशोदितानायासतदन्यसकलवृत्तिक्षयमयीषु नियतासु यास्ववस्थासु स्पन्दनिधानमुन्मुद्रितमभिमुखीभूतमास्ते ता एताः प्रथममुद्योगस्य विषया इत्युपदेष्टुमाह

## TRANSLATION

As the *Spanda* treasure opens up before the awakened one in those particular states in which all the states of mind other than the awareness of *Spanda* have ceased—Spanda which has appeared with ease on account of the firm grip of it by one intent on its discernment, the author teaches that these particular states should, first of all, be the sphere of effort on the part of the partially awakened *yogīs*.

*Text of the 22nd verse*

अतिक्रुद्धः प्रहृष्टो वा किं करोमीति वा मृशन् ।
धावन्वा यत्पदं गच्छेत्तत्र स्पन्दः प्रतिष्ठितः ॥ २२ ॥

Atikruddhaḥ prahṛṣṭo vā kiṃ karomi iti vā mṛśan/
Dhāvan vā yatpadaṃ gacchet tatra spandaḥ pratiṣṭhitaḥ//22

## TRANSLATION

In that state is the *Spanda*-principle firmly established to which a person is reduced when he is greatly exasperated or overjoyed, or is in impasse reflecting what to do, or is running for life.

## COMMENTARY

## TEXT

सर्वत्र तावदुपायमार्गे समस्तेतरवृत्तिप्रशमपूर्वमेकाग्रीभवन्ति योगिनः, एतास्वति-क्रोधाद्यवस्थासु स्वरसत एव समस्तापरवृत्तिक्षयमयीषु यदि स्पन्दतत्त्वविविक्तये सततमुद्युक्ता झटित्यन्तर्मुखीभवन्ति योगिनस्तत्समीहितमचिरेणैव लभन्ते । अयोगिनस्त्वत्र मूढा एवेति तात्पर्यम् । तथाहि समनन्तरविहितदारुणोपघात-शत्रुदर्शनान्मर्मस्पर्शितत्तद्वचनाकर्णनाद्वा प्रथममेवोन्मिषत्संजिहीर्षदेवताबलादन्तर्मु-खीभवद्रश्मिचक्रोऽतिक्रुद्धः, चिरप्रार्थितप्राणेशीवदनेन्दुदर्शनादेव तत्क्षणमे-वोन्मज्जत्पूर्णाभिलाषदेवतावशविकासितानुधावत्समस्तकरणचक्रः प्रहृष्टो वा, बलवदाततायिबलेन सर्वतो वलितत्वात्कान्दिशीकः किं करोमीति मृशन्विकल्प-यन्संशयधाराधिरोहात्मनि पदेऽनुप्रविष्टः क्षीणसकलालम्बनविकसत्संशयसंविन्नि-रालम्बनीकृतवृत्तिप्रसरो वा, मत्तवारणाद्यनुबध्यमानो धावन् शरीरनिरपेक्षमेव

स्वात्मप्रवणीकृतेतरवृत्तिप्रसरवुद्योगदेवीप्रेरणयातित्वरितपलायनक्रियाविष्टो वा; एवमन्यास्वप्येवंप्रायासु सिंहाजगराद्यवलोकनजनितमहात्रासाद्यवस्थासु यद्वृत्तिक्षयात्मकं पदं गच्छेदधितिष्ठेत् स्पन्दतत्त्वविविक्तये सततमुद्युक्तो यो योगिजनस्तस्य तत्र वृत्तिक्षयात्मके पदेऽवस्थाविशेषे स्पन्दः प्रतिष्ठितः स्पन्दतत्त्वमभिमुखीभूतमेव तिष्ठति। तस्मादेतद्वृत्तिक्षयपदं संचेत्य झटिति कूर्माङ्गसंकोचयुक्त्या क्रोधसंशयवृत्तीः प्रशमय्य महाविकासव्याप्तियुक्त्या वा प्रहर्षधावनवृत्तीर्विस्फार्याभिमुखीभूतनिजस्पन्दशक्तिविमर्शवता योगिना भाव्यम् । यथोक्तं श्रीविज्ञानभैरवे

'कामक्रोधलोभमोहमदमात्सर्यगोचरे ।
बुद्धिं निस्तिमितां कृत्वा तत्तत्त्वमवशिष्यते' ॥ (वि० भै० १०१)
आनन्दे महति प्राप्ते दृष्टे वा बान्धवे चिरात् ।
आनन्दमुद्गतं ध्यात्वा तल्लयस्तन्मना भवेत् ॥ (वि० भै० ७१)
क्षुताद्यन्ते भये शोके गह्वरे वारणद्रुते ।
कुतूहले क्षुधाद्यन्ते ब्रह्मसत्ता समीपगा' ॥ (वि० भै० ११८)

इति ॥२२॥

## TRANSLATION

In all the ways of approach to the Divine, the *yogīs* are established in one-pointed concentration after having allayed all the other mental activities. But in these states of vehement anger etc. all the other activities of the mind cease by themselves without any effort on the part of the *yogīs*, and (in such crucial moments) if the *yogīs* who are always on the alert (for grasping the *Spanda* principle) instantly become introverted, they attain their desired object (viz., *Spanda* principle) instantaneously. The purport is that those who are not *yogīs* remain only stupefied (in these states).

*Atikruddhaḥ*, or the greatly exasperated suggests the group of energies becoming introverted under the influence of the goddess 'wishing to destroy' appearing at once after seeing an enemy who has inflicted a terrible wound only a short while before or hearing various heart-rending words of the enemy. *Prahṛṣṭa* (overjoyed) betokens, after the sight of the beloved with moon-like face longed for since long, the entire group of the senses stimulated and running after her, under the influence of the 'goddess of intense longing' emerging at that very moment. *Kiṃ karomi*—'what am I to do' implies a person, encompassed all round by a force of strong desparadoes intent on murder, reflecting-'in which direction may I turn', 'what am I to do'?, thrust in a state of uncertainty, with his mental activities suspended on account of rising uncertainty because of all hopes of help being shattered. *Dhāvan* 'Running for life' denotes one who is attacked by a furious elephant in rut and runs without any regard for his body, and is engaged in a very hasty flight under the influence of 'the goddess of exertion' in full activity, with all other mental activities withdrawn within himself. In this way in all other similar conditions such as great fear generated by the sight of a lion or python, when the *yogī* being always on the alert for discerning the *Spanda* principle, is reduced to any such state in which his other mental activities come to a dead stop, then in that state in which all other mental activities cease, *Spanda* is established, that is the *Spand* principle is turned towards him.

Therefore, considering carefully the cessation of all other mental activities, instantly allaying the states of anger, uncertainty within him, by the device of the tortoise contracting all its limbs within (On the occasion of fear) or by expanding his state of joy, running etc. he should contemplate on the *Spanda* energy which has manifested itself before him. As has been said in *Vijñānabhairava*:

"If one succeeds in immobilizing his mind (in making it one-pointed) when he is under the sway of desire, anger, greed, infatuation, arrogance and envy, then the Reality underlying these states alone subsists" (Verse 101). "On the occasion of a great delight being obtained, or on the occasion of delight arising from seeing a friend or relative after a long time, one should meditate on the delight itself and become absorbed in it, then his mind will become identified with it." (verse 71).

"At the commencement and end of sneeze, in terror, in sorrow, in the condition of a deep sigh or on the occasion of flight from (the attack of) an elephant, during (keen) curiosity, at the commencement or end of hunger, the state of *brahman* approaches near" (Verse 118).

## EXPOSITION

In tense emotional experience, whether of anger, joy, fear or acute mental impasse, all the extroverted mental activities come to a dead stop. We are unable to grasp the inner Reality because of the whirligig of imagination and thought. It is only when this whirligig stops, when the mind is stilled that we are in a fit condition to have an experience of Reality or the *Spanda* principle, if we are properly oriented towards it. *Yogīs*, mystics practise meditation in order to put a stop to all restless mental activities, but intense emotional experiences, of themselves, bring the squirrel-like activities of the mind to a dead halt. That is the psychological moment for catching the vibration of the inner Reality, the Divine *Spanda*, if one is properly introverted to be blessed with its vision. This opportunity is not open to all; it is open only to those who are eagerly waiting for its reception. That is why Kṣemarāja gives the following: warning : एतास्वतिक्रोधाद्यवस्थासु स्वरसत एव समस्तापरवृत्तिक्षयमयीषु यदि स्पन्दतत्त्वविवक्तये सततमुद्युक्ता झटित्यन्तर्मुखी भवन्ति योगिनस्तत्समीहितमचिरेणैव लभन्ते। अयोगिनस्त्वत्र मूढा एव।

"In all these intense emotional states of vehement anger, etc. all other mental activities cease of themselves. If the *yogīs* who are always on the alert for the discernment of the *Spanda* principle instantly become introverted at that psychological moment, they will achieve their desired object instantaneously; the non-*yogīs* even in these states will remain stupefied and bewildered."

Rāmakaṇṭha in his *vivṛti* makes the position clear by the folowing significant remark:

एताश्च प्रबुद्धस्य प्रत्यवमृश्यमानाः सद्यः प्रतिष्ठितस्पन्दोपलब्ध्युपायतां भजन्ते, न तु अनुभूयमानाः। सा हि अवस्था दुःखादिमय्येव। (p. 74)

"These emotional states serve, to the awakened one, as a means for realizing the abiding *Spanda* if they throw him into a reflective recollection of his essential I-consciousness, not if they involve him in their own experience. The experience of these states is only one of pleasure or pain."

*Introduction to the 23rd, 24th and 25th Verses*

TEXT

एवमेतास्ववस्थासूक्तयुक्त्या प्रथमं स्पन्दशक्तिं परिशील्य तदनु तामेवानुसन्दधत्सर्वास्ववस्थासु तद्दार्ढ्यानुप्रवेशमयीं जीवन्मुक्ततामाहरेत्[1] सततोद्युक्त इत्युपदिशति

TRANSLATION

The author now teaches that one, who is always on the alert first of all, closely observes the *Spanda* energy in all these states by the technique already described, and afterwards by constant awareness of that in all the states obtains liberation in life which, in other words, is the realization of its permanent presence(lit., impenetration into its firmness).

*Verses* 23, 24, 25

यामवस्थां समालम्ब्य यदयं मम वक्ष्यति ।
तदवश्यं करिष्येऽहमिति संकल्प्य तिष्ठति ॥ २३ ॥

तामाश्रित्योर्ध्वमार्गेण चन्द्रसूर्यावुभावपि ।
सौषुम्नेऽध्वन्यस्तमितो हित्वा ब्रह्माण्डगोचरम् ॥ २४ ॥

तदा तस्मिन्महाव्योम्नि प्रलीनशशिभास्करे ।
सौषुप्तपदवन्मूढः प्रबुद्धः स्यादनावृतः ॥ २५ ॥

Yām avasthāṃ samālambya yadayam mama vakṣyati/
Tadavaśyaṃ kariṣye'ham iti saṁkalpya tiṣṭhati// 23
Tām āśrityordhvamārgeṇa candrasūryāvubhāvapi/
Sauṣumne' dhvanyastamito hitvā brahmāṇḍagocaram// 24
Tadā tasmin mahāvyomni pralīnaśaśibhāskare/
Sauṣupta-padavan mūḍhaḥ prabuddhaḥ syādanāvṛtaḥ// 25

TRANSLATION

Taking firm hold of that (i.e. *spanda*) the awakened *Yogī* remains firm with the resolution "I will surely carry out whatever

---

१ क० ख० पु० आरोहयेदिति पाठः ।

it will tell me". Resting on the experience of that *Spanda*, both *prāṇa* (*sūrya*) and *apāna* (*candra*) get merged in the *suṣumnā* and by the upward path of *Suṣumnā* they rise up to the great ether of universal consciousness by abandoning the sphere of the body together with the *Brahmarandhra* and are completely dissolved in it. There the unenlightened *yogī* by considering that state a kind of deep sleep remains stupefied, while the one who is not covered with the darkness of infatuation is established in that ether of universal consciousness and abides as fully enlightened. 23, 24, 25.

## COMMENTARY

### TEXT

**अयं-शङ्करात्मा स्वभावो यन्मम वक्ष्यति-अभिव्यक्तं सद् [1]यच्चिदानन्दघनमनुभूतपूर्वं स्वरूपं मां विमर्शयिष्यति तदवश्यमहं करिष्ये बहिर्मुखतां हित्वा तत्प्रवण एव भविष्यामि इति सङ्कल्प्य-निश्चित्य, यामतिक्रोधाद्यवस्थास्वनुभूतचरीं चिदानन्दघनां स्पन्दात्मिकामवस्थामवलम्ब्य[2]-प्राप्यत्वेनाभिसन्धाय तिष्ठति शमितविकल्पगतिमविकल्पामवस्थामविचलत्वेन भजते यो योगी तदीयां तामवस्थां समाश्रित्य चन्द्रसूर्यौ अपानः प्राणश्चोभावपि हृदयभूमौ मिलित्वा युगपदेव सौषुम्नेऽध्वनि ब्रह्मनाड्यामूर्ध्वमार्गेणोदानपथेनास्तमितः शाम्यतः, कथं ब्रह्माण्डलक्षणं गोचरं हित्वा-ब्रह्मबिलाधिष्ठातृब्रह्माधिष्ठितमण्डं मुक्त्वा-ऊर्ध्वकवाटान्तां देहव्याप्तिं त्यक्त्वा तदा चोल्लङ्घितदेहव्याप्तिकेऽत एव प्रकर्षेण लीनावुक्तरूपौ शशिभास्करौ यत्र, तस्मिन्महाव्योम्नि निःशेषवेद्योपशमरूपे परमाकाशे प्राप्तेऽपि यः शिथिलप्रयत्नतया खेचर्याद्यात्मना गुणादिस्पन्दनिःष्यन्देन व्यामोहितत्वात् सौषुप्तपदवद्भवति, सौषुप्तेन च सुप्तमप्युपलक्षितं, तेन च स्वप्नसुषुप्तवत् यः शून्यादिभूमिमेवाधितिष्ठति स योगी सम्यगनभिव्यक्तस्वस्वभावो मूढ इत्युच्यते । यथोक्तं श्रीभट्टकल्लटेन**

'यां स्पन्दात्मिकामवस्थामवलम्ब्य ।'

**इति 'योगिनः' ।**

**इति च**

'यस्य स्वस्वभावाभिव्यक्तिर्न सम्यक् वृत्ता स स्वप्नादिना मुह्यमानोऽप्रबुद्धो निरुद्धः स्यात् ।'

---

१ क० ग० पु० सम्यगिति पाठः ।

२ म० पु० समवलम्ब्येति पाठः ।

इति । यस्तु तत्रापि प्रयत्नपाटवादुद्यन्तृताबलात् क्षणमपि न शिथिलीभवति स तमसानभिभूतत्वात् चिदाकाशमयत्वेनैवावस्थितः प्रबुद्ध उच्यते, अत एव सततोद्योगवतैव योगिना भवितव्यम्,——इत्यादिष्टं गुरुभिः, इति शिवम् ॥२५॥

इति श्रीमहामाहेश्वराचार्यक्षेमराजानकनिर्मिते स्पन्दनिर्णये स्वरूपस्पन्दः प्रथमो निष्यन्दः ॥

## TRANSLATION

'Ayam' ('this') means 'my essential Self which is of the nature of Śaṃkara'. Whatever the previously experienced nature, viz., consciousness-bliss i.e. my essential Self will tell me, i.e. will admonish, that will I surely carry out. i.e. leaving extroverted attitude I will be devoted to it. *Saṃkalpya* means 'having resolved thus'. *Yāṃ samālambya* means 'holding on to that *spanda* state which was previously experienced as consciousness bliss in the state of vehement anger, etc.' *Samālambya* also implies 'having decided that it is a goal worth achieving'. *Tiṣṭhati* (lit., stands remains) implies that 'laying to rest all thought-constructs, he resorts to a state of the absence of thought-constructs (*avikalpaṃ*) firmly'. The *sūrya* and *candra* i.e. *prāṇa* and *apāna* meeting in the stage of *hṛdaya* (centre of the body) and being merged together in the channel of *Suṣumnā* which is otherwise called *Brahmanāḍī*, journeying by the upper i.e. the *udāna* route, get dissolved in the great ether of consciousness, abandoning the sphere of the body presided over by *Brahmā* who specially presides over *Brahmarandhra*. They leave the entire range of the body right up to the gate high up. Thus they get perfectly dissolved in the great ether of consciousness which transcends the entire range of the body and in which the entire objective reality is completely dissolved. The *yogī* who has even attained to the stage of the great ether of consciousness, if he is slack in his efforts, being deluded by the particular emanations of *Spanda* such as *guṇas*, etc. in the form of *Khecarī* and other *śaktis*, experiences it like deep sleep, and thus remains stupefied, because his essential nature is not fully expressed. Therefore, he is called *mūḍha* or the deluded one. The word *sauṣupta* (deep sleep) implies dream also, so this yogi experiences only the state of void, etc. as one does in dream or deep sleep.

As has been said by Śrī Bhaṭṭa Kallaṭa (in his *Vṛtti*)

"Resorting to which state of *Spanda*" and, "That unawakened *yogī* who has not fully realized his essential nature, being deluded by dream etc. is held back (from the state of the great ether of consciousness)".

He, however, who by the intensity of effort and the force of exertion, does not become slack even for a moment, is called *prabuddha* i.e. *suprabuddha*- fully enlightened, and as he is not overcome by the darkness of delusion, he abides as identical with the ether of consciousness.

Therefore, the revered teacher has enjoined that the *yogī* should always make strenuous endeavour. May there be good for all.

Thus ends the first section of the commentary, *Spandanirṇaya*, dealing with *Spanda* which is one's essential nature written by Ācārya Kṣemarâjânaka, devotee of the great Lord.

## EXPOSITION

When the *yogi* catches hold of the *Spanda* principle, his *prāṇa* and *apāna* get merged in *Suṣumnā*, they mount up by the path of *suṣumnā* even beyond Brahmarandhra and get dissolved in the great ether of consciousness. At such an occasion, the *yogī* who is not fully awakened and is not on the alert is simply stupefied, while the *yogī* who is fully awakened is not covered with infatuation by that wonderful experience.

# II SECTION

## SUMMARY OF THE SECOND SECTION:

## TEXT

एवं प्रथमनिःष्यन्देन स्वस्वरूपात्मकं युक्त्युपपन्नं साभिज्ञानं निमीलनसमाधि-प्रत्यभिज्ञेयं स्पन्दतत्त्वं प्रतिपाद्य यथा सततं तत्स्वरूपसमासादनेन सुप्रबुद्धता प्राक्सूचिता भवति तथा इदानीं तस्यैव वैश्वात्म्यमुन्मीलनसमाधिप्रत्यभिज्ञेयं युक्तितोऽपि निर्णेतुं सर्वत्र चिदभेदप्रकाशकं सहजविद्योदयाख्यम् इमं द्वितीयं निःष्यन्दं 'तदाक्रम्य' इत्यादिना 'शिवसद्भावदायिनी' इत्यन्तेन श्लोकसप्तकेन निरूपयति । तत्र विश्वं शुद्धाशुद्धभेदेन द्विधा । तत्र शुद्धं मन्त्रादिरूपं तत एवोत्पन्नं तन्मयं तत्रैव

विश्राम्यति,—इति श्लोकद्वयेनोक्तम् । अशुद्धमपि तन्मयमेव,—इत्यपरेण श्लोकद्वयेनाभिहितम् । तत्संवेदनाधिरूढो जीवन्मुक्तः,—इति श्लोकेनोक्तम् । एतत्तत्त्वसमासादनेनैव साधकानां स्वेष्टसिद्धिः,—इति श्लोकद्वयेनाभिहितमिति संक्षेपः ।

अथ ग्रन्थो व्याख्यायते । यदुक्तम्

'यत्र स्थितमिदं सर्वं कार्यं यस्माच्च निर्गतम् ।' (१।२)

इति, तत्र शुद्धं तावन्मन्त्रादिरूपं, तद्यथा तत एवोत्पन्नं तद्बलेनैव प्रकाशमानं तत्रैव विश्राम्यति तत्प्रथमनिःष्यन्दपरिघटितदृष्टान्तपुरःसरं निरूपयति

## TRANSLATION

Thus, in the first section, the author has first described with significant hint the *Spanda* principle which is one's own essential Self which is conformable to reasoning, and which can be recognized by *nimīlana samādhi* and as he has indicated before how complete enlightenment can come by being constantly united with that essential Self, so now he is going to describe the universality of the same *spanda* principle recognizable by *unmīlana-samādhi* and ascertainable by reasoning. In the second section consisting of seven verses, beginning with 'having recourse to it' and ending with 'bringing about identity with *Śiva*', and entitled 'the rise of innate knowledge' which reveals identity with consciousness everywhere.

The universe is twofold—pure and impure.[1] The first two verses of this section tell us that the pure ones emanate from that *Spanda* principle, are identical with it and finally get merged in it. The next two verses say that the impure ones are also of the same stuff. Another verse says that one who is firmly established in the experience of that principle is liberated in life. The next two verses say that by the realization of this principle alone the practisers of *yoga* achieve their desired object. This is the summary of this section.

## NOTES

1. The *Śuddha* universe consists of 1. Mantra. 2. Mantreśvara, 3. Mantra-Maheśvara, 4. Śiva, and 5. Śakti. The *aśuddha* universe consists of Māyā down to Pṛthvī tattva.

*Introduction to the 1st and 2nd verse*

Now the subject is being explained. In 1,2, it has been said, "in whom this universe rests and from whom it has come forth." The pure aspect of the universe consisting of *Mantra* and others arises from that principle only, is manifest by its force. and is merged in that only. The author describes this fact by means of an example which has already been explained in the first section.

*Text of the first two verses*

तदाक्रम्य बलं मन्त्राः सर्वज्ञबलशालिनः ।
प्रवर्तन्तेऽधिकाराय करणानीव देहिनाम् ॥ १ ॥
तत्रैव संप्रलीयन्ते शान्तरूपा निरञ्जनाः ।
सहाराधकचित्तेन तेनैते शिवधर्मिणः ॥ २ ॥

Tadākramya balam mantrāḥ sarvajñabalaśālinaḥ/
Pravartante 'dhikārāya karaṇānīva dehinām//1
Tatraiva sampralīyante śāntarūpā nirañjanāḥ/
Sahārādhaka-cittena tenaite Śivadharmiṇaḥ//2

TRANSLATION

Resorting to that power (of *Spanda-tattva*), the divinities, *Mantra* etc. together with the sacred formulae which serve as their indicators, being endowed with the power of omniscience proceed to carry out their assigned functions towards the embodied ones just as the senses of the embodied ones by resorting to the power of *Spanda* proceed to carry out their (specific) functions. 1.

Freed of all limitations of office after having performed their assigned duties, (*nirañjanāḥ*),their denotation as particular deities having ceased (*śāntarūpāḥ*) they get dissolved together with the mind of their devotees in that very *Spanda* principle. Hence they are of the nature of *Śiva*. 2.

COMMENTARY

TEXT

तत् स्पन्दतत्त्वात्मकं बलं-प्राणरूपं वीर्यमाक्रम्य अभेदेन आश्रयतया अवष्टभ्य

भगवन्तोऽनन्तव्योमव्याप्यादयो मन्त्राः सर्वज्ञबलेन सर्वज्ञत्वादिसामर्थ्येन श्लाघमाना-जृम्भमाणा अधिकाराय देहिनां प्रवर्तन्ते—सृष्टिसंहारतिरोधानानुग्रहादि कुर्वन्तीत्यर्थः । सर्वज्ञशब्दो भावप्रधानः सर्वकर्तृत्वाद्युपलक्षयति । । यथा देहिनां करणान्युपपादितदृशा तद्बलमाक्रम्य विषयप्रकाशादौ प्रवर्तन्ते इति दृष्टान्तः । तथा निरञ्जनाः कृतकृत्यत्वान्निवृत्ताधिकारमलाः शान्तविशिष्टवाचकात्मस्वरूपास्तत्रैव स्पन्दात्मके बले सम्यगभेदापत्त्या प्रकर्षेणापुनरावृत्त्या लीयन्ते-अधिकारमलान्मुच्यन्ते आराधकचित्तेन उपासकलोकसंवेदनेन सह । यथोक्तम्

'अनुगृह्याणुसंघातं याताः पदमनामयम् ।' (मा० वि० १।४१)

इति । यतश्च तत एवोदितास्तद्बलेन विसृष्टास्तत्रैव लीयन्ते तेनैते मन्त्रमन्त्रेश्वरादयः शिवस्य परमेश्वरस्य सम्बन्धी धर्मः स्वभावो विद्यते येषां ते तथा सामान्यस्पन्दसारा इत्यर्थः । ननु करणानां मन्त्राणां च तत उदयादौ तुल्ये,-किमिति करणानि न सर्वज्ञादिरूपाणि ? । उच्यते परमेश्वरो मायाशक्त्या शरीरकरणानि भेदमयानि निर्मिमीते, विद्याशक्त्या त्वाकाशीयविचित्रवाचकपरामर्शशरीरान्मन्त्रान् । वाचकस्य मायापदेऽपि

'घटोऽयमित्यध्यवसा नामरूपातिरेकिणी ।

परेशशक्तिरात्मेव भासते न त्विदन्तया ॥' (१।५।२०)

इति प्रत्यभिज्ञोक्तनीत्या प्रमातृभूम्यनतिक्रान्तेर्न शरीरपुर्यष्टकादिवद्बोधसङ्कोचकत्वमस्तीति युक्तमेवैषां सर्वज्ञत्वादि । एतच्च

'भेदे त्वेकरसे भाते··········।' (।३।१।८)

इति श्रीप्रत्यभिज्ञाकारिकाटीकायां वितत्य दर्शितम् । एवं विद्यापदावस्थितसृष्ट्यादिकार्यनन्तभट्टारकाद्यपेक्षयैतद्व्याख्येयम् । तथा दीक्षादिप्रवृत्तानामाचार्यादीनां करणरूपाः सर्वे मन्त्रास्तत्स्पन्दतत्त्वरूपं बलमाक्रम्य अनुप्राणकत्वेन अवष्टभ्य आचार्यादीनामेव सम्बन्धिनाराधकचित्तेन सह मोक्षभोगसाधनाद्यधिकाराय प्रवर्तन्ते, तत्रैव शान्तवाचकशब्दात्मकशरीररूपा अत एव च निरञ्जनाः शुद्धाः सम्यक् प्रलीयन्ते-विश्राम्यन्ति । अत्र व्याख्याने 'सहाराधकचित्तेन' इति पूर्वश्लोकेन योज्यम् । एवं च मन्त्राणामुदयप्रलयकोटिव्यापि प्रवृत्तावपि भित्तिभूतमिति अभिहितम् । एवं च दशाष्टादशादिभेदेन भिन्ने शैवे मन्त्राणां स्पन्दतत्त्वसारतैवेत्युक्तं भवति ॥२॥

## TRANSLATION

*Tad balaṃ* means 'that power or energy or vitality of *Spanda*.' '*Ākramya*.' means 'laying hold of it as support' because of their being identical with it, *Mantrāḥ* means gods *Anantabhaṭṭāraka*, *Vyomavyāpins*, etc. *Sarvajñabala-śālinaḥ* means 'having full play by the power of omniscience.' *Adhikārāya dehinām pravartante* means 'proceed to carry out their assigned functions of manifestation, withdrawal, veiling, grace, etc. in respect of the limited souls (*jīvas*).' The word 'omniscient' (*sarvajña*) has been used in the sense of abstract noun, i.e. in the sense of 'omniscience' (*sarvajñatva*) and implies also omnipotence, etc (*sarvakartṛtva*, etc). 'As the senses operate in manifesting objects by obtaining the power of that *Spanda* in the manner (already) described' (in I.6). This is the example (given).

Freed of all limitations of office, after having done their duties, (*nirañjanāḥ*).[1] and their denotation as particular deities having ceased (*śānta rūpā*) or in the case of sacred formulae the specific words which were used to indicate them having come to an end, they are dissolved in the strength of that very *spanda* principle.

In *Sampralīyante* the affix 'śam' means *samyagabhedāpattyā* i.e. by attaining complete identity, the affix *pra* means *prakarṣeṇāpunarāvṛtyā* i.e. 'intensely' or in other words 'without ever returning to their previous state,' *līyante* means 'are freed of the limitations of their office, *Saha ārādhaka-cittena* means 'with the knowledge of the people who were devoted to them.'[2]

As has been said in Mālinīvijaya tantra :

"After conferring grace on the aggregate of *jīvas* (limited experients), they are gone to the state in which there is no longer any trouble." (M. V. I. 41).

As *Mantras, Mantreśvaras*, etc., emanate from that only (i. e. the *Spanda* principle), have come forth from that, and are dissolved only in that, therefore, they have the nature of Śiva i.e. they are one in essence with the generic *spanda* principle.

(*An objection*)

Well, the senses and *Mantras* equally arise from that (the *Spanda* principle), how is it that the senses do not have the power of omniscience, etc.?

(*Reply*) :

The Lord forms by His Māyāśakti the bodies and the senses which are full of difference. By His *Śakti* of *Śuddha Vidyā*, He forms *mantras* out of wonderful expressive śaktis (vācaḥ) which are of the nature of the ether of consciousness add thus non-different from the Lord.

The words used as *mantras* do not transgress the stage of the experient (*pramātṛ*) even at the Māyic stage and have no limitation in knowledge like the body, *puryaṣṭaka*, etc. Therefore their omniscience is perfectly justifiable. This is in accordance with what has been said in *Īśvarapratyabhijñā* in the following verse :—

"The ascertainment (*adhyavasā*) expressed in the form 'this is a jar' is the power of the Highest Lord beyond name and form. It always shines as one with 'I' (Self) and never as this (I, 5, 20). This matter has been explained at length in the commentary on the following verse of Īśvarapratyabhijñā "The power of *Māyā* shows itself in manifesting undiluted diversity etc." (III. 1. 8)

Thus this should be explained in the above manner with reference to Anantabhaṭṭāraka, etc. who abiding in the stage of *śuddha vidyā* bring about manifestation etc. (Another interpretation of the above verses) :

All the *mantras* serving as means of the *ācāryas* (teachers) who are occupied with initiation[3] resorting to the power of the *Spanda* principle i.e. laying hold of it as their life-giver proceed with the mind of the devotees for performing the function of liberation and enjoyment, and after their bodies of articulate sound cease to exist, and are hence purified, they are completely dissolved i.e. they rest (in that *Spanda* principle). In this explanation the phrase 'with the mind of the devotees' should be joined with the previous stanza.

Thus it is meant to be said that the *spanda* principle is the substratum of the *mantras* not only in their stages of manifestation and dissolution but also as regards their functioning. Thus in all the ten, eighteen divisions[4] of the *Śaiva śāstras*, the *Spanda* principle has been declared to be the quintessence of the *mantras*.

## NOTES

1. According to Abhinavagupta, *nirañjanāḥ* means '*na añjyante prakaṭīkriyante* (*prameyarūpeṇa*) *iti nirañjanāḥ*' i.e.

those which can never be known as objects are *nirañjanāḥ*.' The *mantras* are full of I-consciousness; therefore they are always as subjects and can never be reduced to the category of objects.

2. *Sahārādhaka-cittena* : Rāmakaṇṭha explains this as follows: 'तस्यां दशायामभिसन्ध्युपाधि-विरहात् स्वाभाविकमात्रावशेषं यत् साधक-चित्तं तेन सह'। (p. 83). In that state, the mind of the devotee is in its original state, as the purpose for which he resorted to the *mantra* has already been fulfilled. It is with such a mind of the devotee that the *mantra* gets dissolved in *Spanda*.

But a deeper meaning is that the limited knowledge of the devotee is dissolved; it is now transformed into higher consciousness.

3. There are four kinds of initiation in the *Śaiva* system, viz., (1) *Sāmayika dīkṣā* in which the *guru* initiates the disciple into the traditional rules of conduct which he has to observe, (2) *putraka dīkṣā* in which the disciple is adopted as the successor of the *guru* after his death, (3). *Sādhaka dīkṣā* in which the *guru* initiates the disciple into the mysteries of *yoga*, (4) *Ācārya dīkṣā* in which the disciple is initiated for becoming a *guru*.

4. There are three main schools of *Śaiva* thought, viz, (1) *Śiva tantra*, (2) *Rudra tantra* and (3) *Bhairava tantra*. (1) *Śiva tantra* has ten divisions. They all teach *bheda* or duality (difference). (2) *Rudra tantra* has eighteen divisions. They teach *bhedābheda*, unity in diversity. (3) *Bhairava tantra* has sixty-four divisions. They teach *abheda*-non-duality or non-difference.

## EXPOSITION

*Kṣemarāja* has explained the word *mantrāḥ* occurring in verse 1 in two ways, viz., the deities *Mantra*, *Mantreśvara* and *Mantramaheśvara* and also *mantras* as sacred formulae to be recited by devotees. Both derive their power from the *Spanda* principle in its generic sense, and both are dissolved finally in the generic *Spanda*.

Rāmakaṇṭha and Utpalabhaṭṭa have taken the word *mantrāḥ* only in the sense of sacred formulae to be recited by devotees.

*Introduction to verses 3 and 4*

TEXT

एवं मन्त्रमन्त्रेश्वरादिरूपा शुद्धाभिमता सृष्टिः शिवस्वभावेति प्रतिपाद्याधुना अशुद्धाभिमतापि सा मायादिरूपा शिवस्वरूपैव,—इति उपपादयन् श्रीमतशास्त्रादिरहस्यदृष्टिमपि उपक्षिपति

TRANSLATION

Thus having described that the manifestation consisting of *Mantra*, *Mantreśvara*, etc. considered as pure is of the nature of *Śiva*, the author is now going to explain that the manifestation considered as impure also consisting of the form of *Māyā*, etc. is of the nature of *Śiva* Himself. Thus he suggests the esoteric view of *Śrīmataśāstra*, etc.

*Verse* 3 *and* 4

TEXT

यस्मात्सर्वमयो जीवः सर्वभावसमुद्भवात् ।
तत्संवेदनरूपेण तादात्म्यप्रतिपत्तितः ॥ ३ ॥

तस्माच्छब्दार्थचिन्तासु न सावस्था न या शिवः ।
भोक्तैव भोग्यभावेन सदा सर्वत्र संस्थितः ॥ ४ ॥

Yasmāt sarvamayo jīvaḥ sarvabhāva-samudbhavāt/
Tatsaṃvedanarūpeṇa tādātmya-pratipattitaḥ//3

Tasmācchabdārthacintāsu na sāvasthā na yā śivaḥ/
Bhoktaiva bhogyabhāvena sadā sarvatra saṃsthitaḥ//4.

TRANSLATION

Since the limited individual Self is identical with the whole universe, inasmuch as all entities arise from him, and because of the knowledge of all subjects, he has the feeling of identity with them all, hence whether in the word, object or thought, there is no state which is not *Śiva*. It is the experient himself who, always and everywhere, abides in the form of the experienced i.e. it is the Divine Himself who is the essential

Experient, and it is He who abides in the form of the universe as His field of experience.

## COMMENTARY

### TEXT

यतो जीवो ग्राहकः सर्वमयः शिववद्विश्वरूपः, तेन हेतुना शब्देषु वाचकेषु, अर्थेषु वाच्येषु, चिन्तासु विकल्पज्ञानादिरूपासु आदिमध्यान्तरूपा सावस्था नास्ति या शिवो न भवति सर्वमेव शिवस्वरूपमित्यर्थः । यतश्चैवमतो भोक्तैव चिदात्मा ग्राहको भोग्यभावेन देहनीलादिरूपेण सदा नित्यं सर्वत्र विचित्रतत्त्वभुवनादिपदे सम्यगनूनाधिकतया स्थितः, न तु भोग्यं नाम किञ्चिद्भोक्तुर्भिन्नमस्ति । जीव इत्युपक्रम्य शिव इत्युपसंहारेण जीवशिवयोर्वास्तवो न कोऽपि भेदः,—इति देहाद्यवस्थासु न कासुचिदप्यपूर्णंमन्यता मन्तव्या, अपि तु चिद्घनशिवस्वभावतैवेति भङ्ग्योपदिशति । यथोक्तम् 'शरीरमपि ये षट्त्रिंशत्तत्त्वमयं शिवरूपतया पश्यन्ति अर्चयन्ति च ते सिद्ध्यन्ति घटादिकमपि तथाभिनिविश्य पश्यन्ति अर्चयन्ति च तेऽपीति नास्त्यत्र विवादः' इति श्रीप्रत्यभिज्ञाटीकायाम् । भट्टश्रीवामनेनाप्युक्तम्

'आलम्ब्य संविदं यस्मात्संवेद्यं न स्वभावतः ।
तस्मात्संविदितं सर्वमिति संविन्मयो भवेत् ॥'

इति । कस्मात् जीवः सर्वमयः इत्यत्र हेतुः सर्वभावानां समुद्भवादुत्पत्तिहेतुत्वाद् अपादानभावप्रधानश्च निर्देशः ।

'प्रमातृमितिमानमेयमयभेदजातस्य ते
विहार इह हेतुतां समुपयाति यस्मात्त्वयि ।
निवृत्तविवृतौ क्वचित्तदपयाति तेनाधुना
नयेन पुनरीक्ष्यते जगति जातुचित्केनचित् ॥'

इति श्रीज्ञानगर्भस्तोत्रोक्तनीत्या संविद्येव प्रसृतायां जगतः सद्भावात्सर्वभावसमुद्भवत्वं जीवस्य । यतश्च जीवादेव उदयति विभ्रमतोऽयं सर्वमयो विभ्रशक्तिरिति यावत् । निर्णीतं चैतद्द्वितीयसूत्रवृत्तौ । सर्वमयत्वे हेत्वन्तरमाह 'तत्संवेदन' इत्यर्धेन । तस्य सर्वस्य नीलसुखादेर्यत्संवेदनं प्रकाशस्तेन रूपेण स्वभावेन तादात्म्यप्रतिपत्तेः सर्वमयत्वस्योपलम्भात् । एवमनेन श्लोकद्वयेन रहस्यचर्याः सर्वभेदपादपोन्मूलनोपपत्तिपरिघटिताश्च ज्ञानोपदेशकथाः, प्रथमचरमसूत्राभ्यां महार्थतत्त्वं, जाग्रदादिसूत्रेण षडर्धपरमार्थः, 'तदाक्रम्य' इत्यनेन सर्वोपासासारतेत्याद्युपक्षिप्तमिति स्पन्दतत्त्वेनैव विश्वोपदेशाः स्वीकृताः ॥ ४ ॥

## TRANSLATION

Since the experient constitutes the whole universe like *Śiva*, therefore there is no state whether it is the beginning or the middle or the end and whether it is word, or object, or ideation i.e. thought etc. *which* is not *Śiva*. The sense is that every thing is *Śiva*. Since it is thus, therefore the experient himself who is of the form of consciousness that abides wholly i.e. neither less nor more in the form of the experienced, such as the body, blue etc. always and everywhere, i.e. in all the diverse stages of *tattva* (categories), *bhuvana* (worlds) etc. The experienced is nothing different from the experient.

Since this teaching begins with *jīva* (experient), and ends with *Śiva*, it teaches by way of suggestion that there is no essential difference between *jīva* and *Śiva*, that is to say, one should not regard oneself as imperfect in any state like body, etc., rather he should consider himself as of the nature of *Śiva* who is a compact mass of consciousness.

As has been said in *Śrī Pratyabhijñā-ṭīkā*[1]

"Even those who perceive the body consisting of thirtysix categories in the form of *Śiva* and treat it with respect acquire spiritual perfection and also those, who investing even jar, etc. with the form of *Śiva* perceive it in that light and honour it (will acquire spiritual perfection). There is no difference of opinoin on this point."

Bhaṭṭa Śrī Vāmana[2] has also said,

"As all objects are known only when they rest on Consciousness, as support, not by themselves, therefore all things exist only as known. So one should identify himself with Consciousness."

How is it known that the experient is identical with the whole ? In reply to this query, it is said that the reason is because he is the origin or cause of the production of all entities.[3] The ablative case *samudbhavāt* has been used in an abstract sense i.e. in the sense of *samudbhavatvāt* i.e. in the sense of 'being the cause of all productions.

Thy sport becomes in this world the cause of the diversity of the knower, knowing, knowledge and the knowable. Since on thy play being over, that diversity disappears somewhere,[3] thou art seldom seen in that light and only by some."[4] In accordance with the view expressed in the above hymn of Śrī Jñānagarbha,[5] the *jīva* is the source of all entities, because the existence of the world comes about only on the prevalence of consciousness. Since the universe emanates only from the *jīva*, therefore, he constitutes the whole and has all powers. This has been conclusively discussed in my commentary on the second verse. Another reason for the *jīva* being declared as identical with the whole is given in the second half of the first verse above in the phrase "because of the knowledge of all" i.e. the *jīva* is known as identical with all, because he is identical with the knowledge of the whole in the form of blue, pleasure, etc.

Since by means of these two verses, the secret practices and the teachings of wisdom brought about by reasoning which serves to uproot the tree of all differences have been suggested, by the first and the last verses, of I Section *mahārtha tattva*[6] the great Reality, by the verse *Jāgradādivibhede'pi* (I, 3) the highest truth of the Trika system and by the verse *tadākramya* the quintessence of all worship has been suggested, therefore, all instructions are acknowledged to be imparted by *Spanda* principle only.

## NOTES

1. This *ṭīkā* was written by Utpaladeva himself. It is not available now.
2. There have been many writers in Kashmir by this name. It is not known to whom Kṣemarāja is referring here.
3. Somewhere i.e. in thyself in the state of *saṃhāra* or withdrawal.
4. By some i.e. by those who have received thy grace.
5. The writer of this has not yet been traced.
6. *Mahārtha tattva* refers to the *krama* system.

## EXPOSITION

Two important points have been stressed in these two verses. Firstly, the individual is identical with total reality. The reason is that through knowledge (*saṃvedana*) he knows every thing.

Therefore through knowledge he feels his identity with the all-of-reality. As he becomes identified with the whole of Reality, he becomes in the words of Kṣemarāja *viśvaśakti* 'universal power,' and thus all objects are said to arise from him.

Secondly, as he feels his identity with all, there is no state which is not *Śiva* to him. Therefore, the difference between the experient and the experienced disappears for him.

*Introduction to the 5th verse*

TEXT

अथैतत्प्रतिपत्तिसारतैव मोक्ष इत्यादिशति

TRANSLATION

The author now points out that it is the quintessence of the realization of one's identity with the whole universe that constitutes liberation (*mokṣa*).

*Text of the 5th Verse*

इति वा यस्य संवित्तिः क्रीडात्वेनाखिलं जगत् ।
स पश्यन्सततं युक्तो जीवन्मुक्तो न संशयः ॥ ५ ॥

Iti vā yasya saṃvittiḥ krīḍātvenākhilaṃ jagat/
Sa paśyan satataṃ yukto jīvanmukto na saṃśayaḥ//5

TRANSLATION

Or he, who has this realization (viz. identity of his Self with the whole universe), being constantly united with the Divine, views the entire world as the play (of the Self identical with *Śiva*), and is liberated while alive. There is no doubt about this.

COMMENTARY

TEXT

वाशब्दः प्रथमनिःष्यन्दोक्तनिमीलनसमाधिप्रकारं विकल्पयन् अस्याः समापत्तेर्दुर्लभतां ध्वनयति । तेनायमर्थः,–ईदृशी तावत्संवित्तिः दुर्लभा यस्य कस्यचिदेवाप-

श्चिमजन्मनो भवति सोऽखिलं जगत्क्रीडात्वेन पश्यन् निजसंविदुन्मेषनिमेषाभ्यां सृजन् संहरंश्च

'मय्यावेश्य मनो ये मां नित्ययुक्ता उपासते ।' (भ० गी० १२।२)

इति स्थित्या सततसमाविष्टो महायोगी जीवन्नेव प्राणादिमानपि विज्ञानाग्नि-निर्दग्धाशेषबन्धनो देहपाते तु शिव एव जीवंश्चेदृङ्मुक्त एव न तु कथञ्चिदपि बद्धः । 'न संशयः' इत्यनेन इदं ध्वनयति, दीक्षादिना गुरुप्रत्ययतो मुक्तिः, ईदृशात्तु ज्ञाना-त्समाचाराद्वा स्वप्रत्ययत एवेति ॥ ५ ॥

## TRANSLATION

By the use of the word *vā* (or), the author means to suggest that the means of *nimīlana-samādhi* described in the first section is optional, but this realization (of identity with the universe) is essential and difficult to acquire. Hence the sense of the verse is as follows.

Such realization is difficult to acquire and is attained by some such person as has no future birth. He views the whole world as play and by evolution (*unmeṣa*) and involution (*nimeṣa*) manifests or withdraws it. As has been said in the Bhagavadgītā, "Having mentally entered in me, those who are always united with me and wait upon me" (Bh-Gītā XII.2) the great *yogi* has his consciousness always absorbed in the Universal Consciousness, and even while he is living i.e. even while he is exercising the act of maintaining *prāṇa*, his entire bondage is burnt to ashes by the fire of spiritual knowledge and after the fall of the body, he abides as *Śiva* Himself. Even while living, such a person is indeed liberated and can never suffer bondage.

By the phrase 'there is no doubt,' the author suggests that by initiation, liberation comes about by faith in the *guru* (the spiritual guide), but by such knowledge and conduct, it comes about by one's own experience.

### *Introduction to the 6th and 7th verse*

## TEXT

इयमेव महासमापत्तिः साधकाचार्यादीनामभीष्टप्राप्तिहेतुः,—इति श्लोक-द्वयेनाह—

## TRANSLATION

This great realization is the means of the attainment of the desired object of all the *sādhakas* (aspirants) and the *ācāryas* (teachers).

*Verse 6th and 7th*

अयमेवोदयस्तस्य ध्येयस्य ध्यायिचेतसि ।
तदात्मतासमापत्तिरिच्छतः साधकस्य या ॥ ६ ॥

इयमेवामृतप्राप्तिरयमेवात्मनो ग्रहः ।
इयं निर्वाणदीक्षा च शिवसद्भावदायिनी ॥ ७ ॥

Ayamevodayas tasya dhyeyasya dhyāyi-cetasi/
Tadātmatā-Samāpattir icchataḥ sādhakasya yā//6.

Iyamevāmṛtaprāptir ayamev ātmano grahaḥ/
Iyaṃ nirvāṇa-dīkṣā ca śiva-sadbhāvadāyinī//7.

## TRANSLATION

This only is the manifestation of the object of meditation in the meditator's mind that the aspirant with resolute will has the realization of his identity with that (object of meditation).

This alone is the acquisition of ambrosia leading to immortality; this alone is the realization of Self; this alone is the initiation of liberation leading to identity with *Śiva*.

## COMMENTARY

### TEXT

इह 'शिवो भूत्वा शिवं यजेत्' इति यदुद्घोष्यते तत्र ध्यायिनश्चेतसि संवेदने तस्येति 'न सावस्था न या शिवः' इति प्रतिपादितशिवस्वभावस्य ध्येयस्य अन्यस्य वा कस्यचित्तत्तत्सिद्धिहेतोर्मन्त्रदेवताविशेषस्य अयमेवोदयः प्रकटीभावः या साधकस्य ध्यातुराचार्यादेः

'तस्माच्छब्दार्थचिन्तासु न सावस्था न या शिवः ।' (२।४)

इति प्रतिपादितरूपा तदात्मता।समापत्तिः-शिवैक्यावेशो न तु पञ्चवक्त्रादेर्व्यतिरिक्तस्याकारस्य दर्शनं, न तु निश्चयमात्रेण तदात्मतासमापत्तिः अपि तु इच्छतोऽवि-

**कल्पविश्वाहन्तात्मकशिवैक्यरूपेच्छापरामर्शाधिरूढस्य । एतदुक्तं भवति, अहमेव तत्संवेदनरूपेण तादात्म्यप्रतिपत्तितो विश्वशरीरश्चिदानन्दघनः शिव इति सङ्कल्पो यस्याविकल्पशेषीभूतत्वेन फलति, तस्य ध्येयमन्त्रदेवतादि किं न नाम अभिमुखीभवति सर्वस्यैतदद्वयप्रथालग्नत्वात् । यथोक्तमस्मत्परमेष्ठिपादैः**

'साक्षाद्भवन्मये नाथ सर्वस्मिन्भुवनान्तरे ।
किं न भक्तिमतां क्षेत्रं मन्त्रः क्वैषां न सिध्यति ॥' (उ० स्तो० १।४)

**इति । इयमेव च समापत्तिः परमाद्वयरूपस्यामृतस्य प्राप्तिः, अन्यस्मिंस्त्वमृते कतिपयकालशरीरदाढर्यदायिनि प्राप्तेऽपि साधकैर्मरणमवश्यमवाप्यत एवेत्येवकाराशयः । एवं सर्वत्रानेनैवाशयेन श्रीस्वच्छन्दे स्थूलदृष्ट्यामृतप्राप्तिप्रकरणे**

'नैव चामृतयोगेन कालमृत्युजयो भवेत् ।'

**इत्युक्त्योपसंहृत्य तात्त्विकस्तत्प्राप्तिप्रकारः**

'अथवा परतत्त्वस्थः सर्वकालैर्न बाध्यते ॥' (७।२२३)

**इत्यादिना**

'.........सर्वं शिवशक्तिमयं स्मरेत् ।'

**इति मध्येन**

जीवन्नेव विमुक्तोऽसौ यस्येयं भावना सदा ।
यः शिवं भावयेन्नित्यं न कालः कलयेत्तु तम् ।
योगी स्वच्छन्दयोगेन स्वच्छन्दगतिचारिणा ।
स स्वच्छन्दपदे युक्तः स्वच्छन्दसमतां व्रजेत् ।
स्वच्छन्दश्चैव स्वच्छन्दः स्वच्छन्दो विचरेत्सदा । (७।२५८)

**इत्यनेन सहजसन्दर्भेण सप्रशंसं पश्चादुपदिष्टः । अयमेवात्मनो ग्रहो ज्ञानं यदुच्यते 'आत्मा ज्ञातव्य' इति तत्रेदमेव सर्वज्ञसर्वकर्तृस्वतन्त्रशिवस्वरूपतया प्रत्यभिज्ञानमात्मनो ज्ञानं, न तु**

'पुरुष एवेदं सर्वम् ।' (श्वेत० उ० ३।१५)

**इति श्रुत्यन्तविदुक्तं**

'त आत्मोपासकाः सर्वे न गच्छन्ति परं पदम् ।' (स्व०।४।३८८)

**इत्याम्नायोक्तेः । तथा दीक्षावसरे योजनिकाद्यर्थमयमेव शिष्यात्मनोऽनुग्रहः, इमामेव समापत्तिं विद्वानाचार्यः शिष्यात्मानं शिवे योजयन्नाचार्यो भवतीत्यर्थः । इयं स्वप्रत्ययसिद्धा पुत्रकादेः शिवात्मनः सद्भावस्य पारमार्थिकस्वरूपस्य दायिनी निर्वाणदीक्षा । यथोक्तम्**

---

१ गामिनीति मूलपरात्रीशिकापुस्तकस्थः पाठः ।

एवं यो वेद तत्त्वेन तस्य निर्वाणदायिनी ।
दीक्षा भवत्यसन्दिग्धा तिलाज्याहुतिवर्जिता ॥' (प० त्री० २५)

**इति । हौत्री दीक्षापि दीक्षैव, तत्र मा भूत्कस्यचिदनाश्वास इत्याशयेनात्रैवकारो न कृतः श्रीमहागुरुप्रवरेणेति शिवम् ॥**

**इति श्रीमहामाहेश्वराचार्यक्षेमराजानकनिर्मितस्पन्दनिर्णये सहजविद्योदय-स्पन्दो द्वितीयो निःष्यन्दः ॥२५॥**

## TRANSLATION

It is declared here that 'one should worship *Śiva* by becoming *Siva*'. That alone constitutes the manifestation of the object of meditation in the mind of the meditator which leads to the realization of identity with the object of meditation. *Dhyāyinaścetasi* means in the mind of the meditator, *Tasya* means 'of the object of meditation' i.e. 'of the nature of *Śiva*' as described in 'there is no state which is not *Śiva*,' or 'of the particular deity of *mantra* who is the cause of the attainment of some object.' *Ayameva udayaḥ* means 'this is its manifestation,' which brings about identity of the meditator whether he is a *sādhaka* or *ācārya*[1] with that (i.e. with the object of meditation) in accordance with what is described in 'in word, object or thought, there is no state which is not *Śiva*' (II 4) *Tadātmatā samāpattiḥ* means 'identity with *Śiva*', not the perception of some separate form such as the five-headed deity. *Icchataḥ* means 'not simply by determination, but rather by one who is steeped in the will—which is not an idea—of becoming one with Śiva who is the Self of all'.

This is what is meant to be said. "Because everything is associated with this non-dual light (i.e. the *Spanda* principle), which is the deity of the *mantra* contemplated that will not appear before him whose resolute will is 'I am *Śiva*, of compact mass of consciousness and bliss, and the whole universe is my body', which arises from the realization of identity with the awareness of that and which is the result of non-ideation[2] alone."

As has been said by my great grand teacher[3] "O Lord, in this whole world which is thy own manifest form, what is that spot which is not a holy place to thy devotees and where the *mantras* of these devotees will not bear fruit"? (U.Sto I,4).

This alone is his great accomplishment that he acquires the ambrosia of the highest non-duality. The implication of the word 'eva' (alone, only) is that with any other kind of ambrosia, though it may provide stability to the body for some time, the death of the aspirant is inevitable (ultimately). Thus from this point of view, everywhere in Svacchanda tantra in the chapter dealing with the acquisition of ambrosia from a gross point of view, it begins with the statement, "Never by acquisition of ambrosia can there be victory over death which is brought about by time," and in the relevant context based on the experience of *Sahaja* (*sahaja sandarbheṇa*) with the mode of acquisition of the real ambrosia in terms of praise in the following words:

"Or one established in the supreme principle is not harassed by all forms of Time."

In the middle, it says:

"One should regard everything as of the form of *Śiva* and *Śakti* and finally it says 'One who has always this conviction is liberated while living. Time can never throttle him who always contemplates on *Śiva*. The *yogi* functioning freely by means of *Svacchanda yoga*[4] is united with the status of *Svacchanda*[5] and acquires equality with *Svacchanda*. He becoming *Svacchanda* moves about freely, and enjoys full Freedom" (Svacch. (VII, 258)

This, indeed, is the realization of Self. In the statement. "The Self should be realized," what is meant is the recognition of the Self as *Śiva* who is omniscient, omnipotent and fully free, and not the Self mentioned by the Vedantist in the line, "All this is verily Puruṣa"[6] (Śvet. III 15) The sacred text also says, "All those votaries of Self[7] do not reach the highest stage" (Sv. IV, 388).

On the occasion of initiation for the purpose of uniting (the Self of the disciple with the universal consciousness), the impartation of this knowledge is the favour conferred on the disciple. The *ācārya* (teacher) having a knowledge of this attainment justifies his title of *ācārya* by uniting the Self of the disciple to Śiva. This is the initiation for liberation confirmed by one's personal realization which gives to *putraka*[8] etc. the knowledge of the highest nature of Śiva. As has been said:

"He who thus knows in reality has his certain initiation

which bestows liberation without the oblation with sesamum and ghee (clarified butter)", (P.Tri, 25)

Sacerdotal initiation is also initiation. In order that any one may not lose faith in sacerdotal initiation, the chief great teacher[9] has not used the word *eva* (alone) here (i.e. in the description of *Nirvāṇa—dīkṣā*). May there be good to all.

Here ends the second section entitled *Sahajavidyodayaspanda* of *Spanda-nirṇaya* written by Kṣemarājānaka, the devotee of the great Lord.

## NOTES

1. Vide Note No. 2 on the first two verses of this section.
2. The author means to say that this realization does not come by way of ideation, but of will.
3. This refers to Utpaladeva.
4. *Svacchanda yoga*—This means union with *Svātantrya*, the Divine I-consciousness which is the quintessential nature of *Śiva*.
5. *Svacchanda*—the absolute Free Will of *Bhairava*.
6. By *puruṣa* in the above quotation, the Vedantist does not mean the 25th *Puruṣa tattva* as Kṣemarāja thinks, but *Ātmā*, the Divine Consciousness.
7. According to Trika philosophy, 'ātma-vyāpti' or realization of Self is not the highest ideal. It is *Śivavyāpti*, viz., the realization of both the Self and the universe as *Śiva* which is the highest ideal.
8. Vide note No. 2 on the first two verses of this section.
9. Ths refers to Vasugupta, the author of Spandakārikā.

## EXPOSITION

The second section has been rightly entitled *Sahajavidyodaya* i.e., the rise of *Sahaja vidyā*. *Sahaja* or *Śuddha vidyā* is that state in which in spite of the seeming difference of all that is earth, earthy, there is a running sense of unity, identity, of the Supreme I-consciousness fused with the all-of-reality. As Vasugupta puts it,

"तस्मात् शब्दार्थचिन्तासु न सावस्था न या शिवः"

"Whether it is word or thought or object there is no state which is not Śiva."

In the first section, the emphasis is on the Self-realization or in the technical language of this system on *ātmavyāpti* on the realization of Self as Śiva. In the second section, the emphasis is on the realization of the universe as *Śiva* or in the technical language of this system on *Śiva-vyāpti.*

From the point of view of *yoga*, the emphasis in the first section is on *nimīlana-samādhi*, on introversive meditation, on taking a plunge mentally in the innermost Self and realizing it as *Śiva.* In the second section, the emphasis is on *unmīlana samādhi* or extroversive meditation in which in spite of the senses being open to the onset of external sensation, the world appears as the materialization of the bliss of Śiva. Kṣemarāja rightly calls it *mahāsamāpatti*, the *coup* of supreme realization.

In the two concluding verses of the section, the author depicts, in beautiful words, the mystic significance of the spiritual praxis of the seeker in the light of the rise of *Sahaja vidyā.*

The aspirant meditates over *mantra* in order that the deity embodied in the *mantra* may manifest himself or herself to him. The author says that the realization on the part of the seeker, of his identity with *Śiva* is alone the manifestation of the deity for which he has been spending days and nights of vigil.

Man has been in search of ambrosia that will make him immortal. The author says that the realization of one's identity with *Śiva* is alone the real ambrosia, for it sets one free from the whirligig of birth and death.

The aspirant subjects himself to a tedious ceremony of initiation (*dīkṣā*) for liberation (*nirvāṇa*). The author says that which gives the realization of identity with *Śiva* is alone the real initiation for liberation. Utpalabhaṭṭa quotes the following verse as a definition of *dīkṣā*:

ददाति ज्ञानसद्भावं क्षपयत्यखिलं मलम् ।
बोधानुवेधाद्दीक्षोक्ता दानक्षपणधर्मिणी ॥

*Dīkṣā* is that which gives realization and destroys all impurities. Because it imparts that realization which awakens one from the sleep of ignorance, therefore is it called *dīkṣā*. It has the characteristic of both giving (*dī*) and destroying (*kṣā*)".

## III SECTION

### *Summary of the 3rd Section*

एवं निमीलनोन्मीलनसमाधिद्वयसमाधेय उभयविसर्गारणीभूतः सुप्रबुद्धताभिव्यक्तये स्पन्दतत्त्वसमावेशो निःष्यन्दद्वयेन निर्णीतः । अथेदानीमेतदवष्टम्भाभ्यासेन परापरविभूत्युदयो भवतीत्यभिधाय संक्षेपेण बन्धमोक्षस्वरूपं निरूप्य प्रथमोपक्रान्तं निगमयति—यथेच्छेत्यादिभिः चक्रेश्वरो भवेदित्यन्तैरेकोनविंशत्या श्लोकैरनेन विभूतिस्पन्दाख्येन तृतीयनिःष्यन्देन । तत्र श्लोकद्वयेन जाग्रत्सिद्धस्वातन्त्र्यदृष्टान्तपुरःसरं स्वप्नस्वातन्त्र्यम् । एकेन तद्विपर्ययमभिदधता सततोद्युक्ततैवाश्रयणीयेति तात्पर्येणोक्तम् । द्वितयेनाभीष्टवस्तुज्ञानाविर्भावः । एकेन कर्तृशक्त्याविर्भूतिः क्षुधादिजयश्च । एकेन सर्वज्ञताप्राप्तिः । एकेन ग्लानिनाशश्चेत्यष्टके निरूपितम् । ततः स्पन्दात्मन उन्मेषस्यैकेन स्वरूपं लक्षितम् । एकेन परसमाधिविघ्नभूतानां सिद्धीनां हेयतोक्ता । एकेन द्वितीयनिःष्यन्दनिर्णीतविश्वात्मतास्वभावः समावेश उक्तः । ततः समाविष्टतालाभे युक्तिरुक्तैकेन । त्रयेण पशुपाशनिर्णयः । एकेन स्पन्द-तत्त्वस्यैव बन्धमोक्षोभयपदाक्रांतिरुक्ता । द्वयेनोच्छेद्यत्वेन बन्धस्वरूपमनूदितम् । एकेन तदुच्छित्त्युपायमभिदधतादिसूत्रोक्तार्थो निगमित इति संक्षेपो निःष्यन्दस्य ॥

Thus by the two sections the absorption into Spanda principle for the manifestation of the state of the fully illuminated *yogī* has been conclusively explained which is to be brought about by both introversive (*nimīlana*) and extroversive (*unmīlana*) meditation both of which are to be interpenetrative (*ubhaya-visargāraṇībhūtaḥ*) i.e., the inner experience of the Divine has to be experienced externally also and the external experience of the Divine has to be experienced internally also.

Now in the third section of nineteen verses of entitled *Vibhūti Spanda*, beginning with the verse *Yathecchā* (according to the desire) and ending with *Cakreśvaro bhavet* (he becomes the lord of the group), he (the author) having said that the higher and the lower supernormal powers arise by laying hold of the *Spanda* principle, and having briefly delineated the nature of bondage and liberation, concludes what has begun in the first section.

In this section, by the first two verses, the author mentions the freedom in dream on the analogy of the well-known freedom in the waking state. By the third while talking about its opposite i.e. when he does not have freedom of experience in the waking and dream state, he implicitly states that the *yogī* should maintain strenuous and constant endeavour. The next two verses deal with the manifestation of the knowledge of the desired object. By another verse, he describes the power of effecting things and the control of hunger, etc. By yet another verse, he describes the achievement of omniscience. By the eighth verse, he describes the disappearance of the depression of mind. After that, he defines the nature of *unmeṣa* or the unfoldment of spiritual consciousness which is of the nature of *spanda.* Another verse describes the necessity of rejecting those powers which are an obstacle in the way of the highest meditation. By another verse, the nature of identity with the entire universe as described in the second section has been mentioned for achieving absorption in the divine consciousness.[1] After that the means for achieving that absorption has been described by another verse. The next triad of verses describes the bondage of the limited individual. Another verse says that the *Spanda* principle prevails both in bondage and liberation. By two verses the nature of bondage has again been repeated for the sake of its being destroyed. The last one while describing the means of cutting asunder the bond emphasizes the sense of the first verse (i.e. I.1) in conclusion. This is the summary of this section.

## NOTES

1. *Samāveśa uktaḥ* has to be read as *samāveśe uktaḥ* i.e. *samāveśa* is here in the locative case. The locative case has here to be treated as *naimittikī saptamī* i.e. 'samāveśe' here means for achieving *samāveśa* (absorption).

### *Introduction to the 1st and 2nd verse*

*Text*

अथ ग्रन्थो व्याख्यायते । यदुक्तं 'सुप्रबुद्धस्य सततं स्पन्दतत्त्वोपलब्धिः' इति । तत्र 'अतः सततमुद्युक्त' इत्यनेन जागरायां तत्परिशीलनेन शिक्षा प्रबुद्धस्य सुप्रबुद्धता-प्राप्त्यर्थमुक्ता । यामवस्थामित्यादिना प्रतिपदोपायपरिशीलनपाटवेन योगिसुषुप्तावरणभङ्गः उक्तः ।

इदानीं लौकिकस्वप्नसुषुप्तविदलनेन सुप्रबुद्धतामेव साधयितुं स्वप्नोचितां विभूतिमस्य दर्शयितुमाह

## TRANSLATION

Now begins the commentary on the book.

In I,17, it has been said, "The fully enlightened has always the experience of *Spanda tattva.*" In the same section, it has been said, in I, 21, "One should always be on the alert for the discernment of the *spanda* principle." By this an exhortation has been imparted to the partially enlightened for its constant practice in the waking state in order to attain the status of the fully enlightened one. In I, 23, 24, 25, beginning with 'which state etc'., the *yogī* has been advised to tear the veil of deep sleep by constant, intensive, skilful practice of the means.

Now in order to prove the perfect enlightenment of the *yogī* by his power to rend asunder the condition of ordinary (normal) dream and deep sleep. the author is going to show his super-normal power in relation to dream.

### *Text of the verse 1 and 2*

यथेच्छाभ्यर्थितो धाता जाग्रतोऽर्थान् हृदि स्थितान् ।
सोमसूर्योदयं कृत्वा सम्पादयति देहिनः ॥ १ ॥
तथा स्वप्नेऽप्यभीष्टार्थान् प्रणयस्यानतिक्रमात् ।
नित्यं स्फुटतरं मध्ये स्थितोऽवश्यं प्रकाशयेत् ॥ २ ॥

Yathecchābhyarthito dhātā jāgrato'rthān hṛdi sthitān
Somasūryodayaṃ kṛtvā sampādayati dehinaḥ// 1

Tathā svapne 'pyabhīṣṭārthān praṇayasyānatikramāt/
Nityaṃ sphuṭataraṃ madhye sthito' vaśyaṃ prakāśayet// 2

## TRANSLATION

As the sustainer of this universe (i.e. *Śiva*) when eagerly entreated with desire accomplishes all the desires abiding in the heart of the embodied *yogī* who is awake after causing the rise of the moon and the sun. 1

So also in dream, by appearing in the central *nāḍī* (*madhye*), does He surely reveal always and more vividly his desired objects to him who never desists from his zealous prayer. 2

## COMMENTARY

### TEXT

**धत्ते सर्वमात्मनीति धाता-शङ्करात्मा स्वभावः। स यथा जाग्रतः-जागरायामभिव्यक्तस्वस्वातन्त्र्यस्य देहिनो देहभूमिकायामेव प्रकटीभूतपिण्डस्थज्ञानस्य योगिनः सम्बन्धिन्येच्छयाभ्यर्थितोऽन्तर्मुखस्वरूपविमर्शबलेन प्रसादितो हृदि-चेतसि स्थितानर्थानिति विन्दुनादादिज्ञानपुरस्सरं क्षोभप्रतिभाचालनबोधस्तोभज्ञानसञ्चारादिप्रयोजनानि सम्पादयति। कथं सोमसूर्ययोर्ज्ञानक्रियाशक्त्योरुदयं कृत्वा, ज्ञानशक्त्या भास्यमानं हि तत्तत्क्रियाशक्त्योन्मील्यते। समावेशोन्मिषत्प्रतिभात्मकमूलावष्टम्भयुक्तिस्फारितज्ञानक्रियाव्याप्तिसारसव्येतरमरीचिविस्फारणक्रमेण तत्तद्वेधसङ्क्रमणादि सम्पादयति योगिशरीरानुप्रविष्टः परमेश्वरः। यथा चैवं तथा**

अनागतायां निद्रायां विनष्टे बाह्यगोचरे ।
मावस्था मनसा गम्या परा देवी प्रकाशते ॥ (वि० भै० ७५)

**इति**

पीना च दुर्बला शक्ति ध्यात्वा द्वादशगोचरे ।
प्रविश्य हृदये ध्यायन् स्वप्नस्वातन्त्र्यमाप्नुयात् ॥ (वि० भै० ५५)

**इति सम्प्रदायस्थित्या वमनग्राससक्ततदुभयविसर्गारणिचितिशक्तिपरामर्शमुखेन नित्यं प्रणयमनतिक्रामतो भगवत्प्रार्थनापरस्य योगनिद्रारूढस्य स्फुटतरमनाच्छादितरूपतया मध्ये-सौषुम्नधामनि स्थितो धाता स्वप्नेऽप्यभीष्टानेवाणवशाक्तशाम्भवसमावेशादीनन्यानपि समावेशाभ्यासरसोन्मृष्टमतिमुकुरस्य जिज्ञासितानर्थान्नवश्यं प्रकटीकरोति, नास्य योगिनः स्वप्नसुषुप्तयोर्व्यामोहो भवतीत्यर्थः। स्वप्नेन सौषुप्तमप्युपलक्षितम्। अत्राभीष्टार्थप्रकाशे आवृत्त्या अयमेव हेतुः, प्रणयस्य प्रार्थनाया अन्तर्मुखस्वरूपपरिशीलनोपासासम्पाद्यस्य मायाकालुष्योपशमलक्षणस्य प्रसादस्य भगवतानतिक्रमात्। परमेश्वरो हि चिदात्मा यद्यन्तर्मुखोचित-**

सेवाक्रमेणार्थ्यंते तत्तत्सम्पादयत एव, जाग्रतः-इति परतत्त्वे जागरूकस्य जागरावस्था-स्थस्य चेति श्लेषोक्त्या व्याख्येयम् ॥२॥

## TRANSLATION

*Dhātā* is one who holds everything within Himself i.e. *Śiva's* own being. *Jāgrataḥ* means 'of one who is waking' i.e. to whom his freedom has manifested itself in the waking state. *Dehinaḥ* means of the embodied *yogī* or 'of the *yogī* who has knowledge in the waking condition,[1] *Icchābhyarthitaḥ* means 'pleased on account of his discernment of the inner nature'. He brings about the objects abiding in the heart of the *yogi* e.g. by means of *jñāna* (vindu) and *kriyā* (nāda)[2], the *yogī* produces agitation (kṣobha) of the mind in others, the scattering of other's knowledge hither and thither, (pratibhācālanena), immobilising another's knowledge (bodhastobha), and transmission of knowledge into another (jñānasañcāra) etc.

How does He do so? By causing the rise of the moon and the sun[3] i.e. of *jñānaśakti*, the power of knowledge, and *kriyāśakti*, the power of action. All that is thought about by the cognitive power (*jñānaśakti*) is actualized by the operative power (*kriyāśakti*). The great Lord entering the body of the *yogī* brings about various sorts of powers, e.g., transference through penetration etc. by the expansion of his *apāna* and *prāṇa* Śakti of which the quintessence is the expansion of *jñāna* and *kriyāśakti* which are brought about by laying hold of the root (i.e. the *spanda* principle) intuitive knowledge of which is unfolded by his compenetrative meditation (*samāveśa*).

According to the tradition expressed in the following verse.

"When sleep has not yet fully appeared, i.e. when one is about to fall asleep, and all the external objects (though present) have faded out of sight, then the state (between sleep and waking) is one on which one should concentrate. In that state, the Supreme Goddess will reveal Herself."

"If *prāṇaśakti* which is gross and thick i.e., which is expressed with sound; is made frail and subtle i.e., is expressed slowly and if a *yogī* meditates on such *śakti* in *dvādaśānta*,[4] then by entering mentally in between waking and dream condition, he gains freedom of having dream experiences i.e., the dream is entirely under his control. He will have only that dream which he wants to experience" (V. Bh. 55). Thus in accordance with tradition, the sustainer (Śiva) appears in the region of the *Suṣumnā* of the *yogī* who is always intent on praying to God with the awareness of *citi śakti* which is present in both the practice of *prāṇa* (*visarga*) and *apāna* (*araṇi*) which are connected with exhalation (*vamana*) and inhalation (*grāsa*) and who is enjoying the sleep in which *yoga* is being carried on (*Yoganidrā*). He abiding in the *suṣumnā* region even in dream surely reveals the objects desired such as *āṇava*, *śākta*, or *śāmbhava samāveśa* (absorption) or other desired objects, in the mirror of his mind polished by the sap of compenetrative meditation. This *yogi* never suffers from infatuation in dream and deep sleep. The word dream implies deep sleep also.

In the matter of revelation of desired objects by repetition,[5] this is the reason. The Lord never neglects to confer the grace which is the outcome of the cessation of the turbidity of Māyā and a result of his prayer which, in other words, is only the devout practice of the inner (divine) nature.

The great Lord who is of the nature of consciousness surely brings about all those things for which one prays with real inner sincerity. The word *jāgrataḥ* should be treated as having double meaning and should be interpreted both in the sense of 'one who is in the waking state and one who is alert about the highest principle'.

## NOTES

1. *Piṇḍasthajñānasya*—One who has knowledge during the waking condition. The word for waking condition for the common man is *jāgrat*, the word of the *yogī* for the waking condition is *piṇḍastha*, the word of the *jñānī* for the same condition is *sarvatobhadra*.

2. *Vindu* and *nāda* are symbolic terms of the system. From the point of view of *āṇava upāya*, *vindu* and *nāda* symbolize *prāṇa* and *apāna*; from the point of view of *Śākta upāya*, they symbolize *pramāṇa* and *prameya*, from the point of view of *Śāmbhava upāya*, they symbolize *jñāna* and *kriyā*, and from the point of view of *anupāya*, they symbolize *prakāśa* and

*vimarśa*. Here they symbolize *jñāna* and *kriyā*.

3. *Somasūryodayaṁ kṛtvā*—Lit. by causing the rise of the moon and the sun. *Soma* and *Sūrya*, the (the moon and sun) are symbolic terms. *Soma* or moon symbolizes the *apāna śakti* which is expressed in us in the form of inhalation and *sūrya* or sun symbolizes the *prāṇa śakti* which is expressed in us in the form of exhalation. This symbolism holds good in *āṇavopāya*. In connexion with *Śāktopāya*, *soma* or moon symbolizes *jñāna śakti*, (the power of knowledge) and *sūrya* or sun symbolizes *kriyāśakti* (the power of action). In the present context *soma* and *sūrya* mean *jñāna-śakti* and *kriyāśakti*.

In connexion with *Śāmbhavopāya*, *soma*, symbolizes *Vimarśa* and *sūrya* symbolizes *prakāśa*.

4. This *dvādaśānta* (distance of 12 fingers) refers to *antaradvādaśānta* i.e. inner *dvādaśānta*. This has three stages, viz. *hṛdaya* or centre of the body, *Kaṇṭhakūpa* or the small depression below the throat, and *bhrūmadhya* or the middle of the eye-brows.

5. 'By repetition' means *Sauṣupt epyabhīṣṭārthān prakāśayet* i.e. 'in deep sleep also He reveals the desired objects'.

*Introduction to the 3rd verse*

TEXT

यदि पुनरेवं सावधानो न भवति तदा नास्य योगितेत्याह

TRANSLATION

Now the author says that if a person is not thus concentrated, then he is not fit to be a *yogī*.

*Text of verse* 3

अन्यथा तु स्वतन्त्रा स्यात्सृष्टिस्तद्धर्मकत्वतः ।
सततं लौकिकस्येव जाग्रत्स्वप्नपदद्वये ॥ ३ ॥

Anyathā tu svatantrā syāt sṛṣṭis taddharmakatvataḥ/
Satataṁ Laukikasyeva jāgratsvapnapadadvaye//3

TRANSLATION

Otherwise, the Creative power of the Divine according to its characteristics, is free in manifesting always all kinds of things (usual and unusual) (to the *yogī* also) both in waking and dream states as in the case of the common people of the world.

## COMMENTARY

यद्युक्तयुक्त्या नित्यं नाराध्यते धाता तदास्य स्वरूपस्थित्यभावे सततं-प्रत्यहं लौकिकस्येव चास्य योगिनोऽपि जागरायां स्वप्ने च साधारणासाधारणार्थप्रकाशनतन्निश्चयनादिस्वभावा पारमेश्वरी सृष्टिः स्वतन्त्रा स्यात्, लौकिकवद्योगिनमपि संसारावट एवासौ पातयेदित्यर्थः । यथोक्तम्

'प्रवृत्तिर्भूतानामैश्वरी ।'

इति । 'तद्धर्मकत्वतः' इति स्वप्नजागराविपदप्रकाशने भगवत्सृष्टेः स्वातन्त्र्यभावादित्यर्थः ॥३॥

## TRANSLATION

If the yogī does not always pray to the sustainer of the universe according to the method described, then, in the absence of his remaining in his essential nature, the Divine Creative Power whose nature is to manifest (an object), to determine, etc. things of the usual and unusual kinds[1] is quite free to show always to *yogī* also similar things both in the waking and dream states, as in the case of the common people of the world. The sense is that this throws the yogī also into the pit of transmigratory existence like the common people. As is said, "The outgoing tendency of creatures is determined by the Lord's Will."

According to its characteristics this means that the Divine Creative Power is quite free to manifest things as it likes both in the waking and dream states.

## NOTES

Usual and unusual—In the waking state the experience of all people is common, it is an objective experience which is common to all. In dreams the experience of each, being subjective, is unusual i.e. is not common to all.

## EXPOSITION

The *yogī* by his prayerful attitude towards the Divine which really means by being established in his divine nature sees both in the waking and dream states what he wills to see. This is not possible for the common people. The experiences of both these states are not under their control. But if the *yogī* becomes unmindful and trips, he becomes subject to the same conditions both in the waking and dream states as the common people.

*Introduction to the 4th and 5th verse*

TEXT

एवं स्वप्नसौषुप्तनिर्दलनोपायं स्वप्रबुद्धतायै संसाध्य स्पन्दतत्त्वसमावेशोपायं सुप्रबुद्धस्य दृष्टान्तयुक्तिपूर्वकं निरूपयति जिज्ञासितार्थज्ञप्तिरपीत्थं भवतीत्यादिशति—

TRANSLATION

Thus having established the means for cleaving asunder the conditions of dream and deep sleep in order to attain the state of the fully enlightened one, the author now elucidates with example and reason the means of absorption in the *Spanda* principle for the fully enlightened one and exhorts that the knowledge of the object desired to be known is also possible in this way.

*Text of the Verse* 4 *and* 5

यथा ह्यर्थोऽस्फुटो दृष्टः सावधानेऽपि चेतसि ।
भूयः स्फुटतरो भाति स्वबलोद्योगभावितः ॥ ४ ॥
तथा यत्परमार्थेन येन यत्र यथा स्थितम् ।
तत्तथा बलमाक्रम्य न चिरात्सम्प्रवर्तते ॥ ५ ॥

Yathā hi artho'sphuṭo dṛṣṭaḥ sāvadhāne' pi cetasi/
Bhūyaḥ sphuṭataro bhāti svabalodyogabhāvitaḥ//4

Tathā yatparamārthena yena yatra yathā sthitam/
Tattathā balam ākramya na cirāt saṃpravartate//5

TRANSLATION

Indeed just as a thing which, in spite of all the attentiveness of the mind, is perceived indistinctly at first, appears more distinctly, later, when observed with the strenuous exercise of one's power.

So when the *yogī* resorts to the power (of *Spanda*), then whatever thing (*yat*) actually (*paramārthena*) exists in whichever form (*yena*), in whichever place or time (*yatra*) in whichever state (*yathā*) that thing (*tat*) becomes at once (*na cirāt*) manifest in that very way (*tathā*).

## COMMENTARY

### TEXT

हिशब्दः किलशब्दार्थे । सावधानेऽपि चेतसि दूरत्वादिदोषैर्यथा किलार्थोऽस्फुटो दृष्टो भूयोऽध्यक्षनिरीक्षणात्मना स्वबलोद्योगेन भावितो-भृशमालोकितो न केवलं स्फुटो यावत्स्फुटतरोऽपि भाति, तथा यत्स्पन्दतत्त्वात्मकं बलं येनानन्दघनतात्मना परमार्थेन यत्रेति-शङ्करात्मनि स्वस्वभावे यथेति-अभेदव्याप्त्या स्थितं तत्कर्तृ तथेति-स्वबलोद्योगेन-अन्तर्मुखतदेकात्मतापरिशीलनप्रयत्नेन सम्भावितं शीघ्रमेव स्फुट-तरत्वेन प्रवर्तते अभिव्यज्यते । कथमाक्रम्याराधकस्य कल्पितदेहादिप्रमातृभूमिं स्वात्मन्येव निमग्नां कृत्वा, अथच स्पन्दात्मकं बलमाक्रम्य स्थितस्य कल्पितदेह-बुद्धिप्रमातृभूमिमसकृदुत्तेजयतः साधकस्य योगिनो यज्जिज्ञासितं निधानादि यत्र देशादौ येन हेमादिना परमार्थेन यथा सन्निवेशेन स्थितं तथा तदचिरादेव प्रकाशते ॥५॥

### TRANSLATION

The word *hi* is used in the sense of 'indeed, verily'. Indeed just as, in spite of the attentiveness of mind, on account of the drawback of distance, etc. a thing appears indistinctly at first, but later when observed again minutely with the full application of one's visual power not only appears clearly but even more clearly, even so whatever power of *spanda* principle (*yat*), exists (*sthitam*) in its highest form in the nature of a mass of consciousness-bliss (*yena-ānandaghanatātmanā paramārthena*), in one's own essential nature which is identical with *Śiva* (*yatra*), in a nondifferent way (*yathā*) that (*tat*) appears instantly (*na cirāt*) more distinctly in that very way (*tatheti*), when observed with the strenuous exercise of one's power i.e. with the strenuous practice of identity with that inner nature. *Tat* i.e. the word 'that' is used in the nominative case.

How? By the votary merging his so-called stage of the experient in the form of the psycho-somatic organism in his inner essential Self.

(Another interpretation of the 5th verse)

To the *yogī* who resorts to the power of *spanda* and who stimulates his so-called state of the experient consisting of the body, *buddhi*, etc. over and over again to the pitch of the highest, essential experient, whatever (*yat*) he desires to know for instance, treasure wherever (*yatra*) i.e. in whichever region, in whichever state (*yena*) e.g. in the state of actual gold, in whichever form (*yathā*), that at once appears.

*Introduction to the 6th verse.*

TEXT

कर्तृशक्त्यादिरप्यमुत एव बलात्प्रादुर्भवतीत्याह

TRANSLATION

Now the author says that his power of action also appears on account of that power (i.e. the power of *spanda*).

*Text of the 6th verse*

दुर्बलोऽपि तदाक्रम्य यतः कार्ये प्रवर्तते ।
आच्छादयेद्बुभुक्षां च तथा योऽतिबुभुक्षितः ॥ ६ ॥

Durbalo 'pi tadākramya yataḥ kārye pravartate/
Ācchādayed bubhukṣāṃ ca tathā yo'ti bubhukṣitaḥ//6

TRANSLATION

Just as a feeble person also by resorting to that power (of *Spanda*) succeeds in doing what has to be done, even so one who is exceedingly hungry overcomes his hunger.

COMMENTARY

TEXT

यथा क्षीणधातुर्मृषिप्रायः सोऽपि स्पन्दात्मकं बलमाक्रम्य स्पन्दसमावेशबलेन प्राणप्रमातृभूमिमसकृदुत्तेज्य कार्येऽवश्यकर्तव्ये कर्मणि प्रवर्तते, अशक्यमपि वस्तु

तद्बलाक्रमणेनैव करोतीत्यर्थः । तथा योऽप्यतिबुभुक्षितः सोऽपि तद्बलाक्रान्त्या क्षुत्पिपासादि शमयति । नहि चिद्घनां भूमिमनुप्रविष्टस्य द्वन्द्वाभिभवः कश्चित्प्राणादिभुव एव तदाश्रयत्वात्तस्याश्चेह चिद्भूमौ निमग्नत्वात् ॥६॥

## TRANSLATION

Just as one, whose essential ingredients of the body have decayed i.e. who is as emaciated as an abstemious sage, also by resorting to the power of *Spanda* i.e. by absorption into *spanda* and by stimulating his state of the experient of *prāṇa* succeeds in doing that which has necessarily to be done i.e. by resorting to that power he does that which was beyond his power to do. So even he who is excessively hungry overcomes hunger, thirst[1] etc. by resorting to that power.

For one who has entered the state of the mass of spiritual consciousness, there can be no subjection to the pairs of opposites (like heat, cold, etc), for the pairs of opposites function only in the stage of *prāṇa*, and this in the case of the *yogī*. gets merged in the stage of the spiritual consciousness.

## NOTES

1 Utpala Bhaṭṭa adds बुभुक्षाशब्दोऽत्रोपलक्षणार्थम् । तेन क्षुत्तृषौ शोकमोहौ जरामृत्यू चेति षडूर्मयोऽपि नश्यन्तीत्यर्थः ॥ i.e. the word hunger has been used here elliptically in a generic sense implying the six waves of existence, hunger and thirst (of *prāṇa*), sorrow and delusion (of mind). old age and death (of body)."

*Introduction to the 7th verse*

## TEXT

यत एवमुक्तसूत्रोपपत्तिक्रमानुसारेणेदृक्सिद्धिसमुदायोऽस्माद्भवतीत्यतः

## TRANSLATION

Since by means of the rational method described in the above verse, he gains a number of supernormal perceptual powers by resorting to the power of Spanda, therefore.

## VERSE 7

### TEXT

अनेनाधिष्ठिते देहे यथा सर्वज्ञतादयः ।
तथा स्वात्मन्यधिष्ठानात्सर्वत्रैवं भविष्यति ॥ ७ ॥

Anenādhiṣṭhite dehe yathā sarvajñatādayaḥ/
Tathā svātmany adhiṣṭhānāt sarvatraivaṃ bhaviṣyati//7

### TRANSLATION

Just as all knowability, etc., in respect of the body occurs when it is pervaded by that *spanda* principle, even so when the *yogī* is established in his essential Self[1], he will have omniscience, etc. everywhere.

## COMMENTARY

### TEXT

अनेन स्वस्वभावात्मना स्पन्दतत्त्वेनाधिष्ठिते व्याप्ते देहे सति यथा तदवस्थोचितार्थानुभवकरणादिरूपाः सर्वज्ञतासर्वकर्तृतादयो धर्मा आविर्भवन्ति देहिनः, तथा यद्ययं कूर्माङ्गसङ्कोचवत्सर्वोपसंहारेण महाविकासयुक्त्या वा स्वस्मिन्ननपायिन्यात्मनि चिद्रूपे अधिष्ठानं करोति उक्ताभिज्ञानप्रत्यभिज्ञाते तत्रैव समावेशस्थितिं बध्नाति तदा सर्वत्रेति शिवादौ क्षित्यन्ते एवमिति शङ्करतदुचितसर्वज्ञतासर्वकर्तृतादिरूपो भविष्यति ॥७॥

### TRANSLATION

When the body is pervaded by this i.e. by the *spanda* principle which is one's own essential Self, then as experiences of things suited to that state (i.e. the bodily state), such as states of all-knowability, all-doership (associated with the body) manifest themselves to the embodied being, so, if the *yogi* gets established in his imperishable Self, viz., the spiritual Consciousness recognized as such by the afore-said token, if he is steadily absorbed in that state, either by withdrawing his sense, etc. within himself (*saṅkoca*) as a tortoise withdraws its limbs within itself or by the device of the expansion of all-embracing consciousness (*vikāsa*)[2], then he acquires omniscience, and omnipotence—powers appropriate to *Śiva* everywhere i.e. from the category of *Śiva* down to earth.

## NOTES

1. *Svātmani* means, as Kṣemarâja puts it, in his imperishable Self. Râmakaṇṭha explains it as स्वस्वभावे देहादिव्यतिरिक्त-विशुद्धाद्वयचिन्मात्रवपुषि i.e. in his essential nature which is pure, spiritual, consciousness distinct from the body.

2. *Saṅkoca* and *vikāsa*—*Saṅkoca* connotes the practice of withdrawing the attention from the activity of the senses and turning it towards the inner reality which is the source and background of all activity.

*Vikāsa* means concentration on the inner reality even while the sense-organs are quite open to the external objects.

*Introduction to the 8th verse*

## TEXT

इदमप्येतत्प्रसादेनेत्याह

## TRANSLATION

The author says that he will have this experience also through its grace (i.e. through the grace of the *Spanda* principle)

## VERSE 8

ग्लानिर्विलुण्ठिका देहे तस्याश्चाज्ञानतः सृतिः ।
तदुन्मेषविलुप्तं चेत्कुतः सा स्यादहेतुका ॥ ८ ॥

Glānir viluṇṭhikā dehe tasyāścājñānataḥ sṛtiḥ/
Tadunmeṣa-viluptaṃ cet kutaḥ sā syād ahetukā//8

## TRANSLATION

Just as a plunderer carries away the valuables of the house, even so depression saps away the vitality of the body. This depression proceeds from ignorance. If that ignorance disappears by *unmeṣa*, how can that depression last in the absence of its cause? 8.

## COMMENTARY

### TEXT

देहे या ग्लानिः अर्थाद्देहाभिमानिनः पुंसो यो हर्षक्षयोऽसौ विलुण्ठिका परसंविद्द्रविणापहारेण पारिमित्यदौर्गत्यप्रदा तस्याश्च ग्लानेरज्ञानतश्चिदानन्दघनस्वस्वरूपाप्रत्यभिज्ञानात्सृतिरुद्भवोऽवस्थितिश्च । तदज्ञानं प्रदर्शयिष्यमाणस्वरूपेणोन्मेषरूपेण चेद्विलुप्तं-निकृत्तं तदासौ ग्लानिरज्ञानात्मनो हेतोरभावात् कुतः स्यान्न भवेदित्यर्थः । ग्लान्यभावे च देहेऽवश्यंभाविन्यो व्याध्यादिसन्तापावस्था अपि यथा यथा योगिनोऽपकृष्यन्ते तथा तथा हेम्न इवातिताप्यमानस्य कालिकापगमे स्वस्वरूपं देदीप्यत एव । एवं च देहावस्थितस्यापि सर्वदा ग्लान्यभाव एव परयोगिनो विभूतिः । यथोक्तं परमयोगिन्या मदालसया बालदारकान् प्रयोगीकुर्वत्या

त्वं कञ्चुके शीर्यमाणे निजेऽस्मि-
　　न्देहे हेये मूढतां मा व्रजेथाः ।
शुभाशुभैः कर्मभिर्देहमेत-
　　न्मदादिभिः कञ्चुकस्ते निबद्धः ॥ (मा० पु० २५।१४)

इति मितसिद्ध्यभिलाषिणो योगिनः समावेशाभ्यासरसेन देहं विध्यतो वलीपलितादिव्याधिजयो भवतीत्यपि भङ्ग्यानेन प्रतिपादितम् ॥८॥

### TRANSLATION

*Dehe yā glāniḥ* means that disappearance of (essential) delight[1] of the person who considers his body to be the self. The plunderer(*viluṇṭhikā*) is that which steals away the wealth of the highest consciousness, and brings about poverty in the form of limitation. It i.e. the depression owes its origin and continuance to (spiritual) ignorance[2] i.e. non-recognition of one's essential nature which is a compact mass of consciousness-bliss. If that ignorance is destroyed by *unmeṣa*, the nature of which will be described later, then how can this depression last in the absence of its cause which is ignorance? That is to say it will disappear.

In the absence of depression, the states of inevitable sufferings to the body, such as illness, etc. will be removed. To the extent to which they are removed to that extent his real nature will shine just as excessively heated gold shines when the dross is removed. Thus constant absence of depression even while he remains in the body is the glory of the great *yogī*.

As has been said by the great *yoginī* Madālasā, while teaching her children:

'Ye child, do not commit the folly of regarding the body as the self,—the body which is like a decaying covering and deserves to be rejected. This body of thine is tied to thee like a covering on account of thy good and evil deeds, and infatuation in the form of self-conceit (Ma. pu.25,14).

This also is hinted in this verse that the *yogī* who is desirous of limited powers when his body is permeated with the elixir of compenetrative meditation, is free from diseases like wrinkles, grey hair etc.

## NOTES

1. *Glāni* or depression in this context means the disappearance of the essential delight (*tāttvikaharṣasya kṣayaḥ*). It is, as Rāmakaṇṭha puts it, *sahajānanda-hānirūpā* (p. 114) the loss of innate bliss. Every body who considers his psychosomatic organism as his Self suffers from this loss. It is only when the empirical self is transcended and one is united to the metempirical Self that he can have real happiness.

2. Ignorance here means, as *Kṣemarāja* puts it, *cidānandaghanasva-svarūpa-apratyabhijñāna* i.e. non-recognition of one's essential nature which is a compact mass of consciousness-bliss. It does not mean 'want of education'.

*Introduction to the 9th verse*

## TEXT

अथ योऽयमुन्मेषः स किंस्वरूपः किमुपायलभ्यश्चेत्याकाङ्क्षायामाह—

## TRANSLATION

In reply to the query "What is the nature of this *unmeṣa* and by what means is it available?" the author says:

*Text of the 9th verse*

एकचिन्ताप्रसक्तस्य यतः स्यादपरोदयः ।
उन्मेषः स तु विज्ञेयः स्वयं तमुपलक्षयेत् ॥ ९ ॥

Ekacintāprasaktasya yataḥ syādaparodayaḥ/
Unmeṣaḥ sa tu vijñeyaḥ svayaṃ tam upalakṣayet// 9

## TRANSLATION

That should be known as *unmeṣa* whence the rise of another thought takes place in the mind of a man who is already engaged in one thought. one should experience it introspectively for oneself. 9

## COMMENTARY

## TEXT

भावे त्यक्ते निरुद्धा चिन्नैव भाषान्तरं व्रजेत् ।
तदा तन्मध्यभावेन विकसत्यतिभावना ॥ (वि० भै० ६२)

**इति नीत्या एकस्यां कस्याञ्चिदालम्बनविशेषनिभृतविकारात्मिकायां चिन्तायां प्रसक्तस्य-एकाग्रीभूतस्य योगिनो यत इति-तदेकाग्रताप्रकर्षोल्लसत्संवित्स्फारतस्तदालम्बननिमीलनाज्झटिति ग्रस्तसमस्तचिन्तासन्ततेरग्नीषोमाविभेदात्मनः स्पन्दतत्त्वादपर एवोदयश्चिच्चमत्कारात्मान्य एव लोकोत्तर उल्लासः स्यात् स तच्चमत्कारोन्मेषकत्वादेवोन्मेषो विज्ञातव्योऽन्वेषणीयः, इत्थमेव योगिना ज्ञातुं शक्यः ततश्च स्वयमिति इदन्ताविषयत्वाभावादकृतकप्रयत्नात्मनावधानेनाहन्तयैवोपेत्यात्मनि लक्षयेत्-असाधारणेन चमत्कारात्मना प्रत्यभिजानीयात् । 'यत एकस्यां विषयविचारादिचिन्तायां प्रसक्तस्य अपरस्याश्चिन्ताया झटित्युदयः स्यात् स चिन्ताद्वयव्यापक उन्मेषः' इत्यन्ये ॥९॥**

## TRANSLATION

When the mind of the aspirant that is to quit one object is firmly restrained (*niruddha*) and does not move towards any other object, it comes to rest in a middle position between the two and through it (i.e. the middle position) is unfolded the realization of pure consciousness which transcends all contemplation." (V.Bh.62)

In accordance with this view, there is the rise of 'another' (*aparodayaḥ*)[1] i.e. there is the manifestation of another superb, transcendental awareness which is full of the bliss of consciousness (*ciccamatkārātmanya eva lokottara ullāsaḥ syāt*).

(In whom does it arise?) it arises in the yogī who is deeply engrossed i.e. deeply concentrated in one thought (*ekasyāṃ cintāyāṃ prasaktasya ekāgrībhūtasya*) (What kind of thought?). Thought of a particular object or matter in which all the fluctuations of the mind are stilled (*kasyāñcid ālambana-Viśeṣa-nibhṛta-vikārātmikāyāṃ cintāyām*).

(From where does that transcendental awareness arise?). It arises from the *Spanda*-principle in which the difference of knowledge and its object has disappeared, (*agnīṣomāvibhedātmanaḥ*)[2] in which the entire multitude of thought-constructs has been suddenly swallowed up (*jhaṭiti grastasamastacintāsantateḥ*) on account of the cessation of the object of thought which is due to the swell of deeper consciousness radiating from excessive concentration on that thought.

Since it is an efflorescence of that bliss of consciousness, it is known as *unmeṣa*. This has to be realized, this has to be sought, this can be known thus by the *yogī*. *Svayaṁ tamupalakṣayet*—This is the meaning of this sentence—Since *unmeṣa* cannot be grasped objectively as 'this', one has to observe it within oneself by approaching it in the form of I-consciousness with an awareness completely free of all artificial effort. It has to be recognized in the form of extraordinary bliss.

Others interpret this verse in this way: In the mind of a person who is deeply engrossed in thinking of one object, that from which another thought arises and which pervades both the thoughts is *unmeṣa*."

## NOTES

1. *Aparodayaḥ* may mean the rise of another awareness or the rise of another thought. These two meanings have led to two interpretations of the verse. Kṣemarāja has taken in the former sense: others have taken it in the latter sense.

2. *Agni* symbolizes *pramātā* or *pramāṇa*—knower or knowledge. Here it symbolizes knowledge *pramāṇa*; *soma* symbolizes *prameya* or object.

3. *Vijñeyaḥ*—has to be interpreted in two ways, viz. *arhārtha*, and *Śakyārtha*. In the first case it means it deserves to be known or recognized, it should be known or recognized. In the latter case, it means, it can be known or recognized. Kṣemarāja has interpreted it in both the senses.

## EXPOSITION

This is a very important *yoga* of this system. There are three important points in this verse which have to be borne in mind. Firstly, *aparodayaḥ* may mean the rise of another awareness or the rise of another thought. Kṣemarāja has taken it in the first sense. In this sense, it means *parapramātṛbhāva*, or the awareness of the met-empirical, the metaphysical Self. Kṣemarāja means to say that when the mind is deeply engrossed in one thought, it is completely stilled, it is restricted from indulging in another thought. It is at such a moment that the met-empirical Self reveals itself. Mind is the slayer of the Real. When the slayer is slain, then the Real reveals itself.

Secondly, one has to be on one's guard in grasping the Real. If he wants to know it as an object, he will fail miserably, for it is the Eternal Subject which can never be reduced to an object. That is why the text says *svayaṃ tamupalakṣayet*. Kṣemarāja rightly interprets it as *idantā-viṣayatvābhāvād akṛtakaprayatnāt-mnāvadhānenāhantayaivopetyātmani lakṣayet*. Since the metaphysical Self cannot be objectified, there has to be an effortless awareness of it as I-consciousness shorn of all its external trappings. Similarly, Rāmakaṇṭha says:

परमार्थ-परमेश्वरः सर्वतो विविक्तः परमकारणं परमात्मा अयमहमस्मि इति प्रतिपद्येत । न हि तस्य शब्दादिवद् इदन्तया स्वरूपमुपलक्षयितुं शक्यम्' ।

"This experience has to be regarded subjectively as 'It is I, the Highest Self, the fount and source of every thing, distinct from everything else. Its nature cannot be grasped objectively as 'this', like sound etc."

Thirdly, a very important point has been stressed by Rāmakaṇṭha in this connexion. He deserves to be quoted in full:

"यस्त्वयं मन्यते—यस्यां चिन्तायां सत्याम् अपरचिन्तोदयः सा चिन्तैव चिन्तान्तरकारणं नान्तरावर्ति वस्त्वन्तरं विद्यते, यच्चिन्ताद्वयस्वरूपव्यतिरेकेण उपलक्षणीयात्मकं द्वितीयचिन्ताकारणं स्याद् इति, तं प्रति कारणभावेन कार्यभावेन च अभिमतस्य पूर्वापरीभूतस्य चिन्ताद्वयस्य एष सम्बन्धो न सिध्यति, अनुसन्धातारं तृतीय विना । पूर्व कारणम् अपरा च कार्यभूता चिन्ता इति योऽनुसन्धत्ते, यश्चासावनपह्नवनीयोऽनुसन्धाता सोऽनुसन्धेयचिन्ताद्वयव्यापकविशुद्धचिन्मात्रस्वरूपः सर्वकारणमात्मैवोन्मेष इत्युक्तः ।

"Some think that the first thought is the cause of the rise of the next, there is nothing intervening between the twc which apart from the two thoughts may be the cause of the second thought. (Rāmakaṇṭha has the Buddhists in mind.)

In reply, it is said that there can be no relation of cause and effect between the first and the second without a third to relate the two as cause and effect. That which relates the previous and the latter as cause and effect, that which is the undeniable relater of the two experiences, that is the pure consciousness that pervades both the thoughts, the fount and origin of every thing, that is the Self. That Self has been called *unmeṣa*.

*Introduction to the 10th verse*

TEXT

इदानीं मितयोगिजनप्रयत्नसाध्यास्वपि तासु तासु सिद्धिषून्मेषपरिशीलनमात्रोदितासु परयोगिनो हेयत्वमेव मन्तव्यमित्यादिशति —

TRANSLATION

Now the author exhorts that a great *yogī* should regard those various supernormal powers as rejectable which arise from the practice of *unmeṣa* and which even inferior *yogīs* can acquire with effort.

*Text of the 10th verse*

अतो विन्दुरतो नादो रूपमस्मादतो रसः ।
प्रवर्तन्तेऽचिरेणैव क्षोभकत्वेन देहिनः ॥ १० ॥

Ato vindur ato nādo rūpam asmād ato rasaḥ/
Pravartante'cireṇaiva kṣobhakatvena dehinaḥ// 10

TRANSLATION

From this (*unmeṣa*) appear (supernormal) light, (supernormal) sound, (supernormal) form, (supernormal) taste, in a short time, to the *yogī* who has not yet done away with the identification of the Self with the body, which, however, are only a disturbing factor (in the full realization of the *Spanda* principle).

## COMMENTARY

### TEXT

अत उन्मेषावुपलक्ष्यमाणावप्रलीयमानस्थूलसूक्ष्मादिदेहाहम्भावस्य योगिनोऽचिरेणैव भ्रूमध्यादौ तारकाप्रकाशरूपो विन्दुरशेषवेद्यसामान्यप्रकाशात्मा, नादः-सकलवाचकाविभेदिशब्दनरूपोऽनाहतध्वनिरूपो, रूपमन्धकारेऽपि प्रकाशनं तेजः, रसश्च-रसनाग्रे लोकोत्तर आस्वादः क्षोभकत्वेन-स्पन्दतत्त्वसमासादनविघ्नभूततावत्सन्तोषप्रदत्वेन वर्तन्ते । यदाहुः

'ते समाधावुपसर्गा व्युत्थाने सिद्धयः ।' (पात० सू० ३ । ३७ )

इति । एवमुन्मेषनिभालनोद्युक्तस्यापि देहात्ममानिनो योगिनो विन्दुनादादयः क्षोभका भवन्तीत्युक्तम् ॥१०॥

### TRANSLATION

From it, i.e. from *unmeṣa* which is being practised appear in a short time experience like the light of a star in the middle of the two eye-brows which is a generic light expressive of the entire objective world, sound which is unstruck (spontaneous) which is generic sound representing all undifferentiated words, (supernormal) form which is a glow shining even in darkness, transcendental taste experienced on the tip of the tongue. All these appear to the *yogi* whose identification of 'I' or the Self with gross, subtle body, etc.[1] has not yet dissolved. They only give him temporary satisfaction, but are a disturbing factor, indeed positive obstacle in the realization of the *Spanda* principle.[2]

As they (the ancient sages) say:

"These are obstacles in the way of meditation and are regarded as occult powers in *vyutthāna* (during normal consciousness after meditative absorption)." (P.Su III,37).

This verse says that supernormal light, sound, etc. are only disturbing factors to the *yogī* who identifies the Self with the body even though he may be intent on the introspection of *unmeṣa.*

### NOTES

1. Et cetera refers to the causal body.
2. These powers are a source of attraction to the *yogī* who has not risen above the level of the psychosomatic organism.

But they are an obstacle in the way of spiritual progress, for this *yogī* gets stuck up in these powers, and misses the real aim of *yoga*, viz., realization of the essential Self or the *Spanda* principle.

*Introduction to the 11th verse*

TEXT

इदानीमत्रोन्मेषात्मनि स्वभावे देहप्रमातृतां निमज्जयति, तदाकारामपि पर-प्रमातृतां लभत इत्याह

TRANSLATION

Now the author says that the *yogī*, who sinks his psycho-physical self in the real nature which is *unmeṣa*, experiences the state of the highest experient in the form of that *unmeṣa*.

*Text of the 11th verse*

दिदृक्षयेव सर्वार्थान्यदा व्याप्यावतिष्ठते ।
तदा किं बहुनोक्तेन स्वयमेवावभोत्स्यते ॥ ११ ॥

Didṛkṣayeva sarvārthān yadā vyāpyāvatiṣṭhate/
Tadā kiṃ bahunoktena svayameva avabhotsyate//11

TRANSLATION

When the *yogī* wishing to see all objects abides in that state pervading them all, i.e. infusing them all with the light of his consciousness, then what is the use of saying much, he will experience for himself (the splendour of that vision).

COMMENTARY

TEXT

यथा पश्यन्तीरूपाविकल्पकदिदृक्षावसरे विदृक्षितोऽर्थोऽन्तरभेदेन स्फुरति तथैव स्वच्छन्दाद्यध्वप्रक्रियोक्तान् धरादिशिवान्तान्तर्भाविनोऽशेषानर्थान् व्याप्येति सर्वम-हमिति सदाशिववत् स्वविकल्पानुसन्धानपूर्वकमविकल्पान्तमभेदविमर्शान्तःक्रोडी-कारेणाच्छाद्य यदावतिष्ठते अस्याः समापत्तेर्न विचलति, तावदशेषवेद्यैकीकारेणोन्मि-

**यत्तावद्वेद्यग्रासीकारिमहाप्रमातृतासमावेशचमत्काररूपं यत्फलं तत्स्वयमेवावभोत्स्यते-स्वसंविदेवानुभविष्यति, किमत्र बहुना प्रतिपादितेन ॥११॥**

## TRANSLATION

Just as at the time of the desire to see by means of indeterminate perception in the case of *paśyantī*, the object desired to be seen gleams internally in an identical form, even so, when the *yogī* abides (*avatiṣṭhate*), pervading all the objects from the earth right up to *Śiva* as described in *Svacchhanda* and other works in the chapter dealing with the way of worlds (*bhuvanādhvā*), that is to say infusing every thing with I -consciousness like *Sadāśiva*, with the thought of I to begin with, relating everything. and finally with thought-free awareness embracing everything within himself, then he will experience that for himself which is the result of the bliss of absorption into the state of the highest (divine) Experient that swallows up all objective phenomena by the consciousness that blossoms out of the unification of all objectivity. *Yadā avatiṣṭhate* means 'when he does not swerve from the perfect accomplishment of meditation.' *Svayamevāvabhotsyate* means he will experience it in his own consciousness. What is the use of expatiation in this matter ?

## EXPOSITION

When the yogī sees every object as an expression of the inner divine Self, then the delusion of diversity disappears and he has the bliss of unity consciousness. He finds *Śiva* both within and without.

*Introduction to the 12th verse*

## TEXT

**तस्योपलब्धिः सततम् इति प्रतिज्ञाय तदनन्तरमुपपादितमुपायजातं परिशीलयतः सततं स्पन्दतत्त्वसमाविष्टत्वं सुप्रबुद्धस्य भवतीति तदनन्तप्रमेयसम्भिन्नत्वादुपदेश्य-हृदये स्मारयन्ननुप्रवेशयुक्त्युपसंहारभङ्ग्याह—**

## TRANSLATION

Having declared that the fully enlightened has the knowledge of *Spanda* principle always and incessantly (in I, 17), the author says that the fully enlightened *yogī* who practises the means that have been explained afterwards always has absorption in *Spanda* principle. As it (*Spanda*) is mixed up with innumerable objects, the author reminds the pupil of it and by way of conclusion describes the means for entrance into it.

*Text of the Verse* 12

**प्रबुद्धः सर्वदा तिष्ठेज्ज्ञानेनालोक्य गोचरम् ।**
**एकत्रारोपयेत्सर्वं ततोऽन्येन न पीड्यते ॥ १२ ॥**

Prabuddhaḥ sarvadā tiṣṭhej jñānenālokya gocaram/
Ekatrāropayet sarvaṃ tato anyena na pīḍyate//12

## TRANSLATION

Observing all objective phenomena by knowledge i.e. by external perception, one should always remain awake, and should deposit everything in one place i.e. see everything as identical with *Spanda* which is our own essential Self. Thus, he is never troubled by another.

## COMMENTARY

## TEXT

**सर्वदा जागरास्वप्नसुषुप्तसंविदादिमध्यान्तपदेषु प्रबुद्धस्तिष्ठेद् उन्मीलितस्पन्दतत्त्वावष्टम्भदिव्यदृष्टिः सुप्रबुद्धतामेव भजेत । कथं ज्ञानेन बहिर्मुखेनावभासेन सर्वं गोचरं नीलसुखादिरूपं विषयमालोक्य**

तस्माच्छब्दार्थचिन्तासु न सावस्था न या शिवः ( २।४ )

**इत्युपपादितदृशा विमृश्य एकत्र-स्रष्टरि शंकरात्मनि स्वभावे सर्वमारोपयेत्-निमीलनोन्मीलनदशयोस्तदभेदेन जानीयात्, पूर्वापरकोटयवष्टम्भदार्ढ्यान्मध्यभूमिमपि चिद्रसाश्यानतारूपतयैव पश्येदित्यर्थः। एवं च न केनचिदन्येन व्यतिरिक्तेन वस्तुना बाध्यते सर्वस्मिन् स्वात्मनः स्वीकृतत्वात् । यथोक्तं श्रीप्रत्यभिज्ञाकारेण**

योऽविकल्पमिदमर्थमण्डलं पश्यतीश निखिलं भवद्वपुः ।
स्वात्मपक्षपरिपूरिते जगत्यस्य नित्यसुखिनः कुतो भयम् ॥
(उ० स्तो० १३। १६ )

**इति ॥१२॥**

## TRANSLATION

*Sarvadā* 'always' means 'one should keep awake in the beginning, middle, and end of awareness in all the states of waking, dreaming and deep sleep. 'keeping awake' means 'one should have full awareness, with divine vision which becomes manifest by getting hold of the *Spanda* principle which has been unfolded.' How? By observing all phenomena, such as blue, pleasure etc. by external perception, one should offer it to the creator, *Śaṅkara* i.e. one's essential nature in the light of the belief expressed in the line, 'Therefore, whether in word, or thing or thought, there is no state which is not *Śiva*.' 'One should offer or deposit everything' means 'one should regard it as identical with that *Spanda* principle whether in introversive or extroversive state, one should, by the firm grip of the initial and the final state, regard the middle state also as the congealment of the sap of consciousness'. Thus, he is not troubled by anything separate, because in everything, he acknowledges his own Self. As has been said by the author of *Śrī Pratynbhijñā* "O Lord, whence can there be any fear to the eternally happy one, in this world filled with his own Self, who, in thought-free state, sees entire objective phenomena as thy own form.[2]" (Utpala sto. XIII.16).

## NOTES

1. This refers to Utpaladeva who wrote Īśvarapratyabhijñā.
2. Utpaladeva also wrote a number of hymns which have been collected in a book named *Utpala Stotrāvalī*.

## EXPOSITION

Two points have been emphasized in this verse—firstly, the awakened one should be *en rapport* with the *Spanda* principle which is his essential Self in all the states of waking, dream and deep sleep and in all conditions—the initial, the middle and the end of those states. Secondly, he should view all objective phenomena only as a manifestation of the inward Light of Consciousness and thus identical with it. Since now there is nothing which is different from his Self, he will have no trouble on any account.

*Introduction to the 13th verse*

TEXT

'ततोऽन्येन न पीडयते' इति यदुक्तं तत्र कोऽसावन्यः पीडकः कश्च पीड्यः, यतः शिवात्मकमेव विश्वमुक्तमित्याशङ्क्य पाशानां पशोश्च स्वरूपं निर्णेतुमाह

TRANSLATION

It has been said (in the previous verse), "Thus, he is never troubled by another." "Since the whole universe is said to be the form of *Śiva*, who is it that gives trouble, and who is it that is troubled? In order to remove this doubt, the author, in order to ascertain the nature of the bonds and the bound. says:

*Text of the 13th Verse*

शब्दराशिसमुत्थस्य शक्तिवर्गस्य भोग्यताम् ।
कलाविलुप्तविभवो गतः सन्स पशुः स्मृतः ॥ १३ ॥

Śabdarāśi-samutthasya śaktivargasya bhogyatām/
Kalāvilupta-vibhavo gataḥ san sa paśuḥ smṛtah//13

TRANSLATION

Being deprived of his glory by *kalā*, he (the individual) becomes a victim of the group of Powers arising from the multitude of words, and thus he is known as the bound one (*paśu*).

COMMENTARY

TEXT

इह योऽयं प्रकाशात्मा स्वस्वभावः शाङ्कर उक्तः, असौ
व्यवस्थितः करोत्येष विश्वकारणमीश्वरः ।
सृष्टिं स्थितिं च संहारं तिरोधानमनुग्रहम् ॥
इति श्रीस्वच्छन्दशास्त्रदृष्टया निजशक्त्याश्लिष्टः सदा पञ्चविधकृत्यकारी स्वतन्त्रः स्पन्दललितेश्वरादिशब्दैरागमेषूद्घोष्यते । स्वातन्त्र्यशक्तिरेवास्य सनातनी पूर्णाहन्तारूपा परा मत्स्योदरी महासत्ता स्फुरत्तोर्मिः सारं हृदयं भैरवी देवी शिखा इत्यादिभिरसङ्ख्यैः प्रकारैस्तत्र तत्र निरुच्यते । पूर्णाहन्तैव चास्यानुत्तरानाहत-

**शक्तिसंपुटीकारस्वीकृतादिक्षान्तवर्णभट्टारिका तत एव स्वीकृतानन्तवाच्यवाचकरूपषडध्वस्फारमयाशेषशक्तिचक्रक्रोडीकारान्तःकृतनिःशेषसर्गप्रलयादिपरम्पराप्यक्रमविमर्शरूपैव नित्योदितानुच्चार्यमहामन्त्रमयी सर्वजीवितभूता परा वाक्। एषैव भगवत इयद्विश्ववैचित्र्यचलत्तामिव स्वात्मनि प्रथयन्ती स्पन्दते इत्यर्थानुगमात् स्पन्द इति इहोच्यते। एवं चेयद्विश्वशक्तिखचितपराशक्तिसुन्दरस्य स्वात्मनः स्वरूपगोपनक्रीडया स्वात्मभित्तावेवांशांशिकया निर्भासनं भगवान् यावच्चिकीर्षति तावदेकैवाभिन्नाप्यसौ तदीया विमर्शशक्तिरिच्छात्वं प्रतिपद्य ज्ञानक्रियारूपतया स्थित्वा शिवशक्तिपरामर्शात्मकबीजयोनिभेदेन द्विधा भूत्वा वर्गभेदेन तत्कलाभेदेन च नवधा पञ्चाशद्धा च स्फुरन्ती तद्विमर्शसारैरघोरघोरघोरतरैः संवित्तिदेवतात्मभिः रूपैः प्रथमाना भगवतः पञ्चविधकृत्यकारितां निर्वहति। यथोक्तं श्रीमालिनीविजयोत्तरे**

या सा शक्तिर्जगद्धातुः कथिता समवायिनी।
इच्छात्वं तस्य सा देवी सिसृक्षोः प्रतिपद्यते॥ (३।५)
सैकापि सत्यनेकत्वं यथा गच्छति तच्छृणु।
एवमेतदिति ज्ञेयं नान्यथेति सुनिश्चितम्॥
ज्ञापयन्ती जगत्यत्र ज्ञानशक्तिर्निगद्यते।
एवं भवत्विदं सर्वमिति कार्योन्मुखी यदा॥
जाता तदैव तद्वस्तु कुर्वत्यत्र क्रियोच्यते।
एवमेषा द्विरूपापि पुनर्भेदैरनन्तताम्॥
अर्थोपाधिवशाद्याति चिन्तामणिरिवेश्वरी।
तत्र तावत्समापन्ना मातृभावं विभिद्यते॥
द्विधा च नवधा चैव पञ्चाशद्धा च मालिनी।
बीजयोन्यात्मकाद्भेदाद्द्विधा बीजं स्वरा मताः॥
कादयश्च स्मृता योनिर्नवधा वर्गभेदतः।
पृथग्वर्णविभेदेन शतार्धकिरणोज्ज्वला॥
बीजमत्र शिवः शक्तिर्योनिरित्यभिधीयते।
वर्गाष्टकमिति ज्ञेयमघोराद्यमनुक्रमात्॥
तदेव शक्तिभेदेन माहेश्वर्यादि चाष्टकम्।
शतार्धभेदभिन्ना च तत्संख्यानां वरानने॥
रुद्राणां वाचकत्वेन कल्पिता परमेष्ठिना।
तद्वदेव च शक्तीनां तत्संख्यानामनुक्रमात्॥

**इत्यादि। तथा**

विषयेष्वेव संलीनानधोऽधः पातयन्त्यणून्।

रुद्राणूत्याः समालिङ्गय घोरतर्योऽपरास्तु ताः ॥
मिश्रकर्मफलासक्तिं पूर्ववज्जनयन्ति याः ।
मुक्तिमार्गनिरोधिन्यस्ताः स्युर्घोराः परापराः ॥
पूर्ववज्जन्तुजातस्य शिवधामफलप्रदाः ।
पराः प्रकथितास्तज्ज्ञैरघोराः शिवशक्तयः ॥ (३।३३)

**इति । एवं शब्दराशेः समुत्थितो वर्गनवकरूपो यो ब्राह्म्यादिदेवतावर्गः शिवसहितस्तस्य भोग्यतां-पाश्यतां गतः सन् स एव शंकरात्मा स्वभावः पशुः स्मृतः-आगमेषु तथोक्तः । ननु कथं भोक्ता महेश्वर इमामवस्थां प्राप्तः, इत्याशङ्काशान्त्यै विशेषणद्वारेण हेतुमाह कलाविलुप्तविभव इति । कलयति-बहिः क्षिपति-पारिमित्येन परिच्छिनत्तीति कला मायाशक्तिः, तया विलुप्तविभवः स्वमायया गूहितैश्वर्यः स्थित इत्यर्थः । अथ च कलया किञ्चित्कर्तृत्वोपोद्बलनात्मना शक्त्या तदुपलक्षितेन कलाविद्याकालनियतिरागात्मना कञ्चुकेन विलुप्तविभवः स्थगितपूर्णत्वकर्तृत्वादिधर्मः । भवत्वेवं, भोग्यतां तु कथमसौ शक्तिवर्गस्य गतः इत्यत्रैतदेवोत्तरम् । कलाभिरकारादिवर्गाधिष्ठायिकाभिर्ब्राह्म्यादिभिस्तद्वर्णभट्टारकाधिष्ठातृभूताभिश्च श्रीमालिनीविजयोक्तदेवतारूपाभिः कलाभिरकारादिवर्णैर्विलुप्तविभवः-संकुचितोऽस्मि, अपूर्णोऽस्मि, करवाणि किञ्चिदिदमुपाददे, इदं जहामि इत्यादिविचित्रविकल्पकाविकल्पकप्रतिपत्तिकदम्बकान्तरनुप्रविष्टस्थूलसूक्ष्मशब्दानुवेधकदर्थितो हर्षशोकादिरूपतां नेनीयमान इव क्षणमपि स्वरूपस्थितिं न लभते यतः, अतोऽसावुक्तरूपः शक्तिवर्गेण भुज्यमानः पशुरुक्तः । कलया अख्यात्यात्मनांशेन विलुप्तविभवः संकुचित इव, न तु तत्त्वतः शिवात्मा स्वभावोऽस्य क्वापि गतः, तदभावे हि स एव न स्फुरेत् । तथावभासमानैरेव कलाभिः संकुचितैः शब्दैर्ज्ञानैश्च विलुप्तविभवस्तथारूपमात्मानं न विमर्ष्टुं क्षम इत्यर्थः ॥१३॥**

## TRANSLATION

That which is said to be one's real nature which is, in essence, *Śaṅkara*, of the nature of Light, is proclaimed in the traditional treatises by such words as *Spanda*, *Lalita*, *Īśvara* etc.

In accordance with the view expressed in the followng lines in Svacchanda Śāstra, being embraced by His *Śakti*, He is absolutely free in carrying out five (creative) acts.

"The Lord, who is the cause of the universe, endowed with His *Śakti* carries out the acts of manifestation (*sṛṣṭi*), maintenance (*sthiti*), withdrawal (*saṃhāra*), concealment (*tirodhāna*), and grace (*anugraha*).

The Power of Absolute Freedom of the Lord which is eternal and of the form of perfect I-consciousness is, in different scriptures, called in various, innumberable ways, such as, *Parā* (the Highest), *Matsyodarī* (fish-bellied i.e. full of creative throb), *Mahāsattā* (the Highest Being), *Sphurattā* (the glimmer of Light), *Ūrmi* (wave, the great Manifestation), *Sāra* (the Quintessence of existence), *Hṛdaya* (the Heart, the Creative Centre), *Bhairavī* (the *Śakti* of *Bhairava*), *Devī* (Goddess), *Śikhā* (the Flame). The perfect I-consciousness of the Lord (*Aham*) consisting of the Highest 'A' Power and the innate 'ha' Power encloses within itself as in a bowl all the venerable letters from *a* to *kṣa*. That (*aham*) constitutes the *śakti-Parā Vāk*, the Highest Sound which is ever risen, i.e. eternal but unutterable, the great *Mantra*, the *Life* of all, which is successionless awareness that contains within itself uninterrupted series of manifestation and dissolution, which encloses within its embrace all the groups of *śaktis* consisting of the course of the six (*ṣaḍadhvā*),[1] the outcome of innumerable words and their referents.

The same supreme I-consciousness of the Lord manifesting within itself this universe of diverse objects as if moving is here referred to as *Spanda*, according to the etymological derivation-*spandate iti spandaḥ*—'that which throbs (with life) is *spanda*.' Thus when the Lord, veiling by way of sport the real nature of His Self adorned with the Highest Power (*parāśakti*) endowed with universal energy, desires to display manifestation in different forms, on the screen of His own Self, then His Power of Absolute Freedom (which is the Power of His I-consciousness) becomes Will which assumes the power of cognition and action. As such that Power of Absolute Freedom becomes two in the form of seed (vowel) and matrix (consonant) which respectively indicate *Śiva* and *Śakti*. It also appears as ninefold according to the division of letter-groups (*vargabhedena*), and fiftyfold according to the division of letters of these groups. Appearing in the form of the goddesses *Aghorā*, *Ghorā*, and *Ghoratarī* who comprehend those letters, it brings about the fivefold act of the Lord. As has been said in the Mālinīvijayottara. "That *Śakti* (in the form of I-consciousness) of the Creator of the world who is said to be constantly co-inhering in Him (*Śiva*) becomes Icchā (Will power) when He wants to create. Listen, how She, though one, becomes many. 'This object is like this (as I have willed), not otherwise'—announcing this with perfect definiteness, she is said to be *jñānaśakti* (the power of knowledge) in this world. When she is oriented towards action, and decides 'let all this become like this', then creating that thing then and there, she is said to be *kriyāśakti* (the power of execution). Thus, though of two forms, she becomes innumerable, according to the conditions of the objects to be created. Indeed, this goddess is like a thought-gem (cintāmaṇi). Then when she assumes the aspect of mother, she is divided in two ways, nine ways, and becomes a wearer of a garland of fifty letters.

With the division of *bīja* (vowels) and *yoni* (consonants), she is of two kinds. The vowels are considered to be the *bīja* (seed). 'Ka' and other letters are considered to be *yoni* (consonants; lit. matrix). According to the division of the groups of the letters, she is of nine kinds. According to the division of letters, separately she shines with the rays of fifty (letters). In this context, *bīja* (the vowel) is called *Śiva*, and *yoni* (the consonant) is called Śakti.

The eight groups of letters are to be known as *Aghora*, etc. in succession. The same eight groups of letters have eight goddesses, such as Māheśvarī and others. from the standpoint of the division of *śaktis*.[2]

O beautiful-faced one, the greatest lord has made her fifty-fold as descriptive of the Rudras[3] of that number as well as the *śaktis* of that number in succession (M.V. III, 5-13).

Further,

'The Ghoratarī Śaktis are those who, while they embrace *Rudras*, the elevated souls, push down and down those souls who are engrossed in the pleasure of sense-objects. They are known as *aparā śaktis*.

The *Ghorā śaktis* are those who cause, as before, attachment to the fruit of actions of mixed character and who block the path to liberation. They are known as *parā-parā śaktis*.

The *Aghorā* are those powers of *Śiva* who are aptly called *parā* by those who know the reality. They grant to the creatures the boon of *Śiva*-state as before. "(M.V. III, 33). Thus becoming a victim to the groups of goddesses such as Brāhmī, etc.

along with *Śiva* who are represented by the nine groups[4] of letters that have arisen from the mass of sound, he, though of the nature of *Śiva* is regarded as bound (*paśu*) in the traditional texts.

A question arises here. "How is it that the Experient who is the great Lord is reduced to this state ?" In order to remove this doubt, the author mentions the reason by means of an adjectival phrase, 'because he is deprived of his glory by *kalā*.'

Etymologically *kalā* (from the root '*kala*'—to throw out) means 'one that throws out, that circumscribes to definite limits i.e. the power of Māyā'. The Lord thus continues in a state in which His glory is veiled by His own Māyā. This is the meaning of the phrase *kalāviluptavibhavaḥ*.

(Second Interpretation of *Kalāviluptavibhavaḥ*)

Moreover, the word *Kalā* also means the power of limited activity. So by *kalā* would mean 'by the power supported by limited activity'. This power implies also *kalā*, *vidyā*, *kāla*, *niyati* and *rāga*. So, the adjectival phrase *kalāviluptavibhavaḥ* would ultimately mean one whose characteristics of perfection, unrestrained activity, etc. are veiled by the coverings of *kalā*, *vidyā*, *kāla*, *niyati* and *rāga*.[6]

This may be granted. The question is 'How does he become a victim to the group of powers ?' This is the reply to this question.

(Third Interpretation of *Kalāviluptavibhavaḥ*)

Because, he does not rest in his real nature even for a moment, being exploited by the group of powers, therefore is he called a bound soul. He is deprived of his glory by the goddesses Brāhmī and others presiding over the groups of letters, such as vowel-group, etc. or by the goddesses presiding over individual letters, such as 'a' (अ) etc., as indicated in Mālinīvijaya. As such, he is tormented by gross and subtle words which penetrate within all kinds of definite and indefinite ideas, and he feels "I am limited. I am imperfect; I may do something; this I take, this I reject, etc.," and he is thus led to joy or sorrow.

Thus he, as described above, being exploited by the group of *śaktis* is called *paśu* or bound soul.

(Fourth Interpretation of *Kalāviluptavibhavaḥ*)

*Kalā* may be taken in the sense of a part. Being deprived of his glory by a part, i.e. the innate ignorance of his real nature, he becomes limited as it were. In fact, his real nature in the form of *Śiva* has not gone anywhere. In absence of that, his manifestation itself would not be possible.

Being deprived of his glory by words and ideas which are narrowed down by *kalās* appearing in those ways, he is unable to consider himself in his real nature. This is the gist of the verse.

## NOTES

1. The *Ṣaḍadhvā* (the course of the six) referred to consists of three aspects on the subjective or *vācaka* (word) side and three on the objective or *vācya* (referent) side. They are the following :

| *Vācaka or Śabda.* The Subjective order; the temporal order; the phonematic manifestation. | *Vācya or Artha (Referent)* The objective order: the spatial order; the cosmogonic manifestation. | |
|---|---|---|
| *Para* or *abheda* level | *Varṇa* | *Kalā* |
| *Parāpara or bhedābheda* or *Sūkṣma* (subtle) level. | *Mantra* | *Tattva* |
| *Apara* or *bheda* or *sthūla* (gross) level. | *Pada* | *Bhuvana* |

2. The presiding deities over the groups of letters are the following :

| *Group of letters* : | *Presiding deities* |
|---|---|
| 1. 'A' varga (the group of vowels) | Yogīśvari or Mahālakṣmī |
| 2. 'Ka' varga (ka, kha, ga, gha, ṅa) | Brāhmī |
| 3. 'Ca' varga (ca, cha, ja, jha, ña) | Māheśvarī |
| 4. 'Ṭa' varga (ṭa, ṭha, ḍa, ḍha, ṇa) | Kaumārī |
| 5. 'Ta' varga (ta, tha, da, dha, na) | Vaiṣṇavī |
| 6. 'Pa' varga (pa, pha, ba, bha, ma) | Vārāhi |
| 7. 'Ya' varga (ya, ra, la, va) | Aindrī or Indrāṇī |
| 8. 'Śa' varga (śa, ṣa, sa, ha, kṣa) | Cāmuṇḍā |

3. The fifty *Rudras* are the following :

1. Amṛta, 2. Amṛtapūrṇa, 3. Amṛtābha, 4. Amṛtadrava, 5. Amṛtaugha, 6. Amṛtormi, 7. Amṛtasyandana, 8. Amṛtāṅga,

9. Amṛtavapu, 10. Amṛtodgāra, 11. Amṛtāsya, 12. Amṛtatanu, 13. Amṛtasecana, 14. Amṛtamūrti, 15. Amṛteśa, 16. Sarvāmradhara. All these arise from *bīja* or vowel. The remaining thirtyfour arise from *yoni* or constant. They are the following :

1. Jaya, 2. Vijaya, 3. Jayanta, 4. Aparājita, 5. Sujaya, 6. Jayarudra, 7. Jayakīrti, 8. Jayāvaha, 9. Jayamūrti, 10. Jayotsāha, 11. Jayada, 12. Jayavardhana, 13. Bala, 14. Atibala, 15. Balabhadra, 16. Balaprada, 17. Balāvaha, 18. Balavān, 19. Baladātā, 20. Baleśvara, 21. Nandana, 22. Sarvatobhadra, 23. Bhadramūrti, 24. Śivaprada, 25. Sumanāḥ, 26. Spṛhaṇa, 27. Durga, 28. Bhadrakāla, 29. Manonuga, 30. Kauśika, 31. Kāla, 32. Viśveśa, 33. Suśiva, 34. Kopa (Total 16+34=50). The Rudrāṇis are the same in number and their names are the feminine gender of the above names, e.g. Amṛtā, Amṛtapūrṇā, etc.

4. According to the nine groups of letters, the goddesses are as given below. The goddess of '*A*' varga (i.e. vowels, is Śiva-Śakti; the goddess of '*Kṣa*' varga is *yogīśvari*. The other goddesses are the same as given under Note No. 2.

5. Such an adjective as gives the reason is known as *hetugarbha viśeṣaṇa*. So 'Kalāvilupta-vibhavaḥ' is to be understood as *Kalāvilupta-Vibhavatvāt* (because of his glory being deprived by kalā).

6. These are the five *kañcukas* or coverings of *Māyā*.

(i) *Kalā* reduces *Sarvakartṛtva* or omnipotence of *Śiva* to *kiñcitkartṛtva* or limited efficacy in the case of the *paśu* or the empirical individual.

(ii) *Vidyā* reduces the *sarvajñatva* or omniscience of *Śiva* to limited knowledge.

(iii) *Rāga* reduces the *pūrṇatva* or fulness of Śiva to desire for particular things.

(iv) *Kāla* reduces the *nityatva* or eternity of *Śiva* to limitation in respect of time.

(v) *Niyati* reduces the *vyāpakatva* (all-pervasiveness) or Svātantrya (absolute Freedom of Śiva) to limitation in respect of space and cause.

*Introduction to the 14th verse*

## TEXT

अधुना पशुः संकुचितदृक्छक्तिबाध्यः पाश्यश्चेत्येतद्विभजति

## TRANSLATION

Now the author shows in detail how the bound soul is bound and trapped by limited knowledge.

*Text of the verse 14*

**परामृतरसापायस्तस्य यः प्रत्ययोद्भवः ।**
**तेनास्वतन्त्रतामेति स च तन्मात्रगोचरः ॥ १४ ॥**

Parāmṛtarasāpāyas tasya yaḥ pratyayodbhavaḥ/
Tenāsvatantratām eti sa ca tanmātragocaraḥ// 14

## TRANSLATION

The rise, in the bound soul, of all sorts of ideas marks the disappearance of the bliss of supreme immortality. On account of this, he loses his independence. The appearance of the ideas has its sphere in sense-objects.

## COMMENTARY

## TEXT

तस्य पशोर्यं प्रत्ययानां-लौकिकशास्त्रीयविकल्पानां तदधिवासितानां भिन्नार्थ-ज्ञानानां विकल्पानामप्युद्भवः विनाशाग्रात उत्पादः स परस्यामृतरसस्य-चिद्घन-स्यानन्दप्रसरस्यापायो निमज्जनम् । उदितेषु भिन्नार्थेषु प्रत्ययेषु चिद्भूमिः स्थिताप्य-परामृश्यमानत्वादस्थितेव लक्ष्यते, तत एवमुक्तम् । तेन च प्रत्ययोद्भवेनायमस्वत-न्त्रतामेति-तद्वशः सम्पद्यते । यदुक्तं श्रीशिवसूत्रेषु 'ज्ञानं बन्धः' (१।२) इति । श्रीमद्व्यासमुनिनापि 'मातापितृमयो बाल्ये' इति । श्रीमदालसयापि

तातेति किञ्चित्तनयेति किञ्चिद्
अम्बेति किञ्चिद्दयितेति किञ्चित् ।
ममेति किञ्चिन्न ममेति किञ्चिद्
भौतं संघं बहुधा मा लपेथाः ॥ (मा० पु० २५।१५)

इति । प्रत्ययस्योद्भवस्तन्मात्राणि तीव्रातीव्रभेदसामान्यवृत्तयो गोचरो यस्य तथाभूतो भिन्नवेद्यविषय इत्यर्थः । अनेनेदमाह—यावदियं भिन्नवेद्यप्रथा तावद्बद्ध एव, यदा तूक्तोपदेशयुक्त्या सर्वमात्ममयमेवाविचलप्रतिपत्त्या प्रतिपद्यते तदा जीवन्मुक्त इति । यथोक्तम् 'इति वा यस्य संवित्तिः' ( २ । ५ ) इत्यादि । एवं च यत्पूर्वमुक्तं 'तस्माच्छब्दार्थचिन्तासु न सावस्था न या शिवः ।' ( २ । ४ ) इत्यादि, न तेन सह 'परामृतरसापायस्तस्य यः प्रत्ययोद्भवः' ( ३ । १४ ) इत्यस्य वैषम्यं किञ्चित् ॥ १४ ॥

## TRANSLATION

The rise in that bound soul of ideas whether pertaining to this world or the scriptures and of the knowledge of different objects associated with them leads to ruination. That marks the disappearance or subsidence of the bliss of supreme immortality i.e. of the flow of the bliss of the mass of consciousness. Though the state of supreme consciousness is present even when the ideas conveying the sense of different objects arise yet because it is not noticed, it appears to be absent. Hence it has been said that the bliss of supreme immortality disappears. By the rise of those ideas, he (the bound soul), loses his independence i.e. comes under their clutches. As has been said in *Śiva-sūtra*, 'Limited knowledge is the cause of bondage". (I, 2) The sage Vyāsa also says, "In childhood, he is dependent on his parents."

Madālasā also has said, "Do not indulge frequently in your association with material assemblage, by prating sometimes with 'O father', sometimes with 'O daughter', sometimes with 'O mother' sometimes with 'O beloved', sometimes with 'mine', sometimes with 'not mine'. (Ma. Pu. 25-15).

The rise of ideas is said to be 'tanmātragocaraḥ', because the sphere of these ideas is *tanmātras* which are the generic features either intense or moderate of all objects. So the phrase means 'which have different objects as their sphere'.

By this the author says: As long as there is the appearance of different objects, so long the individual is surely bound. When by means of the teaching imparted before, he has the unswerving knowledge that every thing is identical with Ṣelf, then he is liberated while alive, as has been said before, 'One who has this knowledge' etc. (II, 5).

Thus there is no inconsistency whatsoever between what has been said before, viz., "Therefore, whether it is word or object or thought, there is no state which is not *Śiva* and "The rise, in the bound soul, of all sorts of ideas marks the disappearance of the bliss of supreme immortality."

## EXPOSITION

As the empirical individual becomes subject to words and ideas that are the product of sensori-motor experiences, he becomes their prisoner and loses the power of creative thinking and is thus banished from the realm of immortal bliss, for that is the reality of a different dimension which is not within the province of thought-constructs. He thus becomes a bound soul.

### *Introduction to the* 15*th verse*

## TEXT

ननु यदि प्रत्ययोद्भवोऽप्यस्य परामृतरसापायः तत्कथमुक्तं शक्तिवर्गस्य भोग्यतां गतः,–इत्याशङ्कां परिहरति

## TRANSLATION

A doubt arises here 'If the rise of ideas in the bound soul means the disappearance of the bliss of immortality then how has it been said that he falls a victim to the group of Powers?" The author removes this doubt in the following verse :

### *Text of verse* 15

स्वरूपावरणे चास्य शक्तयः सततोत्थिताः ।
यतः शब्दानुवेधेन न विना प्रत्ययोद्भवः ॥ १५ ॥

Svarūpâvaraṇe câsya śaktayaḥ satatotthitāḥ/
Yataḥ śabdânuvedhena na vinâ pratyayodbhavaḥ// 15

## TRANSLATION

Brâhmī and other Powers are ever in readiness to conceal his real nature, for without the association of words, ideas cannot arise.

*Text of the Commentary*

चः शङ्कां द्योतयन् तत्परिहाररूपं प्रमेयान्तरं समुच्चिनोति । अस्य-पशोः स्वस्य शिवात्मनो रूपस्यावरणे-भित्तिभूतत्वेन प्रथमानस्यापि सम्यगपरामर्शने तन्निमित्तं, व्याख्यातरूपाः शक्तयः सततमुत्थिताः, यावद्धि परामृतरसात्मकस्वस्वरूपप्रत्यभिज्ञानमस्य न वृत्तं तावदेताः स्वस्वरूपावरणायोद्यच्छन्त्येव । यतोऽस्य यः प्रत्ययोद्भवो विकल्पकाविकल्पकज्ञानप्रसरः स शब्दानुवेधेन 'अहमिदं जानामि' इत्यादिना सूक्ष्मान्तःशब्दानुरञ्जनेन स्थूलाभिलापसंसर्गेण च विना न भवति,—इति तिरश्चामप्यसाङ्केतिकः निर्देशः प्रख्यः, स्वात्मनि च शिरोनिर्देशप्रख्योऽन्तरभ्युपगमरूपः शब्दनविमर्शोऽस्त्येव, अन्यथा बालस्य प्रथमसंकेतग्रहणं न घटेत अन्तरूहापोहात्मकविमर्शशून्यत्वात् । स्थूलशब्दानुवेधमयस्तु विकल्पः सर्वस्य स्वानुभवसिद्धः ॥ १५॥

## TRANSLATION

The particle 'ca' expressing a doubt adds another conclusive statement to remove it. The Powers which have been delineated before are ever in readiness to conceal the real nature of this bound soul, that nature which is identical with *Śiva*. They (the powers) are instrumental in not allowing him to discern that nature properly, though it serves as the basis of his life. As long as he is unable to recognize his real nature which is the same as the bliss of supreme immortality, so long they are definitely active in concealing it. (It is these Powers presiding over words that conceal his real nature), because the ideas that arise in him, that lead to the diffusion of knowledge, whether definite or indefinite, are not possible without the association of words, such as 'I know this.' These ideas may be either tinged with subtle internal words or may be expressed in gross speech. Even lower creatures have a hang of ideas involved in sound (serving as natural words), which is non-conventional indicative sign, something like the nod of head, in oneself indicative of inward approval. Otherwise the child cannot catch the first conventional sign being devoid of the power of inwardly thinking out the pros and cons of a matter. Ideas associated with gross words are a matter of selfexperience for all.

## EXPOSITION

Verses 13, 14 and 15 describe how the empirical individual

becomes bound and forgets his essential nature. The individual becomes a tool of ideas. His ideas are oriented towards sense-objects and the pleasure derived from them. The ideas are entirely governed by words. Words have a tremendous power over his life.

Thought-constructs and verbalization become the governing influences of his life. He becomes totally oblivious of the essential Self, for that can never be known as an object. The ideas and words toss him about and do not allow him to introspect within and have an awareness of the inward haven of his life. Ideas and words are all conditioned. The essential Self is unconditioned. The life of the empirical individual is confined within the prison of the conditioned. The unconditioned cannot be known by the conditioned. It is only when the individual frees himself from the shackle of ideas and words that he is free to have an immediate, direct awareness of Self.

*Introduction to the 16th Verse*

TEXT

श्लोकत्रयोक्तमर्थमुपसंहरन्नियतः प्रमेयस्य सामान्यस्पन्दतत्त्वादभिन्नतां प्रागुक्ता-मनुबध्नन् तत्प्रत्यभिज्ञानाप्रत्यभिज्ञानमयौ बन्धमोक्षौ, इति लक्षयति

TRANSLATION

Concluding what has been said in the previous three verses and strengthening the previously described identity of this extensive objectivity with the generic *Spanda* principle, the author defines in the following verse liberation as identical with the recognition of that (*Spanda*) and bondage as identical with its non-recognition.

*Text of the 16th Verse*

सेयं क्रियात्मिका शक्तिः शिवस्य पशुवर्तिनी ।
बन्धयित्री स्वमार्गस्था ज्ञाता सिद्ध्युपपादिका ॥ १६ ॥

Seyaṃ kriyātmikā śaktiḥ śivasya paśuvartinī/
Bandhayitrī svamārgasthā jñātā siddhyupapādikā// 16

## TRANSLATION

That afore-mentioned operative power of Śiva existing in the bound soul is a source of bondage; the same when realized as residing in him as the way of approach to one's own essential reality brings about success (i.e. the achievement of liberation).

## COMMENTARY

### TEXT

सेति श्लोकत्रयनिर्णीतत्वात्, इयमिति-प्रमेयपर्यन्तेन रूपेण स्फुरन्ती-स्वस्वभावरूपस्य चिदात्मनः शिवस्य सम्बन्धिनी स्पन्दतत्त्वात्मिका पराभट्टारिकैव विश्ववैचित्र्यावस्थितिकारित्वात् क्रियाशक्तिः प्राङ्निर्णीतदृशा शिव एव गृहीतपशुभूमिके वर्तमाना प्राणपुर्यष्टकरूपममुं कर्तृतात्मनाहन्ताविप्रुषा प्रोक्षितं कुर्वाणा तथारूपेणाप्रत्यभिज्ञाय स्वरूपावारकत्वाद्धानादानादिपरिक्लेशहेतुत्वाच्च बन्धयित्री भवति । यदा तु स्वस्य शिवात्मनो रूपस्य यो मार्गः

'शक्त्यवस्थां प्रविष्टस्य निर्विभागेन भावना ।
तदासौ शिवरूपी स्याच्छैवी मुखमिहोच्यते ॥' (२०)

इति श्रीविज्ञानभट्टारकोक्तनीत्या प्राप्त्युपायः पराशक्तिस्तदात्मतयासौ क्रियाशक्तिर्ज्ञायते योगिना, यदा वा विकल्पकाविकल्पकप्रसरेऽपि शिवस्वरूपस्य स्वात्मनोंऽशभूतमेवाशेषवेद्यमनेनेक्ष्यते तदास्यासौ परानन्दमयीं परां सिद्धिमुपपादयति॥ १६ ॥

## TRANSLATION

'That'-this has been defined by the previous three verses. Iyam—This one, the operative power which is one's own real nature i.e. of the nature of consciousness identical with *Śiva*. She has been called 'this,' because she manifests herself in the form of objectivity. She is the venerable *Spanda* principle. She is known as operative power (*kriyā śakti*), because she brings about the state of variety of the universe. As described before, she exists in *Śiva* who has assumed the role of a bound soul. She besprinkles this bound soul who is identified with *prāṇa* and *puryaṣṭaka* with a drop of I-consciousness which makes him an agent or doer. Reduced to this state, he does not recognize his real nature which is veiled by her and gets involved in the misery of seizing and relinquishing. Thus she becomes a source of bondage. When the *yogī* recognizes this operative power as the Supreme power, (*parā śakti*), the means of approach to his real nature which is *Śiva*, then according to the view of *Vijñānabhaṭṭāraka* expressed in the following lines, she brings about the highest achievement full of supreme bliss :

"When in one who enters the state of Śakti (i.e. who is identified with *Śakti*), there ensues the feeling of non-distinction[1] (between *Śakti* and *Śiva*), then he acquires the state of *Śiva*, (for) in the *āgamas* (*iha*), she (*śakti*) is declared as the door of entrance (into *Śiva*) (V. Bh. 20)" or when he, in spite of the dispersion of definite and indefinite ideas, regards the entire objectivity as an aspect of his own Self[2] which in its nature is *Śiva*, then also she (*śakti*) brings about the same achievement.

## NOTES

1. The non-distinction between *Śiva* and *Śakti* referred to in the verse quoted from Vijñānabhairava means in *yogic* terms the meeting point or junction between two polarities. In *āṇava-upāya*, the meeting point is between *prāṇa* and *apāna* in the centre or *hṛdaya* as it is called in this *yoga*. This centre in the body is the depression a little above the diaphragm. It is here that *prāṇa* and *apāna* meet. At this point, *śakti* becomes the door of entrance to *Śiva*.

In *Śāktopāya*, the central point between *pramāṇa* and *prameya* and in *Śāmbhava upāya*, the central point between *jñāna* and *kriyā* constitute the *nirvibhāga* or non-distinction of *Śiva* and *Śakti*.

2. This is the *Śāmbhava* form of realization.

## EXPOSITION

The power of ideation and verbalization is an aspect of the *kriyā śakti* of *Śiva*. When the empirical individual considers *kriyāśakti* as a power of his psycho-somatic organism, he is bound by its limitations and suffers. When he regards this *kriyāśakti* only as an aspect of *parāśakti*, the meeting point of *prāṇa* and *apāna*, *pramāṇa* and *prameya*, *jñāna* and *kriyā*, human and divine, then he is liberated.

*Introduction to the 16th and 17th verses.*

TEXT

इत्थंकारं पशुरत्र बध्यते, वक्ष्यमाणोपायपरिशीलनेन च मुच्यते, इति प्रति-
पादयन् बन्धस्वरूपमुच्छेद्यत्वेनानुवदति ।

TRANSLATION

Thus explaining how the individual is bound and is liberated by pursuing the means to be described, the author again describes the nature of bondage for its extirpation.

*Verse* 17 *and* 18

तन्मात्रोदयरूपेण मनोऽहंबुद्धिवर्तिना ।
पुर्यष्टकेन संरुद्धस्तदुत्थं प्रत्ययोद्भवम् * ॥ १७ ॥
भुङ्क्ते परवशो भोगं तद्भावात्संसरेदतः ।
संसृतिप्रलयस्यास्य कारणं संप्रचक्ष्महे ॥ १८ ॥

Tanmātrodaya-rūpeṇa manohaṃ-buddhivartinā/
Puryaṣṭakena saṃruddhastaduttham pratyayodbhavam//17
Bhuṇkte paravaśo bhogaṃ tadbhāvāt saṃsared ataḥ/
Saṃsṛti-pralayasyāsya kāraṇaṃ sampracakṣmahe// 18

TRANSLATION

Besieged by *puryaṣṭaka* which rises from *tanmātras* and exists in mind, I-feeling, and the determinative faculty, he (the bound soul) becomes subservient and undergoes the experiences that arise from it in the form of ideas about certain objects and the pleasure or pain that accrues from them. Owing to the continuance of the *puryaṣṭaka*, he (the bound soul) leads transmigratory existence. We are 'therefore' going to explain what causes the extirpation of this transmigratory existence. 17-18

COMMENTARY

TEXT

पुर्यष्टकोत्थितं भोगं भुङ्क्ते । यत एव प्रत्ययेषु-सुखादिप्रत्ययोद्भवः, अत एवासौ प्रत्ययोद्भवात् पशुः परवशः शब्दानुवेधक्रमेण पदे पदे ब्राह्म्यादिदेवीभिराक्षि-

* अस्य श्लोकस्य टीका नोपलब्धा ।

प्यमाणः, न तु सुप्रबुद्धवत् स्वतन्त्रः । तस्य पुर्यष्टकस्य भावादेव पुनःपुनरुद्बोधितविचित्रवासनः संसरेत्-तत्तद्भोगोचितभोगायतनानि शरीराण्यर्जयित्वा गृह्णाति चोत्सृजति च । यतश्चैवमतोऽस्य पुर्यष्टकसंरुद्धस्य या संसृतिस्तस्या यः प्रकृष्टो लयः पुर्यष्टकात्मकमलोच्छेदेन विनाशः तस्य कारणं-सम्यक् सुखोपायं प्रचक्ष्महे समनन्तरमेव ब्रूमः, तथा संप्रचक्ष्महे प्रकरणेऽस्मिन् स्वयं प्रतिपादितवन्तः । 'वर्तमानसामीप्ये वर्तमानवद्वा' (पा० सू० ३।३।१३१) इति वर्तमानप्रयोगः ॥ १८ ॥

## TRANSLATION

He undergoes the experiences arising from the *puryaṣṭaka.* Since there arises the experience of pleasure, etc. through the ideas, therefore, on account of the emergence of these ideas, the bound soul becomes subservient i.e. through the association of words, he is, at every step, driven hither and thither by *Brāhmī* and other goddesses. He is not independent like the fully awakened *yogī.*

Owing to the continuance of that *puryaṣṭaka,* the residual traces of cravings and desires lying submerged in it are awakened again and again and thus he transmigrates from one form of life to another, getting bodies suited for the appropriate experiences of those lives. Thus he assumes and gives up body after body (i.e. at each birth he assumes a body and at each death, he gives it up).

As it is so, therefore we are going to explain immediately the cause i.e. the easy means of the extirpation of the transmigratory tendency of this individual besieged by the *puryaṣṭaka* through the total extermination of the impurities inherent in it. The author has himself described the means in this treatise. The use of the present tense here conveys the sense of both 'past' and 'future' according to the *sūtra* of pāṇini, "The present tense is optionally used to indicate the near (immediate) past or future."

## EXPOSITION

These two verses are very important inasmuch as they give the rationale of the transmigratory life of the bound soul. The previous verses say that on account of the play of *Māyā śakti,* the soul loses its pristine *jñāna* and *kriyā śakti* and comes to have only limited knowledge and limited power of action. Secondly, he falls a prey to the veiled powers that arise from the multitude of words. In his present life, he acquires ideas through his experience of sense-objects, and education, but these ideas are not possible without words. So ultimately words come to acquire tremendous influence over his life.

Now verses 17 and 18 tell us how the future destiny of the individual is determined. In this the *puryaṣṭaka* plays the most important role. Man is a very complex being. He has not only a physical body but also a subtle one known as *puryaṣṭaka* which consists of the five *tanmātras* or the subtle aspects of the gross physical objects and *buddhi*, *manas* and *ahaṁkāra*. The impressions of our desires and thoughts are deposited in this *puryaṣṭaka*. When a man dies, it is only his physical body that is dissolved. The *puryaṣṭaka* remains as the subtle vehicle of the soul after his death. As has already been said, it contains the residual traces of the desires, etc. of the previous life. The desires and ideas deposited in the *puryaṣṭaka* are not inert elements but tremendous psychic forces seeking expression. So in the next life, man gets a body suited for the expression of the desires, etc., deposited in the *puryaṣṭaka* and is born in an environment suited for that expression.

The *puryaṣṭaka* plays a double role. In the present life, our ideas are formed according to our interests, and desires. The *puryaṣṭaka* is the repository of our interests and desires. As verse 17 says, *taduttham pratyayodbhavam*, i.e. our ideas are largely determined in the present life by the constitution of our *puryaṣṭaka*, and our future life is wholly determined by our *puryaṣṭaka*. That is why Kṣemarāja says, *Puryaṣṭakātmakama-locchedanena tasya (samsṛteḥ) vināśaḥ* i.e. 'The transmigratory existence can be stopped by the extermination of the impurities of the *puryaṣṭaka*."

*Introduction to the 19th Verse*

TEXT

एतत् प्रतिपादयन् आद्यं सूत्रोक्तमर्थं निगमयति—

## TRANSLATION

While substantiating the above, the author sums up the sense of what has been said in the first verse :

### *Verse* 19

यदा त्वेकत्र संरूढस्तदा तस्य लयोदयौ ।
नियच्छन्भोक्तृतामेति ततश्चक्रेश्वरो भवेत् ॥ १९ ॥

Yadā tvekatra saṃrūḍhas tadā tasya layodayau/
Niyacchan bhoktṛtām eti tataścakreśvaro bhavet// 19

## TRANSLATION

When, however, he is firmly rooted in that supreme *Spanda* principle, then bringing the emergence and dissolution of the *puryaṣṭaka* entirely under his control, he becomes the real enjoyer and thenceforth the lord of the collective whole of the *Śaktis*.

## COMMENTARY

### TEXT

यदा पुनरयमुक्ताः परतत्त्वसमावेशोपदेशयुक्तीः परिशीलयन् एकत्र पूर्णाहन्तात्मनि स्पन्दतत्त्वे सम्यगविचलत्वेन रूढः समाविष्टस्तन्मयो भवति, तदा तस्येति पूर्वसूत्रनिर्दिष्टस्य पुर्यष्टकस्य तद्द्वारेणैव विश्वस्य निमीलनोन्मीलनसमावेशाभ्यां लयोदयौ नियच्छन् प्रथमसूत्रनिर्णीतदृशा एकस्मादेव शङ्करात्मनः स्वभावात् संहारं सर्गं च कुर्वन् भोक्तृतामेति धरादिशिवान्तसमग्रभोग्य-कवलनेन परमप्रमातृतां सतीमेव प्रत्यभिज्ञानक्रमेणावलम्बते । ततश्च प्रथमसूत्रनिर्णीतस्य शक्तिचक्रस्य स्वमरीचिनिचयस्येश्वरोऽधिपतिर्भवेत् । अनेनैव च देहेन महेश्वरत्वमवाप्नोत्येवेति यावत् । एवं चोपक्रमोपसंहारयोर्महार्थसम्पुटीकारं दर्शयन् तत्सारतया समस्तशाङ्करोपनिषन्मूर्धन्यतामस्याविष्करोति शास्त्रस्य श्रीमान्वसुगुप्ताचार्यः, इति शिवम् ॥

इति श्रीस्पन्दनिर्णये विभूतिस्पन्दस्तृतीयो निष्पन्दः समाप्तः ।

## TRANSLATION

When, however, he, by constant practice of the means that have been taught of entering into the highest principle, becomes fully and unswervingly established in the *Spanda* principle, which is the perfect I-consciousness i.e. when he becomes identical with it, then he can bring under his control the emergence and the dissolution of the *puryaṣṭaka* referred to in the previous verse and through it also of the universe by means of the introversive and extroversive meditation, and in accordance with the principle established in the first verse, he, by bringing about the manifestation and dissolution of the universe by means of the one essential nature which is *Śaṅkara* becomes the Supreme Enjoyer, and thus by assimilating to himself all the objective categories from the earth upto *Śiva* by the process of recognition rises to the status of the Supreme Experient that he was already (*satīm eva*). Thenceforward he becomes the lord of the *śaktis* referred to in the first verse i.e. of the collective whole of the rays of his essential Self. In other words, he attains to the highest lordship in this very body.

Thus the glorious *Vasugupta*, showing the sameness of the great reality both in the beginning and end of the book, brings out the importance of this *Śāstra* as the essence and crown of the entire secret doctrine of *Śaivism*. May there be good to all.'

In this *Spandanirṇaya*, this is the third section entitled *Vibhūtispanda*.

## EXPOSITION

This verse describes the end of the journey. A spark of the Divine flame descends into matter and forgets its divine origin. Like an exile it wanders into distant lands and in different forms. At the human stage, it acquires the gift of speech and mentation. It has now reached a definite station in the evolutionary march. The human being as now known sows his wild oats, reaps the consequences and learns the inexorable laws of life in the bitter school of experience. A time comes when he is filled with nostalgia, and now begins his journey homeward. He has not to go far. He has only to throw off the mask of the pseudo-I and enter his essential, real I, which is the *Spanda*, the heart-beat of *Śiva*. He now becomes what he always was. The universe is no longer a foreign land. The I and the This, the Subject and the object become one. That is an experience for which there is no word in the human language.

### *Section IV*

## INTRODUCTION

ग्रन्थान्ते परमां स्पन्दभूमिं गुरुगिरं च श्लेषोक्त्या स्तौति

## TRANSLATION

In the end of the book, the author, by means of a *double entendre* lauds the *Spanda* state as well as the power of the word of his *guru* (teacher).

### *Verse* 1

अगाधसंशयाम्भोधिसमुत्तरणतारिणीम् ।
वन्दे विचित्रार्थपदां चित्रां तां गुरुभारतीम् ॥ १ ॥

Agādhasaṃśayāmbhodhi-samuttaraṇatāriṇīm/
Vande vicitrārthapadāṃ citrāṃ tāṃ gurubhāratīm// 1

## TRANSLATION

I pay my homage to that wonderful speech of my *guru* which is like a boat for crossing the fathomless ocean of doubt and is full of words which yield wonderful meaning (in the case of the *guru*).

I offer my reverential prayer to *Spanda* in the form of *parā vāk*, the Supreme divine I-consciousness which is full of wonderful transcendental bliss, and which acts like a boat in crossing the fathomless ocean of doubt regarding my essential nature (in the case of *Spanda* in the form of *parāvāk*).

## COMMENTARY

## TEXT

तामसामान्यां भगवतीं गुरुं 'शंवी मुखमिहोच्यते' (वि० भै० २०) इति स्थित्या शिवधामप्राप्तिहेतुत्वादाचार्यरूपाम् । अथच गुरुं पश्यन्त्यादिक्रोडीकारात् महतीं भारतीं परां वाचम्, तथा गुरोराचार्यस्य सम्बन्धिनीमुपदेष्ट्रीं गिरं चित्रां-लोकोत्तरचमत्काररूपां वन्दे-सर्वोत्कृष्टत्वेन समाविशामि । अथ च सर्वावस्थासु स्फुरद्रू-

पत्वादभिवदन्तीमुद्यन्तृताप्रयत्नेनाभिवादये-स्वरूपविमर्शनिष्ठां तां समावेष्टुं संमुखीकरोमि । कीदृशीमगाधो दुरुत्तरो यः संशयः—पूर्णाहन्तानिश्चयाभावात्मा विचित्रः शङ्काकलङ्कः स एव विततत्वेनाम्भोधिस्तस्य सम्यगुत्तरणे या तारिणी नौरिव तामित्युभयत्रापि योज्यम् । तथा विचित्रार्थानि नानाचमत्कारप्रयोजनानि पदानि विश्रान्तयो यस्यां परस्यां वाचि तां विचित्राणि रम्यरचनानुप्रविष्टानि अर्थपदानि वाच्यवाचकानि यस्यां गुरुवाचि ताम् ॥ १ ॥

## TRANSLATION

'Tām' (that) means that uncommon goddess who, in accordance with the view that "*Śakti* is the door of entrance into *Śiva,*" acts as an *ācārya* (teacher), inasmuch as she is the means of entry into the state of *Śiva.* Moreover 'gurum' means *mahatīm* or supreme, *mahatīṃ bhāratīm* therefore, means *parā vāk*, the Supreme Power of Sound (of the Divine). She is called 'supreme' inasmuch as she encloses within her embrace *paśyantī* etc.

*Gurubhāratī* also means 'the exhortative speech of the teacher'. '*Citrām*' means 'wonderful' in the case of the teacher, and 'of the form of transcendental bliss' in the case of *parāvāk.* 'Vande' means 'I pay homage' in the case of the teacher, and 'I enter it, because it is the Supreme' in the case of *parāvāk.* And I make my reverential salutation to her with all eagerness who, because of her gleaming presence in all states (i.e. *paśyantī, madhyamā* and *vaikharī*) throws a hint of essential reality and I make her favourably disposed towards me in order that I may enter into her who is always immersed in the awareness of the essential nature.

How is that Bhāratī ? Who is like a boat for crossing successfully the fathomless, uncrossable ocean of stains of doubt viz. 'the absence of certainty regarding the Supreme I'. This doubt is called ocean because of its expansiveness. She is like a boat because she enables one to cross this ocean in the right manner. This simile is applicable in both cases.

*Vicitra-arthapadām* in the case of *parāvāk* means 'one whose stages of rest (in the form of *Samādhi*) display wonderful states of bliss'; in the case of the teacher's speech, it means "that which has wonderful words and meanings arranged in a pleasant order".

*Introduction to the 2nd Verse*

TEXT

प्रसिद्धप्रभावस्वनामोदीरणात्सम्भावनाप्रत्ययेनार्थिनः प्रवर्तयन् गूहनीयतया महाफलतामस्य शास्त्रस्य निरूपयति शास्त्रकारः

TRANSLATION

By mentioning his name celebrated owing to his greatness, encouraging the seekers (of knowledge) by their respectful regard for him, the author describes the great reward which this *Śāstra* yields when it is kept secret.

*Verse* 2

लब्ध्वाप्यलभ्यमेतज्ज्ञानधनं हृद्गुहान्तकृतनिहितेः ।
वसुगुप्तवच्छिवाय हि भवति सदा सर्वलोकस्य ॥ २ ॥

Labdhvāpy alabhyam etaj jñānadhanaṃ hṛdguhantakrtanihiteḥ/
Vasuguptavac chivāya hi bhavati sadā sarvalokasya// 2

TRANSLATION

As on the attainment of this treasure of knowledge which is difficult of attainment, and on its being well preserved in the cave of the heart, it has been for the good of Vasugupta, so also on the attainment of this treasure of knowledge difficult of attainment and on its being well preserved in the cave of the heart, it would always be for the good of all.

COMMENTARY

TEXT

एतच्छास्त्रोक्तमेतज्ज्ञानमेव पुरुषार्थप्राप्तिहेतुत्वाद्धनमलभ्यमपि-दुष्प्रापमपि लब्ध्वा-शङ्करस्वप्नोपदेशसारं शिलातलादवाप्य प्रकाशविमर्शात्मकं हृदयमेव विश्रान्तःप्रवेशावकाशप्रदत्वाद्गुहा तस्यामन्तेन-निश्चयेन कृता निहितिः स्थापना

येन अर्थात्तस्यैव ज्ञानधनस्य, तस्य स्वामिनः श्रीवसुगुप्ताभिधानस्य गुरोर्यथैव तच्छिवाय जातं, तद्वदधिकारिनियमसंकोचाभावात्सर्वलोकस्यापि हृद्‌गुहान्त-कृतनिहितेर्यत्नादसामयिकाद् गोपयतः दृढप्रतिपत्त्या च स्वात्मीकुर्वतः सदा शिवाय भवति नित्यशङ्करात्मकस्वस्वभावसमावेशलाभाय सम्पद्यत इति शिवम् ॥ २ ॥

यद्यप्यस्मिन् विवृतिगणना विद्यते नैव शास्त्रे
लोकश्चायं यदपि मतिमान् भूयसोत्तानवृत्तिः ।
जानन्त्येते तदपि कुशलास्तेऽस्मदुक्तेर्विशेषं
केचित्सारग्रहणनिपुणाश्चेतनाराजहंसाः ॥ १ ॥

अनन्तापरटीकाकृन्मध्ये स्थितिममृष्यता ।
विवृतं स्पन्दशास्त्रं नो गुरुणा नो, मयास्य तु ॥ २ ॥

विशेषलेशः सन्दोहे दर्शितः पूर्वमद्य तु ।
रुद्रशक्तिसमावेशशालिनः शिवरूपिणः ॥ ३ ॥

शूरनाम्नः स्वशिष्यस्य प्रार्थनातिरसेन तत् ।
निर्णीतं क्षेमराजेन स्फारान्निजगुरोर्गुरोः ॥ ४ ॥

येषां नो धिषणोपदेशविशदा सद्दैशिकैर्दर्शिता
श्रीमच्छाम्भवशासनोपनिषदां येषां न भग्नो भ्रमः ।
ये नास्वादितपूर्विणो मृदुधियः श्रीप्रत्यभिज्ञामृतं
ते नात्राधिकृताः परैः पुनरिदं पूर्णाशयैश्चर्व्यताम् ॥ ५ ॥

शिवादिक्षित्यन्तो विततविततो योऽध्वविभवः
स्फुरन्नानासर्गस्थितिलयदशाचित्रिततनुः ।
इयद्विश्वं यस्य प्रसरकणिकासौ विजयते
परः संवित्स्पन्दो लसदसमसौख्यायतनभूः ॥ ६ ॥

समाप्तोऽयं श्रीस्पन्दनिर्णयः ।

कृतिः श्रीप्रत्यभिज्ञाकारप्रशिष्यस्य महामाहेश्वराचार्यश्रीमदभिनवगुप्तनाथदत्तोपदेशस्य श्रीक्षेमराजस्येति शिवम् ॥

## TRANSLATION

This knowledge described by the *śāstra* is a treasure inasmuch as it is the means for the attainment of the highest aim of human existence. Though it is difficult of attainment, *Vasugupta* obtained it on the surface of a rock as the essence of *Śaṅkara's* instruction in a dream.

The meaning of *hṛdguhāntakṛtanihiteḥ* is the following: *Hṛt* or heart is of the nature of *prakāśa* (light) or consciousness and *vimarśa* or awareness of the consciousness. This heart or *prakāśa-vimarśa* is like a cave, for like a cave it provides room for entry into the all-of-reality. The whole phrase means 'of him who has established himself with certainty in this cave of the heart' i.e. of *Vasugupta.* Just as this treasure of knowledge was for the good of the teacher, named Vasugupta, so it will be for the good of all, for there is no restriction of rules governing the recipient of this knowledge. When they preserve it carefully in the cave of their heart and guarding it against those who have not got the same faith, assimilate it fully by firm realization, then it would always be for their good. 'For their good' means 'for the acquisition of the competence of entry into their real nature which is always *Śaṅkara*'. May there be good to all!

## *Concluding Remarks by Kṣemarāja*

Though there is no end to the number of commentaries on this *Śāstra*, and though there are intelligent people, yet they are mostly superficial by nature, but they who are competent, who are intelligent swans and are skilled in grasping the essence, know the special merit of my commentary. My teacher could not put up with being bracketed with the numerous other ordinary run of commentators, so he did not write any commentary on *Spanda-śāstra.* I have previously expressed a bit of my special point of view in *Spanda-sandoha.* Today, owing to the fervent entreaty of my pupil named *Śūra* who has experienced entry into the power of *Rudra*, who is Śiva Himself, I, *Khemarāja*, have given conclusive explanation with the help of the splendid detailed exposition of my teacher.

They are not qualified for the study of this *śāstra* whose intelligence is not purified by the teaching of right sort of teachers, whose doubt has not been shattered by the esoteric teaching of *Śaiva* discipline, and who, being of tender intellect, have not tasted previously the nectar of *Pratyabhijñā*. This may, however, be enjoyed by the other high-souled ones.[5]

All glory to this Supreme Creative Pulsation (*Spanda*) of consciousness which is the abode of flashing, unparalleled delight, whose majesty of path extends to far-reaching areas from the earth up to *Śiva*, which is variegated by the display of various states of creation, maintenance and withdrawal and of whose extension this universe is just a minute particle.[6]

This is the work of *Kṣemarāja* who has received instruction from *Abhinavagupta*, the great devotee of the great Lord, the grand pupil of the author of *Īśvarapratyabhijñā*.

---

## GLOSSARY OF TECHNICAL TERMS

### *A* (अ)

A (अ) : Symbol of Śiva, short form of *anuttara* (the Supreme) the one letter that pervades all the other letters of the alphabet.

Akula ; Śiva or अ

Akrama : Successionless manifestation of the essential nature.

Akṛtrima : Natural; inartificial.

Akhyâti : Primal Ignorance.

Agni (Symbolic) : Pramātā – knower or subject.

Agniṣomamayam : The universe which is of the nature of *pramāṇa* (knowledge) and *prameya* (object).

Ajñānam : The primal limitation (*mala*). Being inherent in Puruṣa, it is known as Pauruṣa Ajñāna, on account of which he considers himself as of limited knowledge and activity.

Being in Buddhi, it is known as Bauddha Ajñāna on account of which one forms all kinds of *aśuddha vikalpas* —thought-constructs devoid of essential Reality.

Aghora : The merciful Śiva.

Aghora śaktis : The *śaktis* that lead the conditioned experient to the realization of *Śiva*.

Adhikāra : Office, prerogative, right.

Adhiṣṭhāna : Substratum, support, base.

Adhiṣṭhātṛ : The superintending, governing, presiding principle.
Aṇu-One that breathes i.e. the limited, conditioned experient.

Adhvā : Course or path. Śuddha Adhvā is the intrinsic course, the supramundane manifestation. Aśuddha Adhvā is the course of mundane manifestation.

Anāśrita-Śiva : The state of Śiva in which there is no objective content yet, in which the universe is negated from Him.

Anantabhaṭṭāraka : The presiding deity of the *Mantra* experients

Antarmukhībhāva : Introversion of consciousness.

Anupāya : Spontaneous realization of Self without any special effort.

Anugraha : Grace.

Anuttara : (1) The Highest; the Supreme, the Absolute.
(2) The vowel 'a' (अ).

Anusandhāna : Repeated intensive awareness of the source or essential Reality; joining the succeeding experience to the previous one; synthetic unity of apperception,

Anusandhātā : One who joins the succeeding experience into a unity.

Anusyūta : Strung together; connected uninterruptedly.

Apāna : Inhalation.

Apavarga : Liberation.

Abuddha (Aprabuddha) : Unawakened one, one who is in spiritual ignorance.

Abhāva : Non-ens; void.

Abhinna : Non-different, identical.

Abhiyoga : Backward reference of awareness.

Amāyīya : Beyond the scope of Māyā.

Amūḍha : Sentient.

Avadhāna : Constant awareness.

Avikalpa (Nirvikalpa) jñāna : Direct realization of Reality without any mental activity.

Avikalpa (Nirvikalpa) pratyakṣa : Sensuous awareness without any perceptual judgement, unparticularised awareness.

Aviveka : Non-awareness of the Real.

Avyakta : Non-manifest.

Aśuddha vidyā : Knowledge of a few particulars, empirical knowledge.

Avasthā : State.

Asat : Non-being.

Aśuddhi : Impurity, limitation.

Ahaṃkāra : I-making principle, I-feeling of the empirical self.

Ahantā : I-consciousness.

## *Ā* (आ)

Āṇava upāya : The *yoga* whereby the individual utilizes his senses, *prāṇa* and *manas* for Self-realization. It is also known as *Āṇava yoga, Bhedopāya* and *Kriyāyoga* or *Kriyopāya.*

Āṇava samāveśa : Identification with the Divine by the above means.

Āṇava mala : Primal limiting condition which reduces universal consciousness to a *jīva* (an empirical experient).

Ātma-lābha : Realization of Self.

Ātma-viśrānti : Resting in the Self.

Ātma-vyāpti : Realization of the Self without the realization of the all-inclusive *Śiva*-nature.

Ānanda : Bliss; the letter 'ā', symbolizing *śakti.*

Ānanda upāya : Realization of *Śiva*-nature without any yogic discipline. Also known as *Ānanda yoga* or *Anupāya.*

Ābhoga : Expansion; *camatkāra* or spiritual delight.

## *I* (इ)

Icchā : Will; Representing the letter 'इ' (i).

Ichhopāya : Śāmbhava upāya, also known as Icchā yoga.

Ichhā-śakti : The inseparable innate Power of Parama Śiva intent on manifestation; that inward state of Parama Śiva in which *jñāna* and *kriyā* are unified; the predominant aspect of Sadāśiva.

Idantā : This-consciousness; objective consciousness.

Indu : Prameya or object; apāna; kriyā śakti.

Īśvara-tattva : The fourth *tattva,* counting from *Śiva.* The consciousness of this *tattva* is 'This am I'. *Jñāna* is predominant in this *tattva.*

Īśvara-bhaṭṭāraka : The presiding deity of the *Mantreśvaras* residing in *Īśvara tattva.*

## *U* (उ)

Uccāra : A particular technique of concentration on Prāṇa śakti under Āṇava Upāya.

Ucchalattā : The creative movement of the Divine ānanda bringing about manifestation and withdrawal.

Udaya : Rise, appearance, creation.

Udāna : The vital *vāyu* that moves upwards. The *śakti* that moves up in Suṣumnā at spiritual awakening.

Udyama : The sudden spontaneous emergence of the Supreme I-consciousness.

Unmeṣa : Lit. Opening of the eye.

(1) From the point of view of *svabhāva* or the essential nature of the Divine, it means the emergence of the Divine I-consciousness.

(2) From the point of view of manifestation, it means the externalizing of Icchā śakti, the start of the world process.

(3) From the point of view of Śaiva yoga, it means the emergence of the spiritual consciousness which is the background of the rise of ideas.

(4) Representing the letter 'u'.

Upalabdhṛ : The Experient, knower or subject.

Upalabdhi : Cognition, awareness.

*Ū* (ऊ)

Ūrdhva mārga : Upward path; suṣumnā.

*Ka* (क)

Kañcuka : The coverings of Māyā, throwing a pall over pure consciousness and converting *Śiva* into *jīva*. They are (1) Kalā, (2) (aśuddha) Vidyā, (3) Rāga, (4) Niyati and, (5) Kāla.

Karaṇa : The means of jñāna and kriyā—
Antaḥkaraṇa, the inner psychic apparatus and bahiṣkaraṇa, the external senses.

Karaṇeśvarī : Khecarī, gocarī, dikcarī and bhūcarī cakra.

Kartṛtva : The state of being the subject.

Karmendriya : The five powers and organs of action—speaking (*vāk*), handling (*hasta*), locomotion (*pāda*), excreting (*pāyu*), sexual action (*upastha*).

Kalā : (1) The *śakti* of consciousness by which all the thirtysix principles are evolved, (2) Part, particle, aspect, (3) Limitation in respect of activity (*kiñcitkartṛtva*) (4) The subtlest aspect of objectivity, viz; Śāntyātītā, Śāntā, Vidyā, Pratiṣṭhā, and Nivṛtti.

Kalācakra ; Mātṛcakra, Śakticakra, Devīcakra, the group of letters from 'a' to 'kṣa'.

Kalā śarīra : That of which the essential nature is activity; Kārma mala.

*Ka* (का)

Kāraṇa : Cause.

Kārya : Effect; objectivity.

Kārma mala : *Mala* or limitation due to *karma*.

Kāla adhvā : Temporal course of manifestation, viz., *Varṇa, mantra, pada*.

Kāla tattva ; Time—past, present and future, determined by the sense of succession.

Kāla Śakti : The power of the Divine that determines succession.

*Ku* (कु)

Kuṇḍalī or Kuṇḍalinī : The creative power of Śiva; a dístinct śakti that lies folded up in three and a half folds in Mūlādhāra.

Kumbhaka : Retention of prāṇa.

Kula : All-transcending light of consciousness; śakti manifesting herself in 36 *tattvas*.

Kulāmnāya : The Śākta system or doctrine of realizing the Supreme by means of all letters from (a) to (kṣa).

Kulamārga : The discipline for attaining to the all-transcending light of consciousness; Śāmbhava upāya.

*Kra* (क्र)

Krama : Realization of the Supreme by means of purification of *vikalpas* (determinate ideas) through successive stages (*Krama*). *Krama* employs śāktopāya. It is also known as Mahānaya or Mahārtha darśana.

Kṛtrima : Constructed by *vikalpa* or determinate idea; pseudo-reality.

Kriyā yoga : Āṇava upāya, also known as kriyopāya.

Kriyā Śakti : The power of assuming any and every form (*Sarvākārayogitvaṃ kriyāśaktiḥ*).

*Krīḍā* : Play or sport of the Divine.

*Kṣa* (क्ष)

Kṣetrajña : The empirical subject.

Kṣobha : Identification of the Self with the gross or the subtle body.

*Kha* (ख)

Khecarī : Sub-species of Vāmeśvarī śakti, connected with the pramātā, the empirical self. Khecarī is one that moves in *kha* or the vast expanse of consciousness.

Khecarī cakra : The *cakra* or group of the śaktis that move in the expanse of consciousness of the empirical subject.

Khecarī Mudrā : The bliss of the vast expanse of spiritual consciousness, also known as *divya mudrā* or *Śivāvasthā* (the state of Self).

Khyāti : Jñāna; knowledge; wisdom.

*Ga* (ग)

Gaganāṅganā : *Cit śakti*, consciousness power.

Garbha : Akhyāti, primal ignorance, Mahāmāyā.

Guṇatraya : The three genetic constituents *Sattva*, *rajas*, *tamas*.

Gocarī : Sub-species of Vāmeśvarī, connected with *antaḥkaraṇa* of the experient. 'Go' means 'sense'. Antaḥkaraṇa is the seat of the senses; hence Gocarī is connected with antaḥkaraṇa.

Granthi : Psychic tangle; psychic complex.

Grāhaka : Knower, Subject; Experient.

Grāhya : Knowable; object of experience.

*Gha* (घ)

Ghorā śaktis : The Śaktis or deities that draw the *jīvas* towards worldly pleasures.

Ghoratarī śaktis : The *śaktis* or deities that push the *jīvas* towards a downward path in *saṃsāra*.

*Ca* (च)

Cakra : The group or Collective whole of *śaktis*.

Cakreśvara : The master or lord of the group of *śaktis*.

Candra : *Prameya* or object of knowledge, the *apāna prāṇa* or *nāḍī* (channel or nerve).

Camatkāra : Bliss of the pure I-consciousness; wondrous delight of artistic experience.

Caramakalā : The highest phase of manifestation known as Śāntyātītā or Śāntātītā kalā.

*Ci* (चि)

Cit : The Absolute; foundational consciousness; the consciousness that is the unchanging principle of all changes.

Citta : The limitation of the Universal Consciousness manifested in the individual mind, the mind of the empirical individual.

Citi : The consciousness-power of the Absolute that brings about the world-process.

Cidānanda : (1) The nature of ultimate Reality consisting of consciousness and bliss (2) The sixth stratum of ānanda in uccāra yoga of āṇava upāya.

*Ce* (चे)

Cetana : Parama Śiva, Self, Conscious individual.

Cetya : Knowable, object of consciousness.

*Cai* (चै)

Caitanya : The foundational Consciousness which has absolute freedom of knowing and doing, of *jñāna* and *kriyā* śakti.

*Cha* (छ)

Cheda : Cessation of *prāṇa* and *apāna* by sounding of *anacka* (vowel-less) sounds.

*Ja* (ज)

Jagat : The world process.

Jagadānanda : The bliss of the Self or the Divine appearing as the universe, the bliss of the Divine made visible.

*Jā* (जा)

Jāgrat avasthā : The waking condition.

Jāgrat jñāna : Objective knowledge common to all people in waking condition.

Jāgrat : Esoteric meaning—Enlightenment, undeluded awakening of consciousness at all levels.

*Jī* (जी)

Jīva : The individual soul, the empirical self whose consciousness is conditioned by the *saṃskāras* of his experience and who is identified with the limitations of his subtle and gross constitution.

Jīvanmukta : The liberated individual who, while living in the physical body, is not conditioned by the limitation of his subtle and gross constitution and believes the entire universe to be an expression of Śiva or his highest Self.

Jīvanmukti : Experience of liberation while still living in the body.

### *Jñā* (ज्ञा)

Jñāna : Spiritual wisdom; limited knowledge (which is the source of bondage).

Jñāna yoga : Śākta upāya.

### *Ta* (त)

Tattva : Thatness; principle; reality, the very being of a thing.

Tattva-traya : The three tattvas, viz; Nara, Śakti and Śiva or Ātmā, Vidyā, and Śiva.

Tatpuruṣa : One of the five aspects of Śiva.

Tanmātra : Lit., that only; the primary elements of perception; the general elements of the particulars of sense-perception, viz., *śabda, sparśa. rūpa, rasa, gandha.*

Tamas : One of the constituents of Prakṛti, the principle of Inertia and delusion.

Tarka śāstra : Logic and Dialectics.

### *Tu* (तु)

Turīya or Turya : The fourth state of consciousness beyond the states of waking, dreaming and deep sleep and stringing together all the states; the Metaphysical Consciousness distinct from the psychological or empirical consciousness; the sākṣī or witnessing consciousness; the transcendental Self.

Turīyātīta or Turyātīta : The state of consciousness transcending the turīya, the state in which the distinction of the three, viz., waking, dreaming and deep sleep states is annulled; that pure blissful consciousness in which there is no sense of difference, in which the entire universe appears as the Self.

*Tri* (त्रि)

Trika : The system of philosophy of the triad—Nara, Śakti and Śiva or (1) para, the highest, concerned with identity, (2) parāpara, identity in difference, and (3) apara, difference and sense of difference.

Trika (Para): Prakāśa, Vimarśa and their Sāmarasya.

Trika (Parāpara): Icchā, Jñāna and Kṛiyā.

*Da* (द)

Darśana : Seeing, insight; system of philosophy.

*Di* (दि)

Dik : Space.

Dikcarī : Sub-species of Vāmeśvarī, connected with *bahiṣkaraṇas* or outer senses.

Divya Mudrā : Khecarī mudrā.

*Dī* (दी)

Dīkṣā : (1) The gift of spiritual knowledge (2) The initiation ceremony pertaining to a disciple by which spiritual knowledge is imparted and the residual traces of his evil deeds are purified.

*De* (दे)

Deśa : Space.

Deśa adhvā : Spatial course of manifestation, viz., *Kalā*, *tattva*, *bhuvana*.

*Dha* (ध)

Dhāraṇā : (1) Meditation, (2) The letters, ya, ra, la, va (य, र, ल, व).

Dhruva : (1) Anuttara stage, (2) The letter 'a' (अ).

Dhyāna yoga : The highest dhāraṇā of āṇava upāya in which pramāṇa (knowledge), prameya (object of knowledge) and pramātā (knower) are realized as aspects of *Saṃvid* or foundational consciousness.

Dhvani yoga : A dhāraṇā of āṇava upāya consisting of concentration on *anāhata nāda* (unstruck sound) arising within through prāṇa śakti, This is also known as *Varṇa yoga*.

*Na* (ण)

Nāda : (1) Metaphysical—The first movement of Śiva-śakti towards manifestation, (2) In yoga—The unstruck sound experienced in suṣumnā.

*Ni* (नि)

Nigraha kṛtya : Śiva's act of Self-veiling.

Nibhālana : Perception; mental practice.

Nimeṣa : Lit., closing of the eye-lids, dissolution of the world; (1) the inner activity of *spanda* by which the object is merged into the subject; (2) the dissolution of the Śakticakra in the Self; (4) the involution of Śiva in matter.

Nimīlana Samādhi : The inward meditative condition in which the individual consciousness gets absorbed into the universal consciousness.

Niyati : Limitation by cause-effect relation; spatial limitation, limitation of what ought to be done and what ought not to be done.

Nirvāṇa : Dissolution in Śūnya; liberation.

Nirvikalpa : Devoid of all thought-construct or ideation.

Nirvyutthāna Samādhi : Samādhi (absorption into the Universal consciousness) which continues even when one is not engaged in formal meditation.

*Pa* (प)

Pañcakṛtya : The ceaseless five-fold act of Śiva, viz. manifestation (*sṛṣṭi*), maintenance of manifestation (*sthiti*), withdrawal of manifestation (*saṁhāra*), veiling of Self (*vilaya* or *pidhāna*), Grace (*anugraha*), or the five-fold act of *ābhāsana*, *rakti*, *vimarśana*, *bījāvasthāpana* and *vilāpana* (See Pratyabhijñāhṛdayam, sūtra 11).

Pañcamantra : Īśāna, Tatpuruṣa, Sadyojāta, Vāmadeva, and Aghora.

Pañcavaktra—Do—

Pañcaśakti : The five fundamental *śaktis* of Śiva, viz., *Cit*, *Ānanda*, *Icchā*, *Jñāna*, and *Kriyā*.

Pati : The experient of Śuddha adhvā; the liberated individual.

Pati daśā : The state of liberation.

Para : The Highest, the Absolute.

Para pramātṛ : The highest experient; Parama Śiva.

Parama Śiva : The Highest Reality, the Absolute.

Parāpara : The intermediate stage, both identical and different, unity in diversity.

Paramārtha : The highest reality, essential truth; the highest goal.

Parāmarśa : Seizing mentally; experience; contemplation, remembrance.

Parāvāk : The vibratory pulsation of the Divine Mind that brings about manifestation, Logos; Cosmic Ideation; Spanda.

Parāśakti : The Highest Śakti of the Divine, Citi.

Pariṇāma : Transformation.

Paśu : The empirical individual bound by *avidyā* or spiritual nescience.

Paśu mātaraḥ : Māheśvarī and other associated śaktis—active in the various letters, controlling the life of the empirical selves.

Paśyantī : The Divine view in undifferntiated form; Vāk-śakti, going forth as seeing, ready to create in which there is no difference between *vācya* (object) and *vācaka* (word).

Pāśa : Bondage.

Pidhāna Kṛtya : The act of Self-veiling, same as *vilaya.*

Puṃstattva or Puruṣa tattva : Paśu pramātā; jīva; the empirical self.

Puryaṣṭaka : Lit; the city of the group of eight i.e. the five *tanmātras, buddhi, ahaṅkāra* and *manas*; the *sūkṣma śarīra* (subtle body).

Pūrṇatva : Perfection.

Pūrṇāhantā : The perfect I-consciousness; non-relational I-consciousness.

Prakāśa : Lit., Light, the principle of Self-revelation; consciousness; the principle by which every thing is known.

Prakṛti or Pradhāna : The source of objectivity from *buddhi* down to earth.

Pramā : Exact knowledge.

Pramāṇa : Knowledge, means of knowledge.

Pramātṛ : Knower; Subject: Experient.

Prameya : Knowable; object of knowledge, object.

Pratha : To expand; unfold; appear; shine.

Prathā : The mode of appearance.

Pratibhā : (1) Ever creative activity of consciousness; (2) The spontaneous Supreme I-consciousness, (3) Parā śakti.

Pratimīlana : Both nimīlana and unmīlana samādhi i.e. turning of the consciousness both within i.e. into Śiva and outside i.e. the Śakti of Śiva, experience of divinity both within and outside.

Pratyabhijñā : Recognition.

Pratyāhāra : (1) Comprehension of several letters into one syllable effected by combining the first letter of a sūtra with its final indicatory letter. (2) In yoga, withdrawal of the senses from their objects.

Pratyavamarśa : Self-recognition.

Pralaya : Dissolution of manifestation.

Pralayākala or Pralayakevalī : One resting in Māyātattva, not cognizant of anything; congizant of śūnya or void only.

Prasara : Expansion; manifestation of *Śiva* in the form of the universe through His *śakti.*

Prāṇa : Generic name for vital power; vital energy; specifically it is the vital vāyu in expiration.

Prāṇa-Pramātā : The subject considering prāṇa to be his Self.

Prāṇa-bīja : The letter *ha* (ह).

Prāṇāyāma : Breath control.

Prāsāda : The mantra *sauḥ* (सौः).

Prthivi : The earth *tattva. Pau* (पौ)

Pauruṣa ajñāna : The innate ignorance of Puruṣa regarding his real Self.

Pauruṣa jñāna : Knowledge of one's Śiva nature after the ignorance of one's real Self has been eliminated.

*Ba* (ब)

Bandha : (1) Bondage, (2) Limited knowledge, (3) Knowledge founded on primal ignorance; (4) Yogic practice in which certain organs of the body are contracted and locked.

Bala : *Cid-bala,* power of Universal Consciousness or true Self.

Bindu or Vindu ; (1) A point, a metaphysical point, (2) Undivided Light of Consciousness, (3) The compact mass of śakti gathered into an undifferentiated point ready to create

(4) Paraḥ pramātā, the Highest Self or Consciousness, (5) Anusvāra or nasal sound in अहं indicated by a dot on the letter ह, suggesting the fact that Śiva in spite of the manifestation of the universe is undivided: (6) A specific *teja* or light appearing in the centre of the eye-brow by the intensity of meditation, (7) A drop of semen.

Bahirmukhatā : Externalization, extroversion.

Brahma : In Śāṅkara Vedānta—Pure foundational consciousness without activity; unlimited knowledge without activity. In Śaiva Philosophy—Pure foundational consciousness full of *svātantrya śakti*, i.e. unimpeded power to know and do any and every thing, *parama Śiva.*

Brahma nāḍī : Suṣumnā or the central prāṇic channel or nerve.

Brahmanirvāṇa : Resting in pure *jñāna tattva,* devoid of activity; the state of Vijñānākala.

Brahmarandhra : The *Sahasrāra cakra.*

Brahmavāda : Śāṅkara Vedānta.

Bīja : (1) The active Light of the highest Śakti which is the root cause of the universe (2) Vowel (3) The mystical letter forming the essential part of the *mantra* of a deity. (4) The first syllable of a *mantra.*

Buddha : One awakened to the light of consciousness.

Buddhi : The ascertaining intelligence; the intuitive aspect of consciousness by which the essential Self awakens to truth.

Buddhīndriya : The five powers of sense-perception, viz., smelling, tasting, seeing, feeling by touch, hearing, also known as jñānendriya.

Baindavī kalā : Baindavī—pertaining to Bindu or the knower, kalā—will power. Baindavī kalā is that freedom of Parama Śiva by which the knower always remains as the knower and is never reduced to the known, *svātantrya śakti.*

Bauddha ajñāna : The ignorance inherent in Buddhi by which one considers his subtle or gross body as the Self on account of *aśuddha vikalpas.*

Bauddha jñāna : Considering oneself as Śiva by means of *śuddha vikalpas.*

*Bha* (भ)

Bhakti (*aparā*) : Devotion; intense feeling and will for being united with Śiva.

Bhakti (parā) the constant feeling of being united with Śiva and the supreme bliss of that consciousness.

Bhava : Transmigratory existence.

*Bhā* (भा)

Bhāva : Existence both internal and external; object.

Bhāvanā : The practice of contemplating or viewing mentally oneself and everything else as Śiva; *jñāna yoga*; Śākta upāya; creative contemplation, apprehension of an inner, emergent divine consciousness.

*Bhu* (भु)

Bhuvana : Becoming; place of existence; abode. There are 108 *bhuvanas*.

*Bhū* (भू)

Bhūta : Gross physical element.

Bhūcarī : Sub-species of Vāmeśvarī, connected with the bhāvas or existent objects.

Bhūmikā : Role.

*Bhai* (भै)

Bhairava (*apara*) : Siddhas who have unity-consciousness and consider the whole world as identical with Self.

Bhairava (*para*) : Parama Śiva; the Highest Reality; This is an anacrostic word, *bha*, indicating *bharaṇa*, maintenance of the world, *ra*, ravaṇa or withdrawal of the world, and *va*, *vamana* or projection of the world.

Bhairava or Bhairavī mudrā : This is a kind of physical condition brought about by the following practice :
"Attention should be turned inwards; the gaze should be turned outwards, without the twinkling of eyes."

Bhairava samāpatti : Identity with Parama Śiva.

*Bho* (भो)

Bhoga : Experience, sometimes used in the narrow sense of enjoyment.

Bhoktā : Experient.

*Ma* (म)

Madhya : (1) The Central Consciousness, the pure I-consciousness, (2) The suṣumnā or the central prāṇic nāḍī.

Madhya dhāma : The central nāḍī, also known as *brahmanāḍī* or *suṣumnā.*

Madhyamā : Śabda or sound in its subtle form as existing in the *antaḥ-karaṇa*, prior to its gross manifestation.

Madhyaśakti : Saṃvit-śakti, the Central Consciousness-power.

Manas : That aspect of the mind which co-operates with the senses in building perceptions, and which builds up images and concepts, intention and thought-constructs.

Mantra : (1) Sacred word or formula to be chanted (2) In Śāktopāya, that sacred word or formula by which the nature of the Supreme is reflected on as identical with the Self. It is called *mantra,* because it induces *manana* or reflection on the Supreme and because it provides *trāṇa* or protection from the whirligig of transmigratory life. In Śāktopāya, the Citta itself assumes the form of *mantra.* (3) The experient who has realized the *śuddha vidyā tattva.*

Mantra-maheśvara : The experient who has realized *Sadāśiva-tattva.*

*Mantra-vīrya* : The perfect and full I-consciousness; Śiva-consciousness; the experience of parāvāk, the energy of the mantra of I-consciousness.

Mantreśvara : The experient who has realized *Īśvara tattva.*

Manthāna Bhairava : Bhairava that churns i.e. dissolves all objects into Self-consciousness; Svacchanda Bhairavaḥ.

Marīci : Śakti.

Mahārtha : The greatest end; the highest value; the pure-I-consciousness, the *Krama* and *Kaula* discipline.

Mahāmantra : The great mantra of pure consciousness, of supreme I-consciousness.

Mahāmāyā (*apara*) : The state below *śuddha vidyā* and above Māyā in which resides the *vijñānākala.*

Mahāmāyā (para) : The lower stratum of *śuddha vidyā* in which reside the *vidyeśvaras* who, though considering themselves as of the nature of pure consciousness, take the world to be different from the Self.

Mahānaya : *Krama* discipline.

Mahāhrada : The highest, purest I-consciousness. It is called mahāhrada or the great lake because of its limpidity and depth.

*Mā* (मा)

Mātṛkā : (1) The little unknown mother, the letter and word-power which is the basis of all knowledge. (2) The *parāvāk śakti* that generates the world.

Mātṛkā-cakra : The group of śaktis pertaining to Mātṛkā.

Mādhyamika : The follower of the Buddhist Madhyamaka Philosophy.

Māyā tattva : The principle that throws a veil over pure consciousness and is the material cause of physical manifestation, the source of the five *kañcukas*.

Māyā : In Śāṅkara Vedānta : The beginningless cause that brings about the illusion of the world.

Māyā śakti : The *śakti* of *Śiva* that displays difference in identity and gives rise to *māyā tattva*; the finitising power of the Infinite.

Māyā-pramātā : The empirical self, governed by Māyā.

Māyīya mala : The limitation due to Māyā which gives to the soul its gross and subtle body, and brings about a sense of difference.

Mālinī : Śakti of letters which holds the entire universe within itself and in which the letters are arranged in an irregular way from 'na' to 'pha'.

Māheśvarya : The power of Maheśvara, the supreme lord.

Māheśvaryādayaḥ : Māheśvarī and other deities presiding over the group of letters.

Mukti : Liberation from bondage; acquisition of Śiva-consciousness, *Jīvan Mukti*—Liberation while living i.e. acquisition of Śiva-consciousness while the physical, biological and psychic life are still going on. *Videha-mukti*-establishment in Śiva-consciousness after the mortal body has been dissolved.

*Mu* (मु)

Mudrā : (1) *Mud* (joy), *rā* (to give); it is called *mudrā*, because it gives the bliss of spiritual consciousness or because it seals up (mudraṇāt) the universe into the being of turīya-consciousness, (2) Yogic control of certain organs as help in concentration.

Mudrā-Krama or Krama-mudrā : The condition in which the mind by the force of samāveśa swings alternately between the internal (Self or Śiva) and the external (the world which now appears as the form of Śiva).

Mudrā-vīrya : The power by which there is emergence of the Supreme I-consciousness; *mantra-vīrya*; *khecarī* state.

*Me* (मे)

Meya (*prameya*) : Object.

*Mo* (मो)

Moha : Delusion by which one regards the body as the self; Māyā.

Mokṣa : Same as *mukti.*

*Yo* (यो)

*Yoga* : (1) Acquisition of what is not yet acquired. (2) Communion. Communion of the individual soul with the Supreme; discipline leading to this communion, (3) (In Patañjali)—Samādhi, cessation of mental fluctuation (*yuji samādhau*).

Yoginyah : The śaktis—*Khecarī, Gocarī, Dikcarī, Bhūcarī,* etc.

Yoni : (1) Womb, source, (2) The nine classes of consonants; in the context of letters, *Śakti* is *yoni,* and *Śiva* is *bīja,* (3) The four Śaktis, viz. Ambā, Jyeṣṭhā, Raudrī, Vāmā, (4) Māyā śakti.

Yonivarga : Māyā and its progeny; mayīya mala.

*Ra* (र)

Rajas : The principle of motion, activity and disharmony—a constituent of Prakṛti.

Ravi : Lit., Sun, in esoteric philosophy and yoga, pramāṇa (knowledge), prāṇa.

*Rā* (रा)

Rāga : One of the kañcukas of Māyā on account of which there is limitation by desire, passionate desire.

*Ru* (रु)

Rudra (Kālāgni) : Rudra residing in the lowest plane of Nivṛtti kalā.

*La* (ल)

Laya : Interiorization of consciousness; dissolution.

*Lo* (लो)

Loka : Plane of existence.

*Va* (व)

Varga : Classes of letters like kavarga, cavarga, etc.

Varṇa : (1) Letter (2) Object of concentration known as dhvani in āṇavopāya; anāhata nāda (unstruck sound experienced in suṣumnā).

*Vā* (वा)

Vācaka : Word, *Varṇa mantra* and *pada*.

Vācya : Object, referent, *Kalā, tattva, bhuvana*.

Vāmā or Vāmeśvarī : The divine Śakti that emits (from 'vam' to emit) or projects the universe out of the Absolute and produces the reverse (vāmā) consciousness of difference (whereas there is non-difference in the Divine).

Vāsanā : Residual traces of actions and impressions retained in the mind; habit energy.

Vāha : Flow, channel. the prāṇa flowing in the *iḍā nāḍī* on the left, and *apāna* flowing in the *piṅgalā nāḍī* on the right of *suṣumnā* are together known as *vāha*.

*Vi* (वि)

Vikalpa : Difference of perception; distinction; option; an idea as differentiated from another idea; fancy: imagination; thought-construct.

Vikalpa-kṣaya : The dissolution of all *vikalpas*.

Vikalpanam : The differentiation-making activity of the mind.

Vikalpa (śuddha) : The fixed idea that I am Śiva.

Vikāsa : Unfoldment; development; expansion.

Vigraha : Individual form or shape; body.

Vigrahī : The embodied one.

Vijñānākala : Experient below Śuddhā Vidyā but above Māyā

who has pure awareness but no agency. He is free of *Kārma* and *māyīya mala* but not free of *āṇava mala.*

Vidyā : (1) Śuddha vidyā tattva; (2) Unmanā śakti, Sahaja Vidyā (3) Limited knowledge, a kañcuka of Māyā.

Vimarśa : Self-consciousness or awareness of Parama Śiva full of jñāna and kriyā which brings about world-process.

Viśva : The universe; the all; all (adjective).

Viśvamaya, Viśvātmaka : Immanent.

Visarga : Emanation, creation.

Visargabhūmi : Two dots, simultaneously representing *śakti*'s external manifestation of the universe and the internal assimilation of the same into Śiva.

*Ve* (वे)

Vedak : Experient.

Vedya : Object.

*Vai* (वै)

Vaikharī : Śakti as gross physical word.

*Vya* (व्य)

Vyāpakatva : All-pervasiveness.

Vyāmohitatā : Delusion.

Vyutthāna : Lit; rising, coming to normal consciousness after samādhi or meditative absorption.

*Śa* (श)

Śakti : (1) The power of Śiva to manifest, to maintain the manifestation and to withdraw it. (2) The *spanda* or creative pulsation of Śiva or foundational consciousness.

Śakti-cakra : The group of twelve *mahākālis*, the goddesses responsible for creation, etc; the group of *Śaktis* of the senses; group of *mantras*; the group of khecarī, etc.

Śakti-tattva : The second of the 36 tattvas.

Śakti-pañcaka : The five foundational śaktis of Śiva. viz., *Cit*, *ānanda*, *icchā*, *jñāna*, and *kriyā*.

Śakti-pāta : Descent of śakti; Divine grace by which the empirical individual turns to and realizes his essential Divine nature.

Śaktimān : Maheśvara; Śiva.

Śabda : Sound, word.

Śabda-brahma ; Ultimate Reality in the form of *cit*-vibration in which state thought and word are identical.

Śabda-rāśi : The group of letters from *a* to *kṣa*.

*Śā* (शा)

Śākta-upāya : The ever-recurring contemplation of the pure thought-construct of oneself being essentially Śiva or the Supreme I-consciousness.

Śāmbhava upāya : Sudden emergence of Śiva-consciousness without any thought-construct (*vikalpa*) by a mere hint that one's essential Self is Śiva; also known as Śāmbhava yoga or Icchopāya or Icchā-yoga.

*Śi* (शि)

Śiva ; The good; the name of the Divine in general; the foundational *prakāśa* or divine light.

Śiva (*parama*) : The Absolute; the transcendent divine principle.

Śiva Tattva : The first of the 36 tattvas, the primal manifestation.

*Śu* (शु)

Śuddha Adhvā : The course of extra-mundane manifestation from Śiva upto Śuddha vidyā.

Śuddha Vikalpa : The thought of one's self being essentially Śiva.

Śuddha Vidyā : The fifth *tattva*, counting from Śiva. In this *tattva* the consciousness of both 'I' and 'This' is equally prominent.

*Śū* (शू)

Śūnya (Bauddha) : A state in which there is no distinct consciousness of knower, knowledge and known; an indefinable state of Reality.

Śūnya (Śaiva) : A state in which no object ls experienced.

Śūnya--pramātā : The experient who is identified with the void, *pralayākala*.

*Śai* (शै)

Śaiva āgama : The ten dualistic śāstras, eighteen *śāstras* which teach identity in difference, and sixty-four non-dualistic *śāstras* expounded by *Śiva*.

*Ṣa* (ष)

Ṣaḍadhvā : The six forms of manifestation—three on the subjective or temporal side, viz., *mantra, varṇa,* and *pada,* and three on the spatial or objective side, viz; *Kalā tattva,* and *bhuvana.*

Ṣaṇḍha-bīja : The four lettets ऋ, ॠ, ऌ, ॡ—which are unable to give rise to any other letter.

Ṣaṣṭha-vaktra : Lit., the sixth organ or *meḍhra-kendra,* near the root of the rectum.

*Sa* (स)

Saṅkoca : Contraction, limitation.

Sandhāna : Lit., joining, union, union of the individual consciousness with the Universal consciousness through intensive awareness.

Saṃghaṭṭa : Meeting; mental union; concentration.

Saṃvit : Consciousness; Supreme consciousness in which there is complete fusion of prakāśa and vimarśa; jñāna śakti; svātantrya śakti.

Saṃvit-devatā : From the macrocosmic point of view, Saṃvit-devatās āre Khecarī, gocarī, dikcarī, and bhūcarī. From the microcosmic point of view, the internal and external senses are said to be *saṃvit-devatā.*

Saṃsāra or saṃsṛti : Transmigratory existence, the world-process.

Saṃhāra kṛtya : The withdrawal or reabsorption of the universe into Śiva.

Saṃsārin : Transmigratory being.

Sakala : All limited experients from gods down to the worm.

Sat : Existence which is consciousness.

Sattva : The principle of being; light and harmony, a constituent of Prakṛti.

Sadvidyā : Śuddha vidyā.

Sadāśiva (Sadākhya tattva) : The third tattva, counting from Śiva. At this stage, the 'I-experience' is more prominent than 'this'-experience.

Samanā : When the unmanā śakti begins to display herself in the form of the universe beginning with *śūnya* and ending with earth, then descending from the highest state of Pramātā (knowing Self), she is known as Samanā inasmuch as she has started the mentation of all phenomena (*aśeṣa-manana-mātra-rūpatvāt samanā*).

Samarasa : One having the same feeling or consciousness.

Samādhi : Collectness of mind in which there is cessation of the fluctuations of the mind; mental absorption.

Samāna : The vital vāyu that helps in the assimilation of food etc., and brings about equilibrium between *prāṇa* and *apāna*.

Samāpatti : Sometimes a synonym of samādhi; consummation; attainment of psychic at-one-ment.

Samāveśa : Being possessed by the Divine, absorption of the individual consciousness in the Divine.

Sarvakartṛtva : Omnipotence.

Sarvajñatva : Omniscience.

Savikalpa jñāna : Knowledge which is acquired by the *manas*.

Sahaja : Innate essential nature.

Sahaja vidyā : Knowledge of the innate essential nature, sometimes used in the sense of *unmanā*-pure divine consciousness in which mental consciousness ceases, pervasion in Śiva-consciousness.

### *Sā* (सा)

Sāmarasya : Unison of Śiva and Śakti; identity of Consciousness; identical state in which all differentiation has disappeared.

Sākṣād upāya : Śāmbhava upāya.

Sākṣātkāra : Direct intuitive experience of the essential Self.

### *Su* (सु)

Sugata : The Buddha.

Suprabuddha : One who has awakened to the transcendental state of consciousness and in whom that consciousness is constantly present.

Suṣupti : Sound, dreamless sleep.
Suṣupti (*savedya*) : Sound sleep in which there remains slight trace of the sense of pleasure, lightness, etc.
Suṣupti (*apavedya*) : Very deep sleep in which there is complete absence of all objective consciousness.
Sūkṣma Śarīra : The inner subtle body, *puryaṣṭaka*.

*Sū* (सू)

Sūrya (symbolic) : Prāṇa, pramāṇa (knowledge), *jñāna śakti*.
Sūrya nāḍī : The Iḍā nāḍī carrying prāṇa.

*So* (सो)

Soma (symbolic) : *Prameya* or object, *apāna*.
Soma nāḍī : The Piṅgala nāḍī carrying apāna.

*Sau* (सौ)

Saugata : Follower of Buddha, a Buddhist.

*Stha* (स्थ)

Sthāna-kalpanā : A mode of āṇava upāya concerned with concentration on external things.
Sthiti kṛtya : Maintenance of manifestation.
Sthūla bhūtam : Gross elements—ether, air, fire, water and earth.
Sthūla Śarīra : Gross physical body.

*Spa* (स्प)

Spanda : Throb in the motionless Śiva which brings about the manifestation, maintenance, and withdrawal of the universe; svātantrya śakti, creative pulsation.

*Spha* (स्फ)

Sphurattā : Gleam; a throb-like gleam of the absolute Freedom of the Divine bringing about the world-process; *spanda*, the light of the spirit.

*Sva* (स्व)

Svatantra : The Absolute of unimpeded will.
Svacchanda : The absolutely Free Being, Śiva, Bhairava.
Svapna : Dream, dreaming condition, *vikalpas* or fancies limited to particular individuals.

Svarūpa : Essential nature.
Svarupāpatti : Attaining one's essential nature or true Self.
Svalakṣaṇa : An object limited in its particular space and time.
Svasaṃvedana : An intuitive apprehension of Self.

*Svā* (स्वा)

Svācchandya ; Absolute Freedom of the Supreme.
Svātantrya : Absolute Freedom of Will; Vimarśa Śakti.
Svātma-sātkṛ : To assimilate to oneself; to integrate to oneself.

*Sve* (स्वे)

Svecchā : *Śiva's* or *Śakti's* own will, synonymous with *svātantrya.*

*Ha* (ह)

Ha : Symbol of Śakti or divine power.
Haṭhapāka : Persistent process of assimilating experience to the central consciousness of the experient.

*Hṛ* (हृ)

Hṛdaya : Lit., heart; the central consciousness which is the substratum of all manifestation, *citprakāśa.*

*He* (हे)

Hetu : Cause.
Hetumat : Effect.

*Hra* (ह्र)

Hrada : Lit; Lake; the supreme spiritual awareness. It is called a lake, because it is clear, uncovered by anything, deep, and infinite.

*Ham* (हं)

Haṃsa : The jiva, the soul.
Haṃsajapa : The consciousness of *nāda-kalā.*

# SUBJECT INDEX

# INDEX TO IMPORTANT SANSKRIT WORDS

## AN ALPHABETICAL INDEX

*To the first pāda of each verse*